It's
All in
Your Head

A DIRECTION DYNAMICS BOOK

IT'S ALL IN YOUR HEAD

Bruce A. Baldwin, Ph.D.

DIRECTION DYNAMICS
Wilmington, NC
1985

Cover design: Kaye Florence

Printed by Carter Printing Company, Richmond, VA

ISBN 0-933583-00-1

Published and distributed by: **DIRECTION DYNAMICS**
309 Honeycutt Drive
Wilmington, N.C. 28412

Manufactured in the United States of America

DEDICATION

To Joyce and Travis and Elissa
who have taught me the meaning
of REAL success.

A SPECIAL
ACKNOWLEDGEMENT

My deepest appreciation is extended to the Managing Editors and staff of Piedmont Airlines' superb inflight magazine PACE in which much of the material in this book was originally published. A special thanks is due to Jane Gibson Brown who first took a chance on an unknown writer. To Leslie Daisey, my heartfelt thanks to you for your patience and many kindnesses over the years.

CONTENTS

REMEMBER: LIFESTYLE MANAGEMENT IS WHAT YOU DO
     . . . AFTER YOU'VE PAID YOUR DUES!!!

Introduction to $\underset{\wedge}{REAL}$ Success!

There's a true story about a man who was about to celebrate his silver wedding anniversary. To express his positive feelings about his long and satisfying relationship with his wife, he decided to send her flowers on their special day. He fondly reminisced about all the years they had shared together and concluded that there had been twenty-two very good ones of the twenty-five they had been married. He went straight to the florist and ordered twenty-two long-stemmed roses, one for each of the good years they had spent together.

On the day of their anniversary, he picked up the bouquet of roses and took them home. With a big kiss and a hug, he gently told his mate that he loved her and presented her with the flowers. He told her that each represented one of the good years they had shared. She graciously accepted the roses, and listened with a little gleam in her eye. Saying nothing, she smiled and separated ten more roses from the bouquet and threw them in the trash can! Then she lovingly placed the remaining dozen roses in a beautiful vase for all to see and admire. The stunned husband was initially at a loss for words, but he got the message.

Obviously, in this case there was a significant difference in perception about how many years of marital bliss there had actually been in this marriage. Deep down, this very successful man had also been unhappy for years, but didn't understand the causes or what to do about them.

This book is about Lifestyle Management. Its goal is to help you create strategies for balancing a productive career and a quality Life After Work. For all his successes, this successful man had been unable to create a satisfying Lifestyle Balance. Looking back, he realized the high price he had paid over the years in terms of diminished personal fulfillment, impoverished relationships, and his current health problems. Understanding and practicing Lifestyle Management now is an excellent way to prevent your own silver anniversary letdown!

Lifestyle Management is your commitment to maintaining a creative balance between work and success on one hand with satisfying involvements in leisure activities, family life, and friendships on the other. It is a much broader approach to health maintenance and career longevity than many of the stress management programs on today's market. Lifestyle Management focuses on restructuring your relationship to your work by helping you to rebuild all the necessary skills to enjoy a quality Life After Work once again. The key to Lifestyle Management lies not only in improving the quality of the relationship to your work, but especially in enhancing your ability to psychologically "get away from it all" on a regular basis. From this perspective, *It's All in Your Head* when it comes to the effective practice (or neglect) of Lifestyle Management strategies.

Lifestyle Management also differs in several other important ways from the usual stress management approach.

1. LIFESTYLE MANAGEMENT IS PREVENTIVE. Most stress management programs seek to diffuse stress *after* it has been created. But taking a more positive approach, Lifestyle Management emphasizes a balanced lifestyle that prevents stress from building to problem levels through *quality* time in leisure activities, family life, and friendships.

2. LIFESTYLE MANAGEMENT BEGINS WITH LIFE AFTER WORK. While many stress management programs focus on strategies to reduce stress in the workplace, Lifestyle Management emphasizes enhancing the quality of Life After Work because that is where you have the most direct control over what happens. Later, you can take your more relaxed attitudes back into your workplace.

3. LIFESTYLE MANAGEMENT IS A MORE COMPREHENSIVE APPROACH. It is a way of life that permits the individual to maintain a strong sense of inner personal control and direction. The practice of Lifestyle Management involves strategies to help you make positive changes in virtually every facet of your life, because every part of your life can be affected easily and negatively by the stress of your success motivation.

This book and its approach to health and career longevity are based on years of observation and clinical experience with career-oriented individuals and their families as they pushed hard for personal success and the "good life." Typically, members of these families are well-educated, inner-directed, goal-oriented, and upwardly mobile, with high aspirations. However, in these same families, early career enthusiasm slowly gives way to a highly stressful, pressure-packed lifestyle that interferes with personal contentment, family cohesion, health, and eventually career advancement.

It is a paradox that amid the trappings of success and relative affluence, the growing tentacles of unhappiness spread into every facet of life. Career involvements and responsibilities slowly take precedence over all else. Intimacy fades. There is less time for leisure and diminished capacity to "let go" and have fun. There is more irritation and anger than ever before, and your communication becomes negative and cynical. You are rushing day and night to keep up. And—you're tired and disappointed. You reach a point when you wonder, "Why am I doing this?" This is not what life is supposed to be like after you "made it." Like the surprised businessman on his silver anniversary, you're successful and unhappy, but you're not sure what to do about it.

Lifestyle Management is the antidote to this all-too-common malady in the family and the individual. Success and happiness have to be teased apart and priorities restructured. As you matured in your career, you became more successful and your standard of living steadily increased. However, as the years have passed, your quality of life *after* work has just as steadily deteriorated by slow increments as your standard of living continued to rise. In the end, you are a successful individual who is making a good living, but who is NOT REALLY LIVING ANYMORE!

In this book, I have tried to create a conceptual framework for understanding how the drive for success needlessly diminishes the lives of so many talented and motivated individuals. It is a book written in the spirit of hope and optimism, because destructive changes can be reversed and, in fact, don't have to occur in the first place. It is easy to give up and plod along, becoming more cynical and jaded by the day. You need not succumb to the ravages of stress. It's a copout to permit unhappiness and disappointment to reign in your life. You have drifted out of control. To reverse this process requires understanding, a commitment to your future, and the skill to rechannel your considerable motivation and energy in new directions.

Look back a moment. Your parents lived in a world of work and leisure that was much less complex than yours. You've become painfully aware just how much the times have changed. To succeed, you don't work much with your hands. Instead, you must constantly use your mind to get your work done and to move towards your personal and professional goals. The mental energy you need each day is very high indeed. And your life beyond your career—successfully maintaining a good marital relationship, successfully raising your children, successfully managing a household, successfully preparing for your future—is immensely complicated. No wonder it is emotionally overwhelming. Because so much of what you do is done between your ears, you need a whole new set of psychologically-oriented skills to insure career longevity and personal satisfaction. These skills are *All in Your Head* if you will only take the time to develop them.

In many respects, the all-too-common unhappiness of the successful career-oriented individual is a "cultural neurosis." A cultural neurosis is a maladaptive pattern of behavior that is so pervasive within a given society that it seems normal. Success motivation, definitely a double-edged sword, has all of the ear-marks of a cultural neurosis as well. In fact, it is not going too far at all to say that society blindly reinforces success and achievement without recognizing their potentially great negative effects on the individual and on the family.

To get the best from success (and leave the rest) and maintain your health and happiness too, you must be able to clearly see the dynamics of success motivation. You must be aware of the values that you have internalized over the years. You must understand the many social and material rewards you have been subjected to on your road to success that have reinforced your achieving behavior patterns. Unless you educate yourself, you will continue to be a typically "normal," quite successful individual who will likely inch toward greater unhappiness with every passing year.

Perhaps without fully realizing it, you have lived out a definite "program for success" that is an ingrained part of our culture. You have been exposed to the sometimes subtle "carrot and stick" effects of this program all of your life. There is no question that if you follow the program guidelines, you will "make it" to a comfortable living— and there is nothing wrong with that. Look at yourself as an example! You have moved through the systems of education, certification, placement, advancement, and "perks" that are all part of the program for success. The catch is that while our cultural formula for success does work, it doesn't follow that health and happiness are also part of it. You're more or less left on your own to find these qualities in your life after success.

Each chapter of *It's All in Your Head* has been written expressly to outline one part of the overall problem with success.

Each chapter also contains specific suggestions for positive lifestyle changes. Key ideas are repeated throughout to reinforce your awareness of them. As you read, you will gain a deeper understanding of how you have changed over the years. At the same time, you will confront parts of yourself. You may see yourself very clearly in some chapters, less so in others. Undoubtedly, you will also begin to clearly see problems as they have developed in the family, with your spouse, with work-related issues, in how you now communicate, even how success has affected you in the bedroom! Success motivation can easily pervade every facet of your life in either positive or negative ways. In this sense, each chapter serves a diagnostic purpose to aid you in pinpointing problem areas and new directions.

To practice Lifestyle Management effectively—and make it stick—there is no room for scapegoating. Because you are in control, you have made success happen in your life. No one can fault you for that! The problems arose because you overdid it. By the same token, because you are in control, you can also make Lifestyle Management happen. The responsibility for your health and happiness lies with you alone. *You are not a victim—except of yourself.* It is not your boss, the organization, the economy, other people, your past, luck, fate, or coincidence. Nor can your unhappiness be attributed to your genes! It is up to you because you are in control. You can have it all. By turning your motivation to succeed in the direction of Lifestyle Management, you will be learning to REALLY succeed! You'll be going to health.

In experiencing the problems stemming from over-involvement in work, remember that you are hardly alone. As I lecture on Lifestyle Management all over the country, a stark and uncomfortable reality emerges. If you begin with a bright and motivated individual bent on "making it" to success and the good life, the same kinds of problems occur no matter what kind of work is being done. Accountants, engineers, teachers, managers, sales personnel, and businessmen and women all confront remarkably similar issues over the years as they slowly succumb to the pressures of their work. No matter what your chosen life's work, if you want to live the good life, you *must* confront the double-edged sword of success.

It is immensely helpful that a strong trend in many businesses and corporations these days is to recognize the importance of Lifestyle Management. There is awareness at the highest levels that the individual who is balancing healthy involvement in a career with equally healthy involvements in a quality Life after Work is also the person who will last longer and have fewer health problems along the way. Such an individual has fewer regrets later in life because life is lived more fully and richly each day. The concepts on which Lifestyle Management are based are supported by more organizations than ever before. Now is the time to make Lifestyle Management work for you, too!

This book is titled *It's All in your Head* because that's where the practice of Lifestyle Management begins and ends. By changing what goes on between your ears, you will be making the necessary changes to make Lifestyle Management an integral part of your life. But, you have to be ready. Change does not occur overnight, nor is it easy. It comes only with strong commitment and the awareness to mobilize your considerable talents in new directions *for you.*

A wit once remarked that "success is knowing the difference between motion and direction." You have been successful so far by focusing on your career. Now it's time for REAL success as you begin to shift into enjoyment by balancing your career with the rest of your life. Again you must be ready, and only *you* can decide when that time has come. In the end, Lifestyle Management is what you do . . . after you've paid your dues. When you decide your dues are paid in full, you're ready to go! You will become even more successful as you learn to live life fully by turning in the direction of Lifestyle Management.

Some time ago I presented a Lifestyle Management seminar to the sales staff of a large corporation. A good friend with a delightful sense of humor introduced me. His opening line was, "Did you hear the joke about the psychologist?" I cringed immediately, expecting to be embarrassed in front of the group. Such was not the case, and what this very successful professional had to say is well worth repeating.

The joke he told was really a riddle: "How many psychologists does it take to change a light bulb?" he asked. The group pondered this weighty question for a few moments, but no one had the answer. "The answer," he quipped, "is simple. It takes just one psychologist to change a light bulb. BUT THAT LIGHT BULB HAS REALLY, REALLY GOT TO WANT TO CHANGE!" His tongue-in-cheek point, I hope, is clear.

The bottom line is that you can read this book and remain a very successful and insightful, but also a quite unhappy, individual. Or, you can take control of your life and begin to make the positive lifestyle changes that will bring the good times and the personal contentment you are seeking. Lifestyle Management is the choice between making a living and really living. In this society we do a much better job with the former than the latter. REALLY LIVING is not just a far-off dream, but something you owe to yourself and to your family for all the blood, sweat, and tears you've shed over the years in your quest for success. The choice is yours. So are the consequences!

Chapter 1

Burning Out in America: When Your Work Is Alive and Well … and Overwhelming!

All your life you've dreamed about the wonderful lifestyle that will be yours with career success. You realized early that success is a game of skill and that luck is where opportunity and solid preparation meet. With that sure knowledge, you've taken the time and energy necessary to develop your talents and hone your skills. You've made many sacrifices, but now it's apparent that you're going to make it. Life is certainly more comfortable than when you were just starting out in your career. Your standard of living has gone up steadily. Your horizon is rosy and you bask in its glow. You have a strong sense that you're close to the fulfillment of the American Dream. It's just around the corner. Life is good.

Some years later, you've moved another notch or two up your career ladder, and your standard of living is higher than ever before. The problem is that you are not the same. You run through life in overdrive. You feel like Atlas under the weight of all the responsibilities that have somehow become yours. Timewise, your focus has narrowed to how you're to get everything done that needs to be done today and how to prepare for tomorrow. You're spread so thin that you are perpetually irritable. You know for a fact that the quality of your Life After Work has deteriorated markedly. You don't feel up to par physically, and you don't like the kind of person you've become either. You've begun to wonder how close you are to cracking up. Cheer up! You're entirely normal. You're Burning Out in America. You're suffering from success.

Just a decade ago, what was known about Personal Burnout was practically nil. Now clearly conceptualized as a very significant career hazard *and* as a preventable problem, Personal Burnout is receiving the attention it deserves. Preventing Personal Burnout is not only a means to enhance career longevity, but also an avenue to upgrade the quality of Life After Work for the talented and motivated men and women it most affects. As a liability for the achievement-oriented individual, Personal Burnout is both insidious and deceptive. It is insidious because it typically creeps into your life by almost imperceptible increments over a span of years. It is deceptive because the real problems, your personal priorities and your relationship to your work, are hidden beneath the more "obvious" stresses of day-to-day living.

Briefly defined, Personal Burnout is "a syndrome resulting from an emotionally destructive relationship to work (or to a career) in which there are experienced a progressive loss of control, the deterioration of nonwork interests, and mixed symptoms reflecting stress overload and depression that result in decreased productivity and general life dissatisfaction." In a nutshell, this syndrome occurs because your work involvements have been permitted to overwhelm everything else in your life. At this unhappy juncture in your career, you have very little Life After Work left for you. The time that you need to emotionally rejuvenate is significantly diminished or nonexistent. Personal Burnout is the result.

The lifestyle issues that are the cause of Personal Burnout must be faced and resolved in healthy directions if this problem is to be reversed. And, it can be reversed. The casual issues are so characteristic among achievement-oriented and motivated individuals that it is a virtual certainty that most such men and women will experience symptoms of Personal Burnout at some point during the course of their working lives. Ironically, there may be little awareness of the real cause: the loss of the ability to maintain a reasonable balance between work responsibilities and satisfying involvements in a quality Life After Work.

By the time that Personal Burnout reaches a serious level, both life at work and life at home have been seriously and negatively affected. You are stressed but you are also depressed. You find little happiness or joy in your life anymore. The American Dream has evaporated. In the midst of your affluence, you're struggling to survive emotionally. And, it's not up to the organization you work for to rescue you from yourself. In the final analysis, you must recreate the Lifestyle Balance you once enjoyed. You can do it because you're in control. You just haven't assumed that control yet. Believe it or not, there's a viable alternative to Burning

Out in America. You don't have to suffer from success. But first, some understanding.

Stage I Burnout: First Danger

Taking a few moments to relate the surprisingly consistent pattern of symptoms of Stage I Personal Burnout to *your* experiences should confront you directly with this creeping career liability that almost every motivated person experiences at one time or another. As have many others, you have given your all for years to "make it" and you have, but the struggle has also taken its toll. You've reached a level of relative economic comfort only to find that you aren't really enjoying life anymore. Although clearly successful, you are disappointed. This is not the way it was supposed to be! Your life of heavy responsibilities and boring, monotonous routines has brought you the "walking depression" that so characterizes Stage I Personal Burnout.

Here is a checklist of symptoms to look for to assess whether or not you are already in the clutches of Stage I Personal Burnout. Note each of the symptoms that is true of you these days. The more of these signs that you see in yourself, the more likely it is that you are moving toward a crisis in your life that will have profound implications for your personal well-being and future career development.

BURNOUT SYMPTOM #1: YOU ASK, "WHY AM I DOING THIS?" Your work used to be professionally challenging and personally interesting. No more! You don't get much out of it now, and you find yourself wondering why you continue to do it. In fact, when you look down the road to see yourself in the same job going through the same routines day after day until you can retire, it's downright upsetting. On the other hand, you're not really sure just what would bring you the life satisfactions that you realize have been missing for some time now.

BURNOUT SYMPTOM #2: YOU HAVE A BAD CASE OF THE "ITS." These days, little things really seem to get under your skin. And, you overreact with anger when you encounter them (which is often). These are your "ITS." You just don't want to deal with any IT in your life anymore. You feel that if you do, you'll scream, bang your head against the wall, strangle someone, or just run away and hide. Examples are many: no sooner do you sit down to dinner than the telephone rings, and someone from the office asks an asinine question; before you're out of town going to visit relatives, one of the kids has to "really go"; just as you're hurrying to an important meeting, the boss stops by to chat and pass the time of day.

BURNOUT SYMPTOM #3: YOU HAVE A DRAGGING, TIRED FEELING. No matter where you are or what you do, you're chronically tired. Further, you can't seem to "catch up," to feel really energetic these days. The root problem is emotional exhaustion due to lack of true relaxation. You just can't sleep this kind of fatigue away. In fact, sleeping more may even make it worse! Even during time off, you're still tired and don't seem to have the energy to be active like you were in the past.

BURNOUT SYMPTOM #4: YOU HAVE A STRONG NEED TO BE LEFT ALONE. Because you're so tired, you don't want to be hassled for any reason by anybody. Your behavior and your words tell others to keep their distance and leave you alone. You resent responding to problems and taking care of other people. You want to withdraw to be by yourself more and more as time passes. You don't reach out to others like you used to and you talk less. Inside you feel very alone. These days, it seems that everyone wants something from you as you struggle for your own emotional survival.

BURNOUT SYMPTOM #5: YOU USE TREMENDOUS ENERGY JUST TO GET THROUGH THE DAY. "One day at a time" is the only way you can function because you have experienced a significant loss of energy. In the past, you used to be able to handle a busy work day easily and have energy left over. Not any more. Just getting through each day takes everything you have in you. When you get home, you have nothing left to give. And, when you do get to the house, you're so tired you don't care much about anything.

BURNOUT SYMPTOM #6: YOU WATCH TELEVISION INDISCRIMINATELY. A hard sign of Personal Burnout, especially for men, is a developing pattern of continous and indiscriminate television watching. You are increasingly inactive at home. You sit night after night in front of the tube, not really enjoying yourself, but staring at it anyway. As time passes, lethargy breeds lethargy and you talk less, and eat, drink, and smoke more while you're sitting there mulling over your growing unhappiness and personal discontent. You sit there hour after hour with a glum look on your face, not reacting to what you are watching.

BURNOUT SYMPTOM #7: YOU DON'T ENJOY LEISURE TIME THESE DAYS. It's practically impossible for you to really relax anymore, even on weekends. When you do get away, you find that you can't "let go" like you used to. You're continually distracted and worried about work, and you can't seem to get problems off of your mind. When you're out with the family, you're there in body, but not in spirit. You don't make plans to do fun things much lately because the hassle isn't worth it. On the other hand, you miss the fun you used to have.

BURNOUT SYMPTOM #8: YOU'RE NOT AS EMOTIONALLY CLOSE AS YOU USED TO BE. You've become much more negative and cynical recently, and it shows in how warmly you relate to others. Deep within, you sense a growing distance from loved ones that troubles you. It's almost as if there is an invisible barrier that has grown between you and the people you care most about. You don't talk much except when you have to, and your conversations often wind up as bickering or an outright fight. Inside, you feel lonely, misunderstood, and resentful. You want others to reach out to you, but when they try, you really don't give them a chance.

BURNOUT SYMPTOMS #9: YOU ARE EXPERIENCING PHYSICAL SYMPTOMS OF STRESS. You are now paying the price for the incessant and unremitting pressures of the years. Your inability to recover emotionally from these stresses has produced your irritability and the physical signals of stress overload. Symptoms may range widely from insomnia to recurring tension headaches to a daily upset stomach. These symptoms may not be serious at this point, but your body is clearly signaling that something is wrong and that lifestyle changes are definitely in order. You're just not feeling as good as you should physically *or* emotionally.

BURNOUT SYMPTOM #10: YOU FEEL OUT OF CONTROL OF YOUR LIFE. You live with a sense that you're swimming upstream against a strong current and slowly losing ground. You are struggling daily to maintain your work output, but it's more a game of "catch up" these days than being firmly in control and on top of things. Over the past several years, your life has become more confusing, chaotic, and complex than you ever thought possible. The feeling that you are not in control serves to compound the inherent stresses of meeting all your responsibilities.

Now that you're aware of the symptom pattern of Stage I Personal Burnout, you can understand why it can be appropriately characterized as the Stage of Withdrawal and Disappointment. You've sacrificed for years and denied yourself willingly because you believed that this was what had to be done so you could enjoy life later. Now that you're successful, the "good life" is elusive. Instead, you live a complicated, pressure-packed existence. Deep down you're angry and disappointed. You're making a good living, but you're not really happy. Society's promise that happiness and contentment would be yours if only you paid your dues and did all the right things has just not panned out. You've burned out instead!

Four Unhealthy Options

If more than a few of the symptoms of Personal Burnout fit you, you're functioning far from your best at work and at home. And, you're more vulnerable than you may realize. The problems you are experiencing could easily get much worse depending on what you do now. When you are deeply disenchanted and highly stressed, it's easy to lose perspective and make costly mistakes. Your objectivity is so clouded that making sound life decisions is difficult. Here are four common errors that only exacerbate the already negative feelings and subjective distress of the individual experiencing Personal Burnout. Each error is a blaming message. Each is a way of saying: "I'm not responsible for my unhappiness. You are!"

NEGATIVE OPTION #1: YOU BEGIN TO JOB HOP. Individuals in the throes of Personal Burnout are sorely tempted to escape by finding a "better" job. However, because the issues of Lifestyle Management and developing healthy coping skills lie within, this is not a solution. It's likely that the same pattern of Personal Burnout will be repeated in a new setting, and it's usually faster the second time around. The "geographic cure" simply doesn't work and the reason is obvious: wherever you go, you must take your head with you and that's where the real issues reside.

It's a far better strategy to stay put and resolve within yourself the issues that led to your present state of Personal Burnout. When that is done, you will be in a much better position to realistically decide if another job is right for you. Then you will know what kind of job to go after. At that point, from a base of strength, you will be going to a position you want, not impulsively running away from one that you can't handle.

NEGATIVE OPTION #2: YOU RETREAT TO A QUIET, SIMPLE LIFE. Those desperately unhappy individuals who are experiencing Personal Burnout often dream of a quiet, simple life free of daily frustrations and stress. A few opt to give up everything to attempt it. This kind of precipitous move usually doesn't work. Highly trained and technically competent individuals may try carpentry, craftmaking, truck driving, or another of the skilled trades. Interestingly, these are usually occupations that involve working primarily with your hands in ways that you can directly control what you are doing. You develop a strong need to respond in a more concrete "hands on" fashion that sharply contrasts with the highly intellectual work of the skilled achiever.

However, such a move leaves you vulnerable in three ways. First, your standard of living may drop drastically. Second, you may eventually miss the "intellectual" side of your work. Finally, if you are highly achievement-motivated, you may soon build your new occupation into one that is equally (or more) stressful and as full of headaches as the one you left behind. Lifestyle Management issues again remain unaddressed and unresolved.

NEGATIVE OPTION #3: YOU ESCAPE THROUGH ALCOHOLISM OR DRUG USE. The possibility of drug abuse grows proportionately with the severity of Personal Burnout. The shift from social or recreational use of drugs to significant dependency occurs in almost imperceptible steps. Drug use becomes a way to "relax," to deal with the ongoing pressures of work, and to cope with life's problems. However, with time the ease of drug use as a coping response leads to more and more dependency.

Gradually, psychological coping skills are lost as reliance on chemicals increases. The end point is inevitable: a severe drug problem develops that further jeopardizes career and family life. The issues involved in Personal Burnout can only be compounded by drug dependency. Nothing at all has been resolved. You've only temporarily escaped. After you "bottom out" on drugs, two sets of problems must still be faced: your dependency on chemicals and Lifestyle Management issues.

NEGATIVE OPTION #4: YOU LEAVE YOUR MARRIAGE. There are at least two ways to leave your marriage. Physically through separation or divorce or emotionally as you progressively withdraw into yourself. Both are frequently seen as a consequence of Personal Burnout. As work pressures have slowly overwhelmed you over the years, your stress has increasingly spilled over into your home and family life. Communication has deteriorated and emotional intimacy has faded. There is less time for leisure and more conflict at home.

These changes too often sound the death knell for your most important relationship. Although the marital relationship may be severely strained, the root problem is your inability to handle work pressures. By confronting Lifestyle Management issues directly instead of running away from them, you may find that your marriage has much more potential than you think. In fact, separation and divorce, or affairs on the side, can easily make matters much worse for you both!

Stage II Burnout: The Cynical Endpoint

Stage II of Personal Burnout occurs when you don't recognize and respond to the danger signals of Stage I. The career-oriented part of you dies and the rest turns into pure jade. Stage II of Personal Burnout might be called the Stage of Terminal Cynicism because you just don't care anymore. It's almost as if your subconscious decides that you have had enough and then turns you completely off. The real danger is that your turned-off, uncaring attitude can easily become permanent. In the beginning, Stage II is like wet cement that hasn't set. It can be changed. With time, though, it sets and hardens into permanent career disinterest. At that point, it may be nearly impossible for you to become excited, challenged, and interested in your career ever again.

Here are the five very negative changes that occur when your subconscious "switch" goes from "ON" to "OFF" in Stage II of Personal Burnout.

TURNOFF #1: YOU CEASE TO BELIEVE IN PERSONAL CONTROL. In other words, you cynically decide that nothing will ever change for you. You feel trapped. You believe that everything — your demanding boss, the contentious clients, the uncaring organization, the daily frustrations — will remain exactly the same forever. Why beat your head against the wall? Why even try? It's easier just to give up and accept defeat than to keep pushing futilely.

TURNOFF #2: YOU FIND IT HARD TO CARE ABOUT PEO-PLE ANYMORE. Because you've decided that nothing will ever change, you withdraw from personal and creative involvement with colleagues, clients, and others in the organization. You are not as empathic as you once were, and your non-caring attitude shows through in many subtle and not-so-subtle ways in your contacts with others, especially at work, but also at home.

TURNOFF #3: YOU RELATE TO YOUR WORK DEFEN-SIVELY. You see the organization as an oppressor, and you are its victim. You must protect yourself from it at all costs. Your over-riding desire is to get through the day as easily as you can with the fewest possible problems. In other words, you place self-protection over getting the job done well. You learn to do the minimum required to get by without being fired.

TURNOFF #4: YOU LIVE WITH A SENSE OF FAILURE WITHIN. You've copped out and you know it, but you can't seem to help it. You see colleagues getting ahead and the youngsters coming up fast. Because you don't care anymore, you don't keep up professionally. Consequently, you are progressively falling behind. One result is that you don't feel part of things anymore either in the organization or in your profession.

TURNOFF #5: YOUR CAREER BECOMES JUST A JOB. Your career used to be not only exciting and challenging, but an important part of your personal identity. Now, it's just an occu-pation. Your chosen life's work has become merely an expedient. You have to do it because you can't afford to stop. It provides few gratifications for you these days. You strive to get away from it and stay away from it as much as you possibly can.

In short, when Stage II of Personal Burnout occurs, your career enthusiasm first weakens and then quickly fades com-pletely away. With a lot of truth and a bit of tongue in cheek, it can be realistically stated that when you reach this stage of Personal Burnout, you retire. The only problem with your retirement is that you typically don't bother to tell the firm you've retired. By giving up, you opt for a plodding day-to-day existence that will go on until you can legitimately retire. A vital part of you has died. As a result, everyone loses — you, the organization, and the clients it serves. A highly skilled professional has become an uncaring, cynical, and resentful drone who goes through the motions day after day just to get a paycheck.

Lifestyle Management: The Strategy

Lifestyle Management is a new approach to preventing or reversing the problem of Personal Burnout. Its dual aim is to enhance productivity and career longevity by promoting the quality of day-to-day living, particularly in Life After Work. It is the responsibility of the individual to protect physical and emotional health by learning to balance a full and productive career with rich and varied non-work experiences. Defined, LIFESTYLE MANAGEMENT IS YOUR COMMITMENT TO MAINTAINING A CREATIVE BALANCE BETWEEN ACHIEVEMENT AND SUCCESS ON ONE HAND AND SATISFYING INVOLVEMENTS IN FAMILY LIFE, LEISURE ACTIVITIES, AND FRIENDSHIPS ON THE OTHER. To regain Lifestyle Balance once it has been lost is difficult, but quite possible. It is also a most worthwhile goal that pays handsome dividends, both in your career and in establishing a quality Life After Work once again.

When Personal Burnout occurs, it is because three fundamental Life Decisions have not been clearly conceptualized nor personal commitments made to them. Your needs for career success and personal achievement have gradually eroded and diminished the Life After Work you used to enjoy so much. Family life, leisure activities, and friendships have also been neglected during your long push to "make it." Your responsibilities have grown by leaps and bounds. Daily frustrations go on and on. You're well aware that a deep dissatisfaction has been welling up within you for years. All of the symptoms of Personal Burnout have become manifest. As the only sensible starting point to reverse this process and to begin the practice of Lifestyle Management, you must make your commitment now to these three major Life Decisions.

LIFE DECISION #1: MAKE YOUR COMMITMENT TO REVERSING "WORK SKEW." Individuals experiencing Personal Burnout have invariably permitted work to dominate everything else in their lives. Enjoyment of life deteriorates as your work becomes an obsession. You are not only spending more time actually working at the office, but you even work at home in the evenings and on weekends. If you're not actually working, then you're thinking about work. The result is that you can no longer psychologically "get away from it all." You're hurried, you're hassled, and you're pressured. Even life's small pleasures don't seem to be there anymore. You've lost the once healthy balance between work and the rest of your life without realizing the serious implications for your health and happiness.

"Work skew" builds slowly and invasively over a period of years. To reverse this destructive encroachment on your time to enjoy life, you must make a commitment to improve the quality of your Life After Work. That is going to take some of the time you are now spending working overtime or worrying about work. You must create and maintain clear boundaries between the work and nonwork spheres of your life. You must leave enough time to learn to enjoy yourself again. This process will not happen overnight. However, just carving out the time, marking the boundaries, and sticking to them is the very best beginning step you can possibly make to effectively practice Lifestyle Management.

LIFE DECISION #2: YOUR COMMITMENT TO DEFINE YOURSELF FROM WITHIN. As you became more successful, it became very easy to begin focusing your self-esteem on various symbols of your success instead of inner resources or who you are as a person. Without realizing it, your good feelings about yourself soon became far too dependent on externals like wealth, power, status, or position. As this process continued, a personal vulnerability has grown. At this point, ask yourself just what your resources are within to cope with the loss of these external symbols of your adequacy. As you have continued to succeed, you may be completely unaware of the slow erosion of the inner strength you need to deal with the failures and setbacks that life has a way of handing almost everyone!

Further, with externally-based sources of self-esteem, there is never enough of what you need to satisfy you. Your life becomes oriented toward status, power, wealth, or position. To get what you need to feel good about yourself, you have to work harder and harder. And the more you get, the more you want. Soon you are in a rat race of your own making, and Personal Burnout is the result. You're moving so fast and so constantly to create the things you need to maintain self-esteem and feel good about you that you no longer have the time to enjoy life anymore. To reverse this process, you must slow down and begin to define yourself once again from within. You must rediscover yourself as a person and feel good about who you are, irrespective of your position or achievements. Then you can work and succeed without a sense of desperation. Then you can fail without vulnerability. Then you will be in control again.

LIFE DECISION #3: YOUR COMMITMENT TO PERSONAL HEALTH. The state of your health, emotional as well as physical, will critically influence whether you ultimately achieve all of your personal and career goals. Your health will also determine how much you enjoy life along the way. In a frequently seen cartoon, a mugger confronts a victim, gun in hand. "Your money or your life!" is the ultimatum. This is the very same ultimatum that confronts highly achievement-oriented individuals each day. It is also the basic issue that must be faced in this third important Life Decision. If you remain oriented only toward money, your life, perhaps its length, surely its quality, may be sorely compromised.

It has been so easy to ignore your physical and emotional health as you drifted onto the fast track. Perhaps you have developed the very bad habit of putting things off until an indefinite "later." You're so busy that it's also easy to rationalize away the time and energy required to take care of yourself. Pleasant diversions, adequate time away, regular exercise, and proper diet are all neglected in lieu of immediate responses to daily work pressures. It is likely you have begun to smoke more, drink too much, or overeat as a way to cope with these same nagging demands. To beat Personal Burnout, you must reestablish your health priority. By taking care of yourself now (it's never too late to start), you will last longer and prevent future problems. By so doing, you will also regain that important sense of inner control and direction that will help you maintain a healthy perspective on how you are living each day and why.

Getting Started: Seven Strategic Tips

You now understand the overall philosophy of Lifestyle Management and the three Life Decisions that are the bedrock of its practice. You are also aware of the ravages of Personal Burnout and its myriad powerful effects on your work and on your ability to enjoy Life After Work. You want to do something about it. You have decided that you deserve more out of life than you've been getting lately. Here are some strategic tips to help you lay the foundation for a sound Lifestyle Management strategy that will work for you.

STRAGETIC TIP #1: BEGIN WITH LIFE AFTER WORK. You have much more control over your life at home than you do at work. At work, you simply can't change the daily frustrations, hassles, pressures, and other "givens." As you begin to practice

Lifestyle Management, focus almost exclusively at first on making positive changes in your Life After Work. Create clean boundaries between the work and nonwork spheres of your life. Your initial challenge is to enhance your enjoyment of Life After Work. To try to modify how you relate to your work in the beginning is an almost overwhelming task. Once you have established better ways of taking care of yourself at home, however, you can more easily bring these relaxed attitudes with you into your workplace and make them stick.

STRATEGIC TIP #2: PROCEED WITH A SERIES OF SMALL CHANGES. As you seek to reverse the destructive lifestyle changes that have occurred over the years, don't make the mistake of trying to do too much at once. Your chances for successful Lifestyle Management are much better if you make a series of small changes, a few at a time. This book is full of suggestions for the kinds of small changes that you can make in various areas of your life. Choose just one or two changes to start with. Practice your new responses until they have become integrated into your lifestyle and are comfortable, almost second nature. Then go on to make a few more changes. As you proceed slowly and carefully, these small changes will soon add up to a major positive shift in your lifestyle and the values on which it is based.

STRATEGIC TIP #3: CREATE A REASONABLE TIME PERSPECTIVE FOR CHANGE. As part of your training for success, you have learned to make things happen and to do them in a hurry. This strong "hurry up and get it done" urge is part of the problem that has produced your Personal Burnout in the first place. And, it will surely sabotage the changes you want to make in your lifestyle. A realistic framework for significant lifestyle changes ranges from about eight months to one year. Making a series of small changes and integrating them takes time. But the time is well spent, because with practice those changes will become part of how you live each day. You'll begin to experience the positive effects of those changes shortly after you make them, but becoming comfortable with them is not an overnight process. Soon, however, one change begins to complement another as your lifestyle evolves in positive directions.

STRATEGIC TIP #4: FOCUS ON CHANGING YOU, NOT OTHERS. One particularly troublesome aspect of Personal Burnout is that you begin to perceive yourself as a victim. In fact, you are a victim — of yourself! It is you who ultimately has control of your life. It is also you who must take responsibility for your health and happiness. Blaming anyone outside yourself or trying to change others to relieve your distress is a waste of time and energy. Work on yourself instead. Tackle the issues within you to change your relationship to work and to leisure. That way, not only will you deal with Personal Burnout, but you will learn to practice Lifestyle Management the right way from the beginning. And, do it for you — because you deserve it!

STRATEGIC TIP #5: BE PERSISTENT DESPITE DIS- COMFORT. You will experience some subjective discomfort with every lifestyle change you make. At first, you may feel guilty for relaxing or taking time off. You may find yourself away from work in body, but not in spirit as you continue to think about problems. It is entirely unrealistic to think that doing anything new just one time will give you real skill. Look at Lifestyle Management as a series of skills that you are relearning. Give yourself a chance. Keep at it. Practice and persistence made you successful in the work world. Now use these same qualities to insure that you effectively learn the skills necessary for Lifestyle Management. These skills also have a way of complementing your successes in the marketplace.

STRATEGIC TIP #6: DEVELOP A SUPPORTIVE ALLY. Change is easier when you have someone to do it with. A spouse, a good friend, or a colleague can all be helpful. You can talk over the changes you're making, and you can support one another through the uncomfortable feelings that will surely come. When you've goofed up, as you undoubtedly will, a supportive ally will help you maintain perspective and get you back on the right track. A spouse as an ally is especially valuable because your Personal Burnout has also negatively affected your family life, including your marriage. Choosing your spouse as an ally symbolizes your deep recommitment to your family. You will begin to grow closer again as you work together toward the positive lifestyle changes that you will both find satisfying.

STRATEGIC TIP #7: DON'T WAIT FOR ANYONE TO GIVE YOU PERMISSION. Now is the time to change for you. Waiting for someone else's approval is futile. No one is going to give you permission except you because you are in control. Accept the fact that there is no right time to begin, nor will there be any time that will be easier than today. By taking control and making a deep commitment to better yourself and to enjoy life once again, you have already taken one big step. Then positive lifestyle changes become a matter of keeping your momentum going. In some respects, you must have the inner strength to resist destructive external pressure to remain exactly as you are. And you will have to fight part of yourself to practice Lifestyle Management. In the end, however, you will win in big ways as you solidify your commitment to enjoying more of the good things in life.

Lifestyle Management Is What You Do ... After You've Paid Your Dues!

Lifestyle Management with its many benefits is simply not for everyone. It is only for those who are ready to make some changes. To be ready, you must decide that you have paid your dues in full. Lifestyle Management also requires that you see yourself as deserving more happiness and good times out of life than you've been getting recently. It means refocusing your considerable talents and energies into seeking inner peace, contentment, and the enjoyment of a full and rich life on a daily basis. Lifestyle Management helps you put all those things you have sought for so long — money, power, image, status, position — into a more realistic life perspective. When you're really ready for Lifestyle Management, it means that you've decided that the good things in life are worth having and that you're worth having them.

You've probably been thinking about making some changes in your lifestyle for some time, but you've made some half-hearted attempts and failed. Maybe you've become discouraged and somewhat pessimistic about ever finding your way to the good life. Lifestyle Management is a philosophy of living that involves a series of eminently practical suggestions for positive change. Following the guidelines contained in IT'S ALL IN YOUR HEAD will give you a reasoned and workable approach to this change process. But change is never easy, and ultimately it's all up to you. There's a lot of truth in the old saying that "after all is said and done, more is said than done!"

As a valid rule of thumb for personal change, perhaps another adage is in order: "It is easier to act your way into a new way of thinking than to think your way into a new way of acting." The bottom line is GO AHEAD AND DO IT whether you are comfortable with the changes you are making or not. Sitting around thinking about change does you no good. Begin to act out the positive changes necessary for Lifestyle Management. It will be initially uncomfortable, but you will soon begin to perceive yourself, your work, and especially your Life After Work in a whole new light. With a new way of defining success, shortly you will find yourself living the "good life" again. Then you'll wonder how you ever let yourself become so miserable in the first place!

Chapter 2

Between Your Ears:
Notes on the Nature of Stress

Jan frequently experiences tight neck muscles that result in headaches. Far too often she must cope with "butterflies" in her stomach. She wishes she knew how to stop these distressing reactions to demanding office responsibilities.

Terry gets so confused under pressure that he barely gets anything done. Ideas spin through his head in overdrive, and he can't seem to slow them down, much less deal with any one issue well. His thoughts become very cynical and negative as the pressure continues.

David's moods go up and down like an elevator when the pressure is on. One minute he's angry and irritable and the next he's down in the dumps. Although he would never admit it, sometimes he just wants to sit down and cry. At other times, he wants to run away.

Jan and Terry and David are all perfectly normal people. What they have in common are stress reactions to pressure. Pressure is the sum total of the demands made on you by the job, by the people around you, and by yourself! Stress, however, is different. Stress is the activation of your neurological, physiological, and sensory systems to meet challenge (*i.e.*, pressure). As an activation response, stress is a form of energy that you need to function well. In fact, you need stress every day. However, stress is a double-edged sword that you can harness to work for you, or it can become a most destructive influence that will impair your physical and emotional health.

It is a fact of life that stress has its origins "between your ears." Pressure can come from external sources or from your own demands on yourself, but how you internally handle that pressure determines the magnitude of stress generated and whether it will have a positive or negative effect on your ability to function. In short, how you handle pressure is an index of the adequacy of your coping skills. Look around you. You will notice some individuals in adverse circumstances who survive and grow. Others (too many) succumb to the cumulative effects of their stress. What makes the difference is what goes on between their ears.

One additional point about stress: almost any individual can handle acute pressure with high levels of stress once in a while. However, never-ending pressure or an ongoing series of acutely demanding situations that continue for a long period of time erode coping skills and produce a negative impact on health, happiness, and productivity. The result is a chronic stress syndrome that can produce not only the symptoms experienced by Jan and Terry and David, but many more besides!

Have you taken some time to think through how *you* cope with pressure? Your reactions to pressure are learned and highly subjective, and can be healthy or unhealthy. Since stress reactions are learned, they can also be unlearned. The reason is that stress comes from between your ears and because *you are in control.* Here is a framework to help you examine and understand your stress reactions to pressure.

Stress Can Be Positive

Stress as internal activation is both necessary and useful to a productive career and to a healthy Life After Work. However, as a harried professional, you may not think so. Kept at optimal levels, stress is a constant source of energy that helps you get things done and then to feel good about what you have accomplished. It generates not only energy, but enthusiasm. Perceived in this way, stress can be a valuable career asset, but it must be managed and used as such. Here are seven signals that you are using your stress in positive ways.

1. You are stimulated each day. Your life is full and rich because you seek out interesting ways of viewing things and you take the time to learn each day. Your career is an exciting and living and developing part of you that you cherish.

2. Your accomplishments are a form of personal expression. You feel good about what you do because it is *you.* You don't perform to prove anything or to beat others, because you already know who you are and like who you are.

3. You are in control from within. You don't have to control everything around you because you have a comfortable sense of direction from inside. Because of these feelings, you are on top of your work, without feeling overwhelmed, victimized, or resentful.

4. You seek personal challenge. You are stimulated to grow, so you take the risks necessary for personal development. Every day you are changing. You grow wiser and more skilled because you seek challenges that you can handle and feel good about.

5. You maintain a positive outlook. You have a well-developed ability to see the bright side of things. You look for and reinforce the positive in yourself and in others. You have kept your pleasant sense of humor, and you can see the funny side of life.

6. You handle setbacks, failures, and frustrations well. You keep problems in perspective, and you maintain your objectivity about them. Mistakes and setbacks, even outright failures, are used as learning experiences. You accept responsibility for your actions and don't blame others.

7. You know how to get away from it all. You have other interests besides work, and you enjoy them. Family life, leisure activities, and relaxation are easy for you, and you make the time for them. You recognize these involvements as necessary to maintain your physical and mental health.

Your Stress Response Pattern

Every adult has developed a patterned response to stress overload. Signs of stress overload show up in three basic realms of experience: physical symptoms, emotional symptoms, and cognitive (or intellectual) symptoms. You will benefit if you become aware of your personal Stress Response Pattern. As a start, here are three basic characteristics of your Stress Response Pattern to keep in mind.

1. Each individual's Stress Response Pattern encompasses all three realms of symptoms, given enough prolonged stress. With a chronic stress syndrome, physical, emotional, *and* cognitive functioning is impaired.

2. Typically, one realm of stress symptoms is dominant over the other two. That is, for any given person, the physical, emotional, *or* cognitive symptoms will emerge earlier and more strongly than stress signals in the other two realms.

3. Your Stress Response Pattern is reasonably stable over time. Your personal pattern may change, but such changes are usually a slow evolution rather than a rapid transition.

To understand in more detail your particular Stress Response Pattern, think about a recent situation that was highly stressful for you. Then ask yourself what superficially seems to be an obvious question: If you experienced high levels of stress in that particular situation, how did you know it? To help you, here are lists of some of the most common signs for each of the three major realms of stress symptoms: physical, emotional, and cognitive. Read each list and check the symptoms that you experience when you are stressed. Some symptoms you will be able to easily associate directly to stress. Others may surprise you.

After you've gone through all three lists once, examine again all the stress symptoms you've marked. Which of them seem to always emerge first when you are highly stressed? Put a big "X" beside these signals. These are your early warning signs of a stress overload. Keep these particular signals firmly in mind so that when you experience them you can immediately take appropriate action to reduce or resolve the stress. In stress management, as with anything else, an ounce of prevention is worth at least a pound of cure (if not more).

STRESS RESPONSE REALM #1: CHECKLIST OF PHYSICAL SYMPTOMS.

_____ 1. Tension or other types of headaches.

_____ 2. Muscle spasms in your shoulders, neck, lower back, or chest.

_____ 3. Inability to get to sleep at night, or sleep that isn't restful.

_____ 4. A lump in your throat that makes swallowing difficult.

_____ 5. Diarrhea or constipation.

_____ 6. Hives or other types of rashes.

_____ 7. An uncontrollably rapid heartbeat.

_____ 8. Increase/decrease in appetite with related weight gain or loss.

_____ 9. Rapid shallow breathing with shortness of breath.

_____ 10. Dizziness or faintness (occasionally actual fainting).

_____ 11. Muscular weakness or a feeling that your legs will collapse beneath you.

_____ 12. Flareups of any chronic condition (arthritis, colitis, asthma, lupus, and many others).

_____ 13. Lowered resistance to colds, flus, and viruses and inability to get rid of them quickly.

_____ 14. Loss of sexual energy (libido). Exception: About 10–15% of men and women experience an *increase* of libido under stress.

_____ 15. Grinding your teeth during sleep (bruxism) or clenching your teeth during the day.

_____ 16. Painful stomach contractions or a nauseous, queasy feeling.

_____ 17. An increase in nervous mannerisms or unconscious facial tics.

_____ 18. Excessive perspiration, including sweaty palms and feet.

_____ 19. Women: Irregular menstrual periods or skipping periods entirely.

_____ 20. Other: _____

Note that each of these physical symptoms of stress overload may also result from physical conditions that require medical treatment. The consistent appearance of any of these symptoms, although they may be clearly associated with stress, should be carefully checked by your physician.

STRESS RESPONSE REALM #2: CHECKLIST OF EMOTIONAL SYMPTOMS.

_____ 1. Persistent sadness or frequent crying episodes.

_____ 2. A gloomy, pessimistic outlook or strong sense of impending doom.

_____ 3. General irritability or unexpected outbursts of anger.

_____ 4. Emotional withdrawal and wanting to be by yourself more than usual.

_____ 5. Strong anxiety with no clear focus or overall tenseness.

_____ 6. Excessive need for emotional support or reassurance from others.

_____ 7. Lethargy, with significant loss of motivation.

_____ 8. Inability to sit still because of nervous energy.

_____ 9. Frequent nervous laughter.

_____ 10. Pushing others away and rejecting their help.

_____ 11. Focusing on vague aches and pains.

_____ 12. Rapid and frequent mood swings.

_____ 13. Impulsive actions motivated by emotional upset.

_____ 14. Feeling overwhelmed or fearing that you will lose self-control.

_____ 15. Other: _____

STRESS RESPONSE REALM #3: CHECKLIST OF COGNITIVE (INTELLECTUAL) SYMPTOMS.

_____ 1. Frequently forgetting things that are usually remembered.

_____ 2. Inability to remember what has been just read or heard.

_____ 3. Loss of objectivity ("making mountains from molehills").

_____ 4. Racing thoughts, but inability to deal with any one of them (flight of ideas).

_____ 5. Increased distractability or lowered attention span.

_____ 6. A critical attitude toward self and others.

_____ 7. Going over and over one thought you can't get off your mind.

_____ 8. Retreat to fantasies or daydreaming.

_____ 9. Over-controlling others or becoming very demanding.

_____ 10. Disorganization, resulting in lack of effective planning.

_____ 11. Feeling that others don't like you or are deliberately making your life difficult.

_____ 12. Stubbornness or rigidity in your positions.

_____ 13. Reduced or absent awareness of personal strengths and assets.

_____ 14. Absent humor or sarcastic and cynical humor.

_____ 15. Other: _____

The Roots: Your Success/Failure Tandem

It is all too easy to just react to pressure without thinking about what you are doing — and generate stress as a consequence. It is also quite easy to blame your stress on external factors — the organization, a manager, the workload, the economy, or all of the above. In truth, however, this is not the case. *You* produce stress. It has its origins between *your* ears. If you examine your stress responses closely and thoughtfully, you will find that at least some of the problem stems from your strong needs to achieve, to advance in your career, and to "make it." You need success to feel good about yourself, and you push yourself to that end.

However, to truly understand the motivational dynamics of stress, you must also examine the flip side of success: your fear of failure. What if you don't "make it"? Part of your drive to do well is created by a fear of failing. In other words, your motivation to succeed is actually a defense against failures you don't know how to handle. The result is that you push yourself long and hard to do well.

Interestingly, failure in many cases is defined very subjectively and personally by the career-minded individual. In fact, failure may be defined so subjectively that it defies reality. It is not uncommon to find individuals experiencing stress overload failing internally *every day*. By all objective criteria, however, they are doing just fine. Organizations routinely promote employees who are doing well in terms of organizational performance, but who are chronically failing because of unrealistic ways of defining personal standards. Keeping your expectations of yourself reasonably in line with organizational reality is one big step in beginning to control your stress responses.

The following are just a few of the ways that individuals unnecessarily create failures for themselves. Each is a psychological set-up that feeds the personal insecurity and professional doubt that generates stress.

- You habitually accept more work than you can possibly get done.
- You create and then don't meet unrealistic personal deadlines.
- You must be Number One in everything that you do.
- You acknowledge only what you do wrong and ignore what you do right.
- You believe that you have disappointed someone important to you with no evidence to that effect.
- You set, then don't meet, perfectionistic standards.
- Every time someone else gets ahead, you feel cheated and insecure.
- You procrastinate.

The Spread of Stress

Striving to succeed, however subjectively defined, interacts with the pressure-packed work environments in which most professionals are immersed each day. Because of the incessant pressures, it is difficult to maintain the necessary skills to prevent stress overload. The result is the Spread of Stress. This is the invasion of work-related stress into non-work areas of life that further erodes your ability to rejuvenate emotionally. As the Spread of Stress becomes more serious, you find it progressively more difficult to "get away from it all" psychologically. The Spread of Stress manifests itself in three ways.

1. The Buildup of Residual Stress. Residual stress is tension that remains with you after you've left work. It may hang on for hours or right up until bedtime. You may not be doing actual work related to your career, but you are doing the next best thing: You are constantly thinking about it. You mull over your many responsibilities, what you didn't get done today, the quality of your work, the mistakes you made, and how you are going to handle that hectic day tomorrow. Accompanying these thoughts (which you can't seem to turn off) is a plethora of negative emotions — anger, guilt, frustration, fear of failing, hopelessness — that further upset you.

2. Anticipatory Stress Responses. The next danger sign of the Spread of Stress is anticipatory anxiety that occurs before you get to work. You might awaken in the morning to notice the beautiful sunlight streaming in through your window. You think: "What a beautiful day it is today." Seconds later you remember that you have to go to work, and that first massive surge of adrenalin streaks through your body. You are stressed and tense from that point onward, anticipating what the day is going to bring to you. At this point, your stress has spread to virtually all your non-work waking hours.

3. Progressive Sleep Disturbance. Finally, your growing inability to relax before and after work begins to interfere with sleep. You are bone tired after a long day and get to bed only to spend an hour (or more) worrying about work-related concerns before sleep comes. You may find yourself drifting into the habit of taking a drink (or two or three) or using sleeping pills or tranquilizers to get to sleep. You may find yourself waking up in the morning extremely tired after a full night's sleep. You have an awareness that you've been thinking all night. No amount of physical labor will produce the same kind of dragging fatigue in the morning or interfere with work performance as much as this kind of sleep disturbance.

Add the Effects of Conditioning

The Spread of Stress is exacerbated significantly by your body's conditioned responses to stress. When it comes to stress, unfortunately, the human body is wonderfully constructed to develop such responses through the long association of stress and certain kinds of stimuli. When a conditioned response is present, such stimuli can trigger a strong global stress response even though, at that moment, the situation is not inherently stressful at all!

Remember Pavlov? He conditioned dogs to salivate when he rang a bell. In like fashion, your body easily learns to respond to stress, without a conscious decision to do so on your part, each time certain stimuli are encountered.

There are two types of conditioned stress responses that occur; you should be aware of both. Remember that, as the Spread of Stress progresses, the likelihood of developing conditioned stress responses increases, making relaxing and truly "getting away from it all" even more difficult.

CONDITIONING MODE #1: STRESS RESPONSES RE-SULTING FROM PHYSICAL STIMULI. Examples:

• Art, director of a suicide prevention center, experiences a strong stress response every time the telephone rings, whether he is in his office, at home, or on vacation.

• Jane, working in a high-pressure advertising agency, feels her anxiety level shoot sky high when she walks into her office, even on a Saturday when no one's there.

• Joe becomes very tense every time he encounters his immediate supervisor who constantly criticizes him, even when the boss is seen at a distance downtown on Joe's day off.

In each of these situations, a strong association between certain kinds of physical stimuli (a telephone, an office, a person) and a stress response has developed. Now, the sight or sound of these key stimuli automatically trigger stress responses without discrimination. That is, the immediate situation does not have to be stressful anymore for your body to respond with stress. The responses occur across the board whenever and wherever the key stimuli are perceived because of their consistent past association with stress. Because of the automatic and indiscriminate nature of these conditioned responses, you are stressed many more times than necessary and in situations where a stress response may be entirely inappropriate.

CONDITIONING MODE #2: STRESS RESPONSES RE-SULTING FROM THOUGHTS OR IMAGERY. Examples:

• Whenever Sue lies down to go to sleep after a long, hard day, her thoughts inevitably turn to the office and all the work problems she encounters there constantly. Her anxiety level rises accordingly.

• George has become aware of a slow, but steady rise in tension as he drives closer to his office. His stress levels are very high long before he gets there, knowing what he has to face when he arrives.

• Linda lies on a beach on a beautiful Carribbean island during her annual vacation. She experiences high levels of stress because unwanted images of a big mistake she made the week before continue to cross her mind.

In this second type of conditioned stress response, your body reacts not to actual physical stimulation, but rather to thoughts or mental images of stressful situations encountered in the past or anticipated in the future.

The problem here results from a quirk of human functioning. Your body cannot tell the difference between actual reality and thoughts or images. When you create thoughts or images that reflect stressful situations, your body responds accordingly. This is the same principle that accounts for your strong stress responses to the frightening imagery of a nightmare. Because of your body's reaction to imagery, your stress responses become one step further removed from actually experiencing a stressful situation. To make matters worse, thoughts or images that trigger stress responses are most likely to occur when your mind is not otherwise occupied, that is, when you are relaxing or want to go to sleep.

When the Spread of Stress is exacerbated by conditioned stress responses, your ability to rejuvenate emotionally is even more seriously compromised. A vicious cycle begins. You're stressed at work and not able to relax at home because of the Spread of Stress. Consequently, your ability to handle work pressure is diminished. Conditioned stress responses grow in number and in strength. Your ability to relax is further compromised, and your ability to cope with work pressure is further eroded. This destructive stress spiral continues to adversely affect your effectiveness at work and the quality of your Life After Work. Over time, the effects on your personal and professional life are often acute.

Emotional Transformations of Stress

When stress overload becomes a personal reality, stress often is internally transformed to be experienced and expressed in different emotional modes. When this occurs, it becomes more difficult, sometimes even confusing, to accurately define the nature of the problem and what remedial steps to take. There are three primary emotional transformations of stress. Each is not only a danger signal, but also acts to further erode the relationships you need for support and emotional nourishment in your present vulnerable state.

The DEPRESSIVE Equivalent. Almost by definition, an individual who is chronically stressed is going to become depressed as well (*i.e.*, burned out). The growing cynicism, the loss of energy combined with emotional fatigue, strong ambivalence about work ("Why am I doing this?"), and feelings of being both overwhelmed and a victim are all depressive symptoms. These feelings produce a slow decline of productivity on the job that seems only to get worse, and that in turn makes you feel like giving up. Add to this your emotional withdrawal from others, even loved ones, along with the shutdown of communication on your part, and the depressive picture is complete. You're too tired to care.

The HOSTILE Equivalent. Anger erupts constantly when this transformation is present. No one — friends, colleagues, your receptionist, your spouse, the kids, even your pet — is immune from your angry outbursts. You try to contain these feelings to be that easygoing person you once were, but when some little event triggers you, the strength and vehemence of your anger surprises even you. These outbursts give you temporary relief from the tension you feel, but the price is very high indeed in terms of loss of good will and closeness in relationships.

The ACTIVATION Equivalent. A continuing restlessness that drives you to constant activity is the hallmark of this transformation. You just can't sit still anymore. You're rushing around, always in a hurry. You are thinking ahead to what you've got to do next before you're done with what you're doing now. No wonder you can't relax: you respond this way twenty-four hours a day. You push others unreasonably to do as much as you do, and you despair that no one is as committed as you are. You can't slow down and take it easy, so you want the world to hurry up to match your pace — and it bothers you when it doesn't happen.

Are You a Stress Carrier?

How is your personal stress like the common cold? If you think about it for a moment, a cold is contagious — and so is your stress. Just as bacteria can be transmitted easily from one person to the next, so can stress responses be communicated to upset and disturb everyone around you. Both your verbal responses and your non-verbal communication lie at the root of this phenomenon. And, unfortunately, your ability to transmit stress contagiously works amazingly well.

When you succumb to stress overload and Personal Burnout, the contagion inevitably begins. You become a "stress carrier." Your stress is always with you. It ripples outward like the wavelets generated by a pebble tossed in a pond, adversely affecting all those around you. The contagion effect is magnified when other individuals cannot easily get away or when they are in a powerless position relative to you. Here are some all-too-typical individuals who have been negatively affected by a Stress Carrier in their midst.

• Patty has been on the receiving end of her husband's bitter and cynical remarks for so long it seems almost "normal." He alternates between angry outbursts and sullen withdrawal. His glaring stares could easily wither the brightest flower. She has learned to cope with him (and preserve her sanity) by removing herself from his presence when he is in one of his very frequent "moods." She's not willing to continue living like this forever, though.

• At the office, Caroline radiates her stress like shock waves. Co-workers never know what to expect from her. At times, she is reasonable and supportive. Too often, some inconsequential frustration triggers an outburst that may have residual effects for days in the office. She is not particularly disliked, but she's certainly avoided. For self-protection and personal comfort, her staff keep a very low profile in relation to her.

• Henry's just a thirteen-year-old kid. For about a year, he's had an upset stomach that really bothers him. At home, his professionally involved and career-oriented parents have marital problems because each is experiencing severe symptoms of Personal Burnout. Tension fills the household and there is very little closeness anymore. Even the family dog seems more withdrawn these days. Henry feels very alone. He responds by getting into trouble.

• At cocktail parties, Tom has noticed that many of his once-close colleagues now politely say hello, quickly pass the time of day, and move on. He is only dimly aware that his nervous mannerisms and sarcasm are the cause. His internal tension is picked up by others. They become uncomfortable and move away to chat with others who are more relaxed.

• Katy is always in motion. If she's not actually up doing something, she fidgets or restlessly tries to carry on a conversation fragmented by constant distractions of her own making. Friends find it extremely difficult to relax with her. The fact is that Katy feels guilty for resting even a moment, and she communicates her discomfort to others. Even her sleep is restless these days. Once good friends don't drop by much anymore.

Each of these individuals has become a Stress Carrier. And, each is experiencing the interpersonal consequences. Whether stress is expressed directly or as depressive withdrawal, irritability, sarcasm, or guilty agitation, the effects are the same. Your personal stress — and the inability to handle it — manifests itself in a wide range of social signals, some of them quite subtle and many out of your conscious control. Your tension causes discomfort for others, and they cope by avoiding you. You are already suffering from too much stress, but the contagion effect isolates you further, making you feel even worse.

It is only natural for other people to seek out friends and colleagues with whom they can relax and be comfortable. You were one of those people once, and you can be so again. Practicing Lifestyle Management helps you learn to handle your stress in better ways. Becoming a Stress Carrier is by no means a permanent affliction. Nor is the contagion effect. When you cope in healthier ways, the "ripple effect" that is feeding your negative feelings will quickly disappear. You will become more easy-going, and those around you will respond to these new "vibes." You will become positively "attractive" again instead of negatively "contagious."

Look Closely at Yourself

Unfortunately, problems with chronic stress are becoming far too common. The destructive effects of stress overload creep up on you in almost imperceptible increments. One day you wake up to find yourself quite successful by most social standards. At the same time, you're very unhappy but not sure why or what has happened. This is the day when you need to carefully examine your lifestyle and how you respond to pressure. Until this day comes, you will find all manner of excuses to continue doing the same things. "I've got to do it to get ahead." "Just this one more project." "My position isn't secure yet." Perhaps there is a grain of truth in each, but there is also in each a denial of the growing problems within you and at home.

In the end, Lifestyle Management is your commitment to creatively balance success and achievements on one hand with satisfying involvements in family life, leisure activities, and friendships on the other. You now know something about the nature of stress and how it affects you physically, emotionally, and intellectually. However, to practice Lifestyle Management effectively, you must also know something about the nature of success. You have been trained throughout most of your life to be successful. You have become capable and skilled in your work. Paradoxically, this same training to "make it" in the marketplace has progressively weakened your ability to relax and enjoy the good life, now that you are successful! But that's the next part of the story. . . .

Chapter 3

The Program for Success: Cultural Mandates for Making It!

To "make it" to comfortable levels of economic success in our society means acquiring considerable technical know-how integrated with a fair share of psychological savvy. You've done it! You've persevered and now you're reaping the rewards of years of relentless effort. For better or worse, you've figured out how the system works and how to use it to your advantage. If you didn't, you wouldn't be where you are now. On the other hand, now that you're successful, you're not as happy or as content as you thought you would be. Part of the problem is that, while you know how to be successful, there are also some critical gaps in your knowledge.

Take a moment for an exercise in awareness. Lean back in your chair and close your eyes. Let your memory drift backward in time. Visualize yourself in elementary school with the friends you knew there. You shared the same school experiences and educational opportunities, and you are all the same age. Now move back to the present. Think about these same individuals in terms of their present career or economic success. A few have undoubtedly reached great heights of accomplishment in their chosen fields. For one reason or another, many others leveled off early and have ceased to move ahead. And, some went nowhere at all. They struggle more than they should at this point in their lives.

What accounts for the differences in these individuals? Luck? Fate? Coincidence? The right breaks? Knowing someone important? Hardly! It's a fact that there are some very definite rules for attaining success in our society. These guidelines are not always taught directly, but their impact on success is a most powerful one. Those individuals who follow the rules for success usually make it. Those who can't, or who choose to ignore them, find significant and sometimes insurmountable barriers to getting ahead. Some of your childhood friends picked up the rules early and followed them as you did. Others never could grasp them, and now their success is proportionately limited.

This chapter is devoted to helping you more clearly conceptualize the program for success in our society and to understand key aspects of your development as well. By understanding the cultural mandates for "making it," you will be in a much stronger position to use them to your advantage in the future. It will also help you become aware of the many liabilities and traps encountered in the process of getting ahead. The fact that you are now successful but unhappy attests to the powerful subtleties in the system that can easily undermine personal satisfaction, health, and, ultimately, success itself.

Intelligence Is a Red Herring!

To succeed, you need only a bit more than average intelligence! At first, this seems to be a most radical statement. The premium placed on measures of raw intelligence or IQ scores as THE gauge of potential is tremendous. However, to assume that a high IQ means ultimate success in the marketplace is erroneous. Think about it: many of the most intelligent individuals you know are simply not the most successful. All communities abound with extremely intelligent people who are not successful by any applicable social standard. Each one attests to the magical mythology of a direct association of intelligence to high levels of career success.

A related "red herring" is the assumption that completing a formal education (college or beyond) will guarantee success. Again, every community has some highly educated individuals who have not really "made it" once they completed their formal education. They couldn't deal effectively with the practicalities of career development because they lacked the critical skills necessary for success. In other words, it is entirely possible to complete high levels of formal education and be extremely intelligent, but still not succeed in the real world if other skills are not present.

What part, then, do intelligence and formal education play in success? A realistic perspective is to view *reasonable* intelligence and a *solid formal education* as necessary, but insufficient conditions for success. In addition you need a constellation of personal qualities such as perseverence, self-discipline, interpersonal skills, a clear sense of purpose, enough trust to work toward future goals, and the ability to deal well with frustration and outright failure in the pursuit of success. Significant liabilities to the attainment of career success are created if these kinds of skills, byproducts of effective parenting and the educational process, have not been developed. In the competitive arena of success, bet on those who have these qualities!

The Ingredients of Success I: A Success Ethic

Virtually everyone who makes it to comfortable levels of success has adopted a personal Success Ethic. Basically, a Success Ethic is a deep belief in your own capabilities to ultimately reach your goals despite setbacks and roadblocks. It's true that there's no such thing as a free lunch. It's just as true that no one will hand you success on a silver platter. In an open society, however, upward mobility is always possible by using available opportunities and by following the cultural guidelines for attaining success. A personal Success Ethic is an integral part of the foundation for success and is made up of two interrelated beliefs.

SUCCESS ETHIC I: YOU CAN MAKE SUCCESS HAPPEN BECAUSE YOU ARE IN CONTROL. This is the land of opportunity. You have personal assets that can be developed. By creatively combining your assets and available opportunities, you make success happen for you. To accomplish this, you must believe in yourself and in your ability to determine your own destiny. Those many individuals who perceive their lives to be dominated by outside influences have a major strike against being successful. Instead, they become victims of external influences (*i.e.*, people, fate, circumstances) rather than using their own control to move steadily toward goals despite hardships and barriers. Those who believe in internal control are much more capable of surmounting obstacles to success. They negotiate their own path through life and ultimately make it because of a deep belief in their personal capabilities and an associated belief in positively influencing their own destinies.

SUCCESS ETHIC II: SUCCESS REQUIRES THAT YOU FOCUS YOUR ENERGIES INTO CULTURALLY PRESCRIBED DIRECTIONS. To succeed, you must channel your efforts into specific areas of endeavor. When you do, you are rewarded as doors to advancement are opened. On the other hand, focusing personal effort into other socially non-productive areas may close those same doors. For example, a child who devotes significant time to studying and making good grades will be rewarded with a sterling transcript and recommendations that will open doors in the job market or to higher education. A child who wants only to play and have fun, while neglecting academics, will not be rewarded socially, and doors to advancement will close. The successful person has a deep belief that hard work will eventually pay off.

Career-involved parents understand the basics of how the success system operates. They spend tremendous amounts of time and energy and money to help their children learn the Success Ethic. "You can do it!" "Go get 'em!" "Be number one!" "Keep studying, it will pay off!" These are all frequently heard mandates from success-oriented parents. Parents provide help with homework, special tutoring, after-school enrichment activities, specialized training, encouragement in sports, and social opportunities as a means to help their children gain confidence and internalize the "you can make it happen" Success Ethic. Parents also model hard work and dedication. Believe in yourself. Do all the right things to open the doors to success. Advance through the system. Push onward and upward. Why? Because the Success Ethic works!

The Ingredients of Success II:
The Information

"Knowledge is power," the saying goes. Having specialized information is the second major key to success. In this technologically advanced society, a great premium is placed on "salable" information. To provide opportunities to gain access to such information, this country has developed one of the finest systems of secondary and higher education in the world. To succeed, then, you must be "educated." In a practical sense, that means possession of highly specialized information that can be sold in the marketplace because not everyone knows what you know. These days, a high school diploma is hardly enough. To provide various kinds of marketable specialized information, post-secondary education is rapidly becoming an absolute necessity.

To attain the high levels of specialized information necessary to succeed these days, each child begins a long educational process that begins in the pre-school years. Once in school, each year of success brings passage to a new grade level and certification that higher orders of information have been mastered. After high school, there is usually technical training or college, and frequently graduate school.

Once a very high level of sophisticated information is gained and understood, that information begins to define you professionally. For example, a lawyer understands certain kinds of information that few others know. When training in law has been completed, the lawyer-to-be is examined by a state board or bar association that then certifies that individual to practice (*i.e.*, to sell legal information). This same process holds true in most professions, including teachers, engineers, nurses, psychologists, and CPA's. Licensing in the skilled trades is also rapidly becoming necessary as plumbers, electricians, and general contractors are all required to take qualifying examinations in most states.

Moving through the educational system to gain the requisite high levels of information for marketability requires a great deal of time. It also requires a deep belief in a personal Success Ethic. Once you have "graduated" and have been certified or licensed, you gain entry into your chosen field of work. Then a process of proving yourself in the practice of your profession begins. The quest for new information is such a powerful, competitive asset that it never ends. Seminars, in-service training, personal reading, learning from experience, and formal continuing education programs are all used to keep your level of "specialized" information up-to-date in order to remain competitive in the marketplace.

The Ingredients of Success III:
The Implementation Skills

Along your path to success, you have undoubtedly met individuals who were unquestionably intelligent, seemed to have a strong Success Ethic, and who were clearly well-educated. Yet, these individuals never really succeeded or fulfilled their considerable personal potential. Often the core of the problem in such talented people is the absence of a number of important success-oriented skills. Together, these interrelated skills constitute the third and perhaps the most critical Ingredient of Success.

In many ways, these essential skills help you to translate your Success Ethic and knowledge into practice on (and off) the job. Without these implementation skills, your ability to succeed is severely limited despite your other qualifications. Interestingly, these essential skills are usually taught quite indirectly. They are a by-product of parenting, of formal education, and of consistently reinforced rules for success on the job. If you understand and learn these skills well, you have a most valuable asset in your quest for success. Neglect of any one of them, on the other hand, produces a significant liability that will make true success correspondingly more difficult.

SUCCESS SKILL #1: THINKING ANALYTICALLY. You must be able to do more than memorize facts and regurgitate them later to succeed (although you *can* get through school on the basis of these skills alone). For professional maturity to develop, you must master other intellectual operations. Common sense and an ability to "think on your feet" are necessary to function well and to advance in your chosen discipline. Your capacity to analyze new information creatively and blend it with prior experience is a prerequisite for becoming wiser and more capable in the practice of your profession. Among the cognitive skills necessary to mature in your work are conceptualizing, abstracting, using inductive and deductive reasoning, extrapolating, and using creative ability to discover innovative ways to translate new ideas into effective practice.

SUCCESS SKILL #2: ANTICIPATING THE FUTURE AND PLANNING AHEAD. No child thinks beyond the present; however, to succeed as an adult, you MUST develop a strong future orientation. Thinking ahead and planning for the responsibilities you must meet tomorrow, next week, next month, and even next year are crucial to ultimate success. No individual can really "make it" by functioning on a completely present-oriented basis. Enjoy today, but at the same time anticipate and prepare for tomorrow. As a professional, your preparation for the near and long-term future never ends, but the training begins early. There is always something "due" or a deadline to meet and you never really "catch up." New responsibilities constantly appear on your calendar, and you are punished if you do not adequately anticipate and prepare for them.

SUCCESS SKILL #3: LEARNING HOW TO COMPETE AND WIN. There is no doubt that both you and your children live in a very competitive world of work. From early childhood on, much of the competition to get ahead is quite overt, but some of it is also very subtle. Remember again your school friends. From the beginning there was attrition. Some students forged ahead; some fell by the wayside. There were fast reading groups in elementary school and slower reading groups. Some of your friends quit in junior high school. Some never made the honor roll. Some of your peers didn't get into college; others never graduated once started. Some managed to get a good job, and some didn't. Some who did, though, never advanced. By this point in your life, the yearly attrition has been in operation for a long time. Only a few of your elementary school peers have made it as far as you have. And, the going gets tougher and more competitive with time. With every advancement now, you're dealing with a more select, knowledgeable, and motivated group of individuals. The competition to get ahead never ends.

SUCCESS SKILL #4: BUILDING A STRONG GOAL-ORIENTATION. The ability to work toward long-term goals with no immediate payoff is critical for success; it also defies human nature. A long-term goal orientation and capacity for self-denial go together. Children operate on the Pleasure Principle — that is, to maximize pleasure and to minimize pain right now. To succeed, however, you must learn to put immediate gratification aside and choose to do something less fun instead. To accomplish this, there must be trust in your own capabilities, trust and perspective in ultimately reaching goals, and trust in the system of success to eventually bring you greater rewards than immediate gratification can provide. The choices involved in self-discipline and a strong goal-orientation are many: to get up and go to work instead of sleeping in, to study for an exam instead of partying, to save for a house down-payment instead of using the extra money for travel, to go to college instead of getting a job and a regular paycheck right after high school. Each of these choices involves self-denial now to work toward a goal with more durable and lasting rewards later. Without a well-developed ability to make these critical choices, real success can become quite elusive.

SUCCESS SKILL #5: PERFORMING TO SURVIVE CONSTANT EXTERNAL EVALUATIONS. From early childhood on, it is a fact of your life that at every level of development your performance will be monitored and evaluated by someone else. Your parents approved of some of your behaviors and disapproved of others. You were regularly graded by your teachers and professors. Throughout your life, you received constant feedback from peers and colleagues. While on the job, you are subject to regular performance evaluations by your superiors. Even if you decide to go into private practice, you don't escape evaluation. Your clientele will either return, or they won't. To be truly successful, it is necessary to discern accurately the needs of the organization (or your clients) and then use the skills you have developed to meet those needs competently. When you do, you survive these periodic external evaluations because you perform up to expectations (or beyond). Because you do, the doors to advancement open. If you fail in this important part of being successful, those same doors will surely begin to swing closed.

SUCCESS SKILL #6: DEVELOPING YOUR CAPACITY FOR PROFESSIONAL OBJECTIVITY. Professional objectivity is your ability to put aside or control your emotions to get the job done. Career success requires that you retain objective perspective and a rational approach to problem-solving. When your emotions begin to reign supreme, objectivity is diminished and mistakes are made as perspective is lost. The result is that your performance is compromised. This is exactly what occurs when Personal Burnout progresses to a serious level. However, being objective does not negate being sensitive, understanding, and empathic in your responses to others. It does require, though, that you develop a professional role through which you relate in your work. Your deeply personal feelings are put aside. This critical skill has both a survival and a performance function. For example, a nurse cannot afford to become too personally involved with seriously ill patients, or there will be severe emotional repercussions. A psychologist cannot be helpful to a client without professional objectivity. On the other hand, a supervisor must evaluate subordinates on the basis of an objective appraisal of performance, not on the basis of blatantly personal biases.

The Five Characteristics of Success-Oriented Functioning

Developing and integrating the three essential Ingredients of Success permit the achievement-oriented individual to respond in ways that bring the rewards of success. And, the formula does work. You may not become fabulously wealthy by following it, but if you apply these lessons, you will surely move into the mainstream, middle-class lifestyle. As you persistently apply your success skills you will move up to an adequate salary, a modicum of economic security, and the fulfillment that goes with feeling good about what you are doing. However, your well-learned, success-oriented style of responding has certain characteristics that you should understand if you are going to preserve health and happiness as you pursue a productive career. Five qualities are important to keep in mind.

CHARACTERISTIC #1: YOUR SUCCESS ORIENTATION IS LEARNED. No child is born with a success-oriented way of relating. This mode of response is the product of our extremely long socialization process to help children develop into productive members of society. Parents, the educational system, middle-class values, and religious doctrine all extol the virtues and rewards of hard work. Exposure to these values begins shortly after birth and never ends. To succeed, a child must relinquish many "childish" qualities to mature and advance through the system to become successful. Literally decades of involvement in success-oriented socialization have molded not only the way you relate to work, but how you relate all experience.

CHARACTERISTIC #2: YOUR SUCCESS ORIENTATION IS HIGHLY INTELLECTUAL. In a nutshell, you don't "feel" your way to the top. Rather, you think your way there. All of the Ingredients of Success are highly cognitive. Success requires you to "use your head" continually. A premium is placed on rationality, logic, effective problem-solving, objectivity, and maintaining perspective unimpeded by the distortions of emotion. Success also requires that you develop an ability to intellectually control or contain your emotions to get the job done no matter how you feel. As you climb the ladder of success, your intellectual skills are constantly reinforced. By the same token, your emotional side gets little recognition or support in the competitive work world. Your personal feelings just don't have much place there.

CHARACTERISTIC #3: YOUR SUCCESS ORIENTATION IS GEARED TO THE FUTURE. A strong characteristic of being successful is your ability to work continually toward your future. You learn to always look ahead and set new goals to strive for. You are taught the value of self-denial in the present and the wisdom of working for rewards that are bigger and better, but that come later. One result of your future orientation is that you may inadvertently begin to neglect living in the present. You are perennially on your way to the top, but you never quite get there. Because of this, you start to put off enjoying life until you get "there," but it never happens. With the years, it becomes progressively more difficult for you to slow down and enjoy life each day because of your future-oriented self-denial. Your success-oriented *modus operandi* skips the "now" for the future.

CHARACTERISTIC #4: YOUR SUCCESS ORIENTATION EMPHASIZES CONTROLLING EXPERIENCES. Your well-developed Success Ethic is a deep personal belief that you are in control of your destiny and that you can make success happen for you. You've demonstrated the validity of this belief to yourself many times. By channeling your energies into particular endeavors (*e.g.*, studying), you create a positive outcome (*e.g.*, better grades). You have learned to strive with dedication toward specific goals, and you do reach them. No small part of your success is your ability to control and direct your responses. To be successful, you learn to control your emotions, control events, control people, and control yourself. With your developed capacity for intellectual control, you work toward attaining personal goals and career success much more efficiently than otherwise could be the case.

CHARACTERISTIC #5: YOUR SUCCESS ORIENTATION REQUIRES TREMENDOUS ENERGY. The mental processes that you constantly use in your quest for success need fuel, and that fuel is your energy. "Using your head" during long hours at work, while not physically demanding, does consume tremendous amounts of energy. In fact, it's far easier to recover from strenuous physical exertion than from the drained feeling resulting from mental fatigue. When your muscles are tired, you rest a while and your energy returns. Mental and emotional exhaustion grow from too much intellectual "work" without relief. It is this kind of dragging emotional fatigue that eventually is transformed into the depressive state so characteristic of Personal Burnout. The only remedy is healthy relaxation (not necessarily more rest). Remember, while you may not actually be in the office working, you may be "working in your head" and consuming valuable energy no matter where you are!

The Sword of Success

Handled well, career success kept in perspective can bring you personal satisfaction, career longevity, and a deep contentment.

On the other hand, untempered success motivation often brings bitter disappointment, immense frustration, personal unhappiness, and health problems. In many individuals, strong achievement motivation is much like the Sword of Damocles. In Greek mythology, Damocles was an ambitious courtier who talked constantly about the happiness that being king would bring to him. Dionysius, the actual king, took notice of this aggressive and upwardly mobile young man and decided to teach him a lesson. He invited Damocles to a banquet and seated him during the long dinner just below a razor-sharp sword hanging by a hair!

Dionysius' point was graphically brought home to Damocles. There is constant peril at the top. But Dionysius' action also made a second, but just as important, point. Wishing to be at the top is a fantasy seen through rose-colored glasses. History does not record whether Damocles learned these valuable lessons or not. However, many centuries later, both are equally relevant to the success-oriented individual who is blinded to everything except the ceaseless drive to be king. Thre are certainly rewards, both personal and professional, that are part of being successful. There are also many hidden dangers. Unless you learn to handle with care the success motivation that you have been taught so well, you may easily become one of the many highly successful, but very unhappy individuals that abound in every community.

The price of success can be very high, but it's also a bill that you don't really have to pay at all. You have concentrated on developing your career for years and the results show. In the meantime, take a close hard look at what has happened to the Life After Work that you once enjoyed so much. It has gone the way of the dinosaurs. Your career has evolved so quickly that your Life After Work simply couldn't keep up. This unhealthy by-product of your success has some potentially serious consequences in the personal suffering that it eventually produces. The sword of Damocles now hangs balanced just above *your* head as you sit at the banquet of your success!

The Problem With Success

There's a big problem with your success orientation. You've learned it too well! While the three Ingredients of Success are *very* functional in your career, they are detrimental when extended into your Life After Work. When you begin to relate to your spouse, your children, leisure activities, free time, friends, and hobbies in that same hard-driving, success-oriented fashion, you lose the ability to relax and enjoy life. Relationships become strained. You don't recover the energy you are constantly expending in the mental "work" that is going on in your mind day *and* night. There is little question that you have learned the success-oriented way of responding very well. The real question, though, is *whether you can turn it off long enough to relax!*

Being "success-oriented" too much of the time has many negative consequences. Among them are stress overload, a negative and cynical attitude, less fun and enjoyment of life, and all the depressive symptoms of Personal Burnout. No wonder you don't feel too well these days. How can you relax if you're always pushing to make things happen, gathering and analyzing information, anticipating and planning, competing, performing up to expectations, and responding in a very professionally objective fashion? The real you is lost in an incessant drive for success that can't be stopped.

Here are some questions to help you decide if your success-oriented way of experiencing has been inappropriately extended into your Life After Work. The more of these statements that you check "True," the more likely it is that you are trapped in a success-oriented way of relating that interferes with your ability to "let go" and rejuvenate each day.

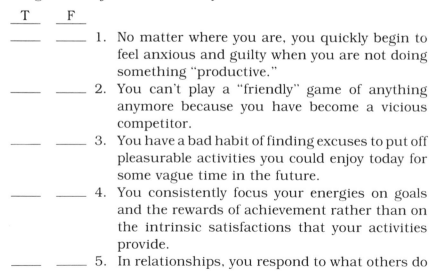

T	F	
___	___	1. No matter where you are, you quickly begin to feel anxious and guilty when you are not doing something "productive."
___	___	2. You can't play a "friendly" game of anything anymore because you have become a vicious competitor.
___	___	3. You have a bad habit of finding excuses to put off pleasurable activities you could enjoy today for some vague time in the future.
___	___	4. You consistently focus your energies on goals and the rewards of achievement rather than on the intrinsic satisfactions that your activities provide.
___	___	5. In relationships, you respond to what others do

T   F

and how well they do it rather than who they are as people.

_____ _____ 6. It is difficult for you to enjoy sensory stimulation because you immediately begin to analyze as data everything you experience.

_____ _____ 7. You find yourself constantly pushed by a never-ending sense of time urgency and always do things rapidly, even when not necessary.

_____ _____ 8. You can no longer "let go" enough to lose yourself in any pleasant activity these days — to the point of losing track of time.

_____ _____ 9. You mentally shift gears to what you are going to do next long before you're done with what you're doing now.

_____ _____10. You are consistently doing two (or more) things at one time so you can get more accomplished.

_____ _____11. You've either given up your hobbies, or you're now competing and trying to make money from an avocational interest.

_____ _____12. With your emphasis on rationality and logical problem-solving, you're not comfortable expressing your deeper feelings anymore.

_____ _____13. Over the years, your work hours have slowly expanded so that you now have little time for leisure activities, and when you do have time, you're too tired to enjoy it.

_____ _____14. You have become very touchy and irritable, and it takes very little to bring forth the anger that seems to be constantly boiling up within you.

_____ _____15. In relationships, you respond to what others have done wrong (in your opinion) and neglect to verbalize support for what has been done well.

In Pursuit of Success

Sitting at a planning meeting, a harried manager remarked: "I'm so busy these days that life is like a never-ending marathon." "Yeah, I know the feeling." replied a colleague. "I think that's why it's called the human race!" A bit of wry humor perhaps, but with more truth for many successful people than it's easy to admit. The fact is that you've been racing in pursuit of success for a long time now. Racing to get everything done. Racing to stay on top of things. To maintain control. To meet your many responsibilities each day. And, success has surely come your way. Deep contentment has been more elusive.

As you've checked yourself on the behavioral signs of an over-developed success orientation, you've begun to realize that success is really a double-edged sword. You understand how your well-learned tendency to "work in your head" without let-up is now limiting your ability to enjoy life while bringing you ever more of the material rewards of your success. Without being fully aware of it, you've been slowly losing your ability to psychologically "get away from it all" for years. However, this loss and the personal dissatisfaction that goes with it is not necessarily permanent at all. The process is entirely reversible by adopting some of the strategies of Lifestyle Management.

Perhaps it's also dawning on you that a big part of what you've lost is perspective. You've had tunnel vision. Your attention has been focused ahead of you as life has passed with blurring speed. You haven't taken time to assess where you are. There's a lot of truth in the saying that "if you want to know where you stand, you've got to stop long enough to see your feet." Perhaps the time has come to slow down and closely examine your life and how you've been living it. Instead of looking ahead, look around you. There are people you care about. There is beauty. There are good times for the taking. With all your external successes, you may find that you've been living in poverty within. When you stop long enough to see your feet, you will find that there is a wealth of rich experience just waiting for you.

Chapter 4

Guilt Drives the Work-Leisure Bind:

If You Can't Beat the Guilt, You Can't Beat the Stress!

Remembering back, some years ago you were busy, but you still had enough time left over to enjoy life. Now you feel overwhelmed all the time and can't seem to catch up. Recently, it has become extremely difficult to separate from your work. In fact, the boundaries between work and your Life After Work have blurred to the point of non-existence. You find yourself always more or less working whether you're at the office or at home. It bothers you that your analytical mind seems to be going constantly. It also scares you that you can't seem to slow down and enjoy life even though you want to. There seems to be a vague something that prevents true relaxation and that keeps pushing you back to work.

The more you think about this situation, the more unfair it seems. You're right! You do deserve to enjoy life more during these prime years. You're aware that you chronically overwork for questionable emotional reasons, but you're not sure why it happens. And, if you look closely at yourself, you find that you have adopted some of the very same behavior patterns as these successful individuals.

- No matter how tired she is, every time Joyce sits down to relax, she quickly finds herself anxious and uncomfortable. These feelings prompt her to get up and get on with her work within minutes.
- John is given ample time off by his company, but he rarely takes it. He becomes so bored with free time anymore that he skips it and packs his schedule instead. He even brags that he doesn't need vacations.

- Ellen has her briefcase close by wherever she is. It's a standing joke with the family that she takes it everywhere, just like a security blanket. The irony is that she never opens it to do a lick of work!

- Dan has a one-track mind, work. These days, he associates primarily with known workaholics, both at the office and socially. Friends he used to enjoy now avoid him because he can't relax *or* converse about anything but work.

What do these very typical behaviors have in common? Examine them closely. First, you might observe that these individuals simply don't know how to relax anymore. You are entirely correct in this perception, but go a bit further. Pondering it a bit more, you might conclude that they can't relax because not one is able to completely separate from work. Each has devised a way to stay connected to work so complete relaxation is impossible. Again, your observations are astute and correct. But this isn't the whole story by a long shot. If you can't spot another powerful issue that impedes relaxation and produces stress, then read on because there is a critical gap in your awareness.

What is easily missed in examining these individuals is the driving force behind these telling behavior patterns. That powerful impetus to overwork is irrational guilt. Guilt for not always being productive. Guilt about relaxing. Guilt because everything isn't done. Guilt because the individual didn't do more. Guilt in the success-oriented man or woman is one of the deepest, but most neglected roots of stress overload. This kind of guilt is both subtle and powerful in its destructive motivational effects. Work-related guilt may slowly invade every aspect of your life. Nothing is immune: your marital relationship, your family life, your productivity at work, your parenting, your self-esteem, and certainly your ability to relax and enjoy life.

Without an understanding of the relationship between guilt and stress, it may be virtually impossible to practice Lifestyle Management and make it stick. Understanding this irrational guilt will also help you face it and resolve it once and for all. When you do, you will have removed a major barrier to becoming a happier person, a more loving spouse, a better parent, and an excited and productive professional once again. But first you've got to confront your guilt. Remember the bottom line: if you can't beat the guilt, you can't beat the stress. Here's how to start doing just that.

Dynamics of the Work-Leisure Bind

To illustrate how guilt blocks relaxation and drives you to work when you could be relaxing, here's a simple exercise. Sit down for one-half hour and do absolutely nothing. Alone. By yourself. No reading, TV, or newspaper. No conversation. Don't think about work. No dozing or sleeping. It's just "you on you" doing nothing productive at all. If the Work-Leisure Bind is present, within minutes you will begin to feel uncomfortable. In fact, several distressing emotions occur in sequence if you remain in non-productive idleness for even a short length of time.

IDLENESS EMOTION #1: VAGUE ANXIETY OR AGITATION. Within a very few minutes after stopping productive work, you feel the first twinges of discomfort. You become restless because you are not actively "working on something." As the minutes pass, these feelings rapidly grow into anxiety.

IDLENESS EMOTION #2: IRRATIONAL GUILT SETS IN. Initial discomfort rapidly turns into overt guilt for remaining "non-productive." It is triggered by your awareness that you have much to do, and you're not doing it. Therefore, you're not only irresponsible, but also bad. You should feel guilty!

IDLENESS EMOTION #3: YOU SLOWLY BECOME BORED AND DEPRESSED. With prolonged non-productivity, your guilt evolves into a depressive state accompanied by boredom because there is nothing "meaningful" (read *work*) to do with your time. Your leisure skills are very rusty; you can't enjoy free time that is legitimately yours.

If you recognize this sequence of emotional events that occurs every time you try to slow down and enjoy life, it's a sure signal that the sticky web of the Work-Leisure Bind has you in its grasp. It is unlikely, however, that you get to the level of bored depression very often. The reason is simple. You go back to work long before that occurs. The bored depression precipitated by the Work-Leisure Bind does occur when there are special circumstances that necessitate prolonged non-productivity. Common examples are a serious illness with a lengthy recuperation, retirement, or the questionable "long vacation" for the over-worked individual who has no leisure skills.

When the Work-Leisure Bind is driving you, you move into productive activity at the first inkling of guilt. The reason is part of the subtle psychology working to limit your health, happiness, and enjoyment of leisure. Here are some of the Emotional Realities that will help explain just how the Work-Leisure Bind operates. You've drifted into all of it with little awareness.

EMOTIONAL REALITY #1: YOU CAN FEEL GOOD ABOUT YOURSELF ONLY WHEN YOU ARE PRODUCING. Early in your career, you were struggling to establish yourself, but there was some time left over for you. As you advanced, productivity became the name of the game. With the years, your responsibilities at work and at home grew. You had more and more to get done each day. Time became a precious commodity that could not be wasted. Every time you slowed down, you began to feel irresponsible and guilty. You were okay only when you were working.

EMOTIONAL REALITY #2: YOU IMPLICITLY CHOOSE TO EXPERIENCE STRESS INSTEAD OF GUILT. With your many responsibilities, the more you persisted in "wasting time" at leisure, the stronger your guilt response became. There is little doubt that guilt is one of the most painful and despised of all the human emotions. You begin to avoid guilt at all costs . . . even at the price of experiencing all the symptoms of stress overload. It's an emotional given that most individuals will choose stress over guilt when there is a choice. You go back to work (and the stress associated with it) to avoid the guilt of leisure.

EMOTIONAL REALITY #3: YOUR GUILT AVOIDANCE RE-SPONSES QUICKLY BECOME AUTOMATIC. As the Work-Leisure Bind develops, two changes occur: your guilt responses are triggered more quickly each time you slow down, and your work response to it becomes an unthinking, subconscious habit. You don't think out what is happening. You just automatically respond by moving toward productive activities to allay the guilt. Interestingly, by the time the Work-Leisure Bind has progressed to this point, it is easier to justify going to sleep than to be "unproductive."

EMOTIONAL REALITY #4: YOU REMAIN ATTACHED TO WORK AT ALL TIMES TO AVOID THE BUILDUP OF GUILT. As guilt becomes more strongly associated with relaxation (there are no tangible "products" to justify the time spent in these activities), you have a choice: either stop such activities completely or seek a compromise. Some individuals stop; most find ways to remain connected to work while at leisure to keep guilt at bay. Carrying your briefcase everywhere, talking about work, wearing a beeper, calling the office, dictating in the car, and many other mechanisms all serve this purpose. Your leisure time dissipates, and what remains is mixed with work-related activities.

EMOTIONAL REALITY #5: YOUR ABILITY TO RELAX AND "GET AWAY FROM IT ALL" DISAPPEARS. Your Work-Leisure Bind has now blossomed into its full destructive maturity. You're driven to work all the time to avoid guilt, and your leisure time (what's left of it) is contaminated by your work connections. How do you spell relief under such circumstances? You don't! You're stressed at work and guilty at leisure. You've become tired, pessimistic, disappointed, and resentful. You're experiencing a stress overload and the symptoms of Personal Burnout are unmistakable. This isn't the way it was supposed to be after you paid your dues. Is this what life as a success really is? No! No! No! A thousand times, No!

Guilt and the Put-Off Pattern

Perhaps the most disappointing long-term effect of the Work-Leisure Bind is the notorious Put-Off Pattern. This easily recognized behavior pattern is signaled by a series of consistently used rationalizations that justify avoiding leisure activities, family involvements, and friendships *right now.* The excuses have a tired familiarity to those who hear them again and again. They all have in common this basic theme: "When I get . . . (you fill in the blank: my next raise, more job security, another promotion, enough money in the bank, etc.), then we'll be able to afford to relax and enjoy life. And we will! I'll slow down, and this family will really start to have some good times together. I just need a little more time."

Do these words sound familiar? They should. They are used by tens of thousands of hard-working men and women to convince themselves and their families that the time just isn't quite right yet to relax, take it easy, and enjoy life. Superficially, the excuses that are the core of the Put-Off Pattern sound reasonable. But there's a catch. These rationalizations are used in a never-ending series that goes on for years, often for decades. "Not right now, but soon" becomes the catchphrase of the individual caught in the trap of the Put-Off Pattern.

Typically, once the individual has reached previously-stated goals, there usually follows some attempt to slow down and develop a quality Life After Work. The problem is that it doesn't last.

Now that you understand the psychological underpinnings of the Work-Leisure Bind, can you figure out why? If you've guessed that taking more time for leisure (that is, "nonproductive" time) leads to a rapid buildup of anxiety, guilt, and even a tad of depression, you are right. When these distressing feelings reach a critical point for the individual, the excuses of the Put-Off Pattern click into play again. The same old promises to make time for family and leisure and friends once new goals are reached are repeated. The Put-Off Pattern continues.

When the Put-Off Pattern is present, the time never seems quite right to begin enjoying life. It's not that you don't want to slow down a bit, but rather you can't because the powerful ir-rational guilt of the Work-Leisure Bind won't permit it. You really don't have much choice in the matter until you decide to face that guilt and resolve it. In the meantime, you deny yourself a priceless gift that can never be recovered: the present. Days become weeks. Weeks become months. The months become years, then decades. At worst, you give up a lifetime of personal fulfillment and pleasant memories. Far too frequently, there is a very sad ending.

THE SADDEST SCENARIO. Day after day, The Retiree sits depressed and dejected in a paid-for home with an entirely ade-quate pension. For the forty years of a very productive career, good times were put off and saved for retirement "when there would be enough time." Now there is nothing. The disappointment is bitter and deep. Few friendships have been nurtured over the years. All along, leisure interests were neglected in lieu of more work and greater success. The children are grown and gone: there wasn't much time for them either. Now they don't have much time for The Retiree. The Retiree is at loose ends all the time, and the marital relationship is strained. After a lifetime of putting off good times for later, The Retiree feels cheated and rightly so. Looking back at a lifetime of over-work and skewed priorities, success has come — but there weren't many good times along the way. Not much to look forward to, either.

THE MORAL OF THE STORY. You can't save up good times for the future like you save money in the bank. On the contrary, the only way you can guarantee the interest on your leisure-time investment is to spend some of it every day. Because of your commitment to balancing success and achievements with leisure activities, family life, and friendships now, you will build lasting power in your career. And, you will be setting the stage for the richest and most fulfilling retirement possible because you will be practicing every day!

First Strategy: Facing the Guilt

Make no mistake about it. This kind of irrational guilt is hard to resolve and eliminate. You know now that it's not healthy guilt. You also realize how it has indirectly influenced and shaped your behavior so that you are suffering at work *and* at home. You don't feel as good as you used to about your chosen career. Your Life After Work isn't much fun anymore because you can't completely relax and rejuvenate. As you contemplate change, you intuitively suspect that dealing with this powerful irrational guilt that has built up over the years will be not only difficult, but emotionally painful. You are right on both counts, *but it can be done.* Your commitment to yourself and to a more balanced lifestyle will be sorely tested in the process.

THE BOTTOM LINE: THE BASIC STRATEGY FOR RESOLV-ING THE WORK-LEISURE BIND REQUIRES THREE NECESSARY STEPS: DECIDING YOU DESERVE MORE, REVERSING THE CHOICE, AND FACING THE GUILT.

It sounds relatively easy, doesn't it? It's not or you would have done it years ago. To accomplish each one of these steps requires self-examination, a deep commitment to change in your priorities, and the intestinal fortitude to stick with them despite initial emotional discomfort. Let's take a moment to examine in more detail each of these not-so-easy changes you must make.

RESOLUTION STEP #1: DECIDING THAT YOU DESERVE MORE. "Why am I doing this to myself?" is the first issue you must face directly. Feeling guilty and irresponsible every time you slow down to relax and enjoy yourself is nothing but a personal put-down. Regardless of your lip service, your behavior says that you deserve little or nothing for yourself. To resolve the Work-Leisure Bind, you must place a high priority on your health and emotional well-being in a very self-centered (but not necessarily selfish) way. You must decide that you deserve more than you are giving to yourself these days. You must also give up the fantasy that con-tentment will somehow magically appear in the vague future if you just persevere. The fact is that you work hard every day, and you deserve more *right now.* Only *you* can give it to you. You are successful, and you've paid your dues. Now decide to accept your success, to relax, and to enjoy yourself.

RESOLUTION STEP #2: REVERSING THE CHOICE. Your unthinking choice to automatically return to work when you sense the first tiny bit of discomfort must be reversed. The strategy for accomplishing this is clearcut. You must take time regularly for relaxation and leisure activities. Force yourself, if necessary, because it won't be easy. You will have to take this time for yourself from a busy schedule. By so doing, however, you will be putting into practice your decision to give yourself more because you count. At the same time, you will be reversing the unthinking choice you've been making as you allowed the Work-Leisure Bind to control your life and diminish it. You will consciously decide what *you* want to do because you're important, too. By reversing the choice consistently, you are taking a major step in asserting control of your life once again.

RESOLUTION STEP #3: FACING THE GUILT. When you begin consistently to reverse the choice, you will not be comfortable at all. By so doing, however, you will lure your subtle adversary, guilt, out into the open. The message of your guilt is that you've got work to do — and you're not doing it. Therefore, you're irresponsible and a bad person. Horsefeathers! You will always have work to do, and you will never get caught up. As you spend more time doing things you enjoy, you will confront this irrational guilt head-on. Why shouldn't you, at this point in your life, have the freedom to enjoy some of the things that you like? As you continue reversing the choice and talking directly to that guilt of yours, you will find that it begins to lose its power. Psychologically, this is an indication that your self-esteem is rising. You will once again enjoy leisure activities as the power of the Work-Leisure Bind is broken.

More Helpful Hints

Now you understand why you can't beat the stress if you can't beat the guilt, and you've begun to change your behavior in ways that will do just that. There are also other specific strategies helpful in reinforcing the changes that are already occurring in your lifestyle. Here are some Helpful Hints to aid your progress in resolving the Work-Leisure Bind permanently. For best results, make one or two small changes and then practice them until they are well-established in your lifestyle. Then make one or two more and repeat the process.

HELPFUL HINT#1: START TO MAKE CHANGES WHERE YOU HAVE MOST CONTROL. It doesn't make sense to start learning anything new at the most difficult level. Rather, you begin where your chances of success are greatest. The fact is that your workplace is filled with many stress-producing "givens" that aren't going to change — ever. You have little control over them. However, you personally own your free time away from work. You have maximum control in your Life After Work, and that's where your chances of successfully resolving the Work-Leisure Bind are greatest. Besides, practicing leisure skills at work is probably quite inappropriate. With a modicum of regular healthy leisure integrated into your Life After Work, you will find that much of the stress and frustration generated each day at work is easily diffused. There will be pleasant diversions to look forward to enjoying. And, because of them, you can return to work refreshed and ready for challenge because you have spent quality time "getting away from it all" in satisfying leisure activities.

HELPFUL HINT #2: MAKE YOUR BREAK FROM WORK VERY CLEAN. Over the last several years, the quantity of your leisure time has progressively diminished. What little is left has been contaminated by work-related activities or by other psychological connections to work. The not-surprising result is that boundaries between work and Life After Work have virtually disappeared. A clearly-needed change is firm and reasonable physical boundaries for work. Decreasing the time you spend at the office to realistic levels will be necessary. Then tackle setting the more difficult psychological boundaries by giving up all those "work connections" that don't permit you to completely get away from it all. At home, put your briefcase in the closet. Don't carry a beeper. Discourage the office from calling you, and don't call them. Don't talk about work. Do take all the vacation and compensatory time due you. Although uncomfortable at first, you will soon feel the positive effects of these changes.

HELPFUL HINT #3: MUTUALLY REINFORCE QUALITY TIME SPENT TOGETHER. Frequently, individuals making a commitment to Lifestyle Management start off strong — but it doesn't last. Their resolve is quickly undone by the never-ending pressures of work, home, children, and everything else that must be done. A major asset is creating support for positive lifestyle changes. Too often, spouses reinforce maladaptive behaviors in one another through constant reminders that there is work to be done that isn't finished. The message is: "We can relax together only after everything else is done. We get what's left over." Lots of luck. Make spending quality time together a consistent priority in your overall Lifestyle Management strategy. Begin to reinforce in one another the value of this time together for personal health and as a way to rebuild some of the closeness you've both lost over the years. And, the work that really needs to get done will get done!

HELPFUL HINT #4: LEARN TO RELAX IN YOUR HOME. It's a given that over-stressed individuals spend long hours at work. Less obvious is that home activities have narrowed to: chronically and indiscriminately watching television, napping or sleeping during time off, or dejectedly doing household chores or home maintenance tasks. The net effect is predictable. Your home is not an enjoyable refuge where you can retreat to relax and enjoy yourself. Instead, it has become a secondary work environment with stress-inducing qualities of its own. If you learn to enjoy your home, you won't have to leave town to relax (as many individuals must). After eliminating napping and television, your options for relearning to enjoy your home are many. Here are just a few suggestions: enjoy leisurely early morning coffee on the patio, sit on the porch to watch the sun go down, begin a before dinner conversation time, invite friends in to casually share fun games.

HELPFUL HINT #5: TAKE TIME OFF IN SMALL BLOCKS IN THE BEGINNING. One easy habit that develops in very busy people is to work evenings and weekends and then save yearly vacations to spend in one long block of time away. This often backfires because you have no practice in using leisure time to best advantage. You may be plagued during such extended time away by anxiety, guilt, boredom, and even depression. You also spend large amounts of time with your family with no practice, and often this causes conflict and stress for everyone involved. You feel let down and disappointed. Long vacations are worth it, but you must prepare for them by increasing your tolerance for enjoying free time away and spending quality time with your family. To do this, consistently start taking small blocks of time off. Day trips on the weekends. An overnighter here and there. Work up to three-day weekends or longer periods. Then you'll really enjoy your next super "getaway" vacation.

HELPFUL HINT #6: START TO FILL THE "LEISURE VOID." As you resolve the Work-Leisure Bind, you have more leisure time, but perhaps little to do with it. This is the "leisure void" that stems from neglecting your relaxation skills for years. You've given up many of the leisure interests you once enjoyed because you became too busy. A vicious cycle started. As you spent less time enjoying personal interests, you emotionally disconnected from them. Now, when you do occasionally have time for these activities, you don't really enjoy yourself as much as you'd like. You go back to work (or sleep or watch TV) by default. The cycle gets worse, and the Work-Leisure Bind has won again. Be persistent in getting back to old leisure interests or finding new ones. In the beginning you may feel that you're just going through the motions. As time passes, you will begin to let go again and really enjoy your leisure diversions. It will take time. Keep going until it happens.

HELPFUL HINT #7: STAY FAR AWAY FROM WORK-AHOLICS. It is well-known that workaholics gravitate to one another and mutually reinforce stressful overwork, intense competitiveness, and avoidance of true leisure. Workaholics also trigger these destructive behaviors in others who are susceptible by making them feel guilty for not keeping up or doing more. One healthy change to put into action immediately is to stay as far away as you can from these "subversive" workaholics. While you may not be able to completely eliminate contact with them at work, you can certainly stop socializing with them or spending your valuable leisure time in their company. Move in the direction of developing new relationships with individuals who are more "laid back" and who have established quality in their Life After Work. You will soon find that their healthy perspective on life and living will rub off. Then you'll continue to maintain a respectable distance from the workaholics who haven't developed the mature values you've adopted.

From Bind to Balance

Have you heard about the workaholic who bragged: "I work just half a day every day. I don't care if it's the first twelve hours or the second twelve hours. I just put in my half day every day." You chuckle. Then you look at how you've been living, and you see the sad truth. You have developed a strong need to be "productive" at all times. Guilt is the "big stick" that drives you back to work each time you start to slow down and do something pleasurable for yourself. Now you understand only too well the powerful dynamics of the Work-Leisure Bind. Your determination to move toward Lifestyle Balance has been strengthened. You know that you deserve more, and now you know how to get it.

As you look back on your life, you realize just how much being "productive" has been emphasized all along the way. And, that's not particularly bad. In a positive vein, your ability to produce has been a major factor in your success to date. On the downside, blind reinforcement for always being productive has probably been overdone. Let's look at your development in broad perspective.

• Your PARENTS modeled and emphasized working hard and diligently because they knew that's the only way to get ahead and be successful.

• Your TEACHERS warned you not to waste time when you were supposed to be working and demanded that you do homework in the evenings and on weekends.

• In your SPIRITUAL TRAINING, the virtue of hard work as the avenue to a personally rich and fulfilled life was a major theme.

• The ORGANIZATIONS that have employed you have given you many responsibilities and expect you to consistently meet them regardless of the time it takes.

• All along the way, you've had to compete with PEERS by working just a bit harder and being more productive so you could advance in your career.

Now ask yourself a question. How many of these people or institutions placed high value on time spent away from work? Time spent in leisure activities. Time spent with good friends. Time spent developing strong family life. Time spent just enjoying yourself, but not doing anything particularly productive. There was probably a bit of lip service here and there for such activities, but not much actual modeling. The over-riding emphasis was on working hard, being productive, and thereby becoming successful. During the course of your development within such heavily work-biased environments, the legitimacy of leisure time wasn't reinforced. The stage was set for the Work-Leisure Bind to spread its tentacles to adversely affect every part of your life as you became busier.

These days, much of your work is cognitive and done "in your head." Because of this, it's not as easy to "get away from it all" as it once was. It's just not as simple as walking away from the office. Yet, to maintain health and happiness, it is necessary to clearly separate work from a quality Life After Work. You now realize that pleasant leisure diversions enjoyed regularly are *not* a bonus for hard work well done. Rather, such activities are necessary to your long-term emotional survival and as such must be highly valued and preserved at all costs. With new perspective, you realize the validity of the old saying (slightly paraphrased): "All work and no play make Jack and Jill dull kids!" Unhappy, unfulfilled, and unhealthy, too. You know because you've been there.

Chapter 5

Shifting into Enjoyment: Lose Your Mind, Come to Your Senses!

The signs that you need to strengthen your ability to relax and "get away from it all" are not difficult to spot. You're successful, but you're also disappointed. It seems that there should be more fun in your life now that you've made it. The days have become consistently hectic, but humdrum. You're tired more than you should be at your age, and it takes just too much energy to get out and do things just for you. In fact, everything that you do do is functional and responsible. There's always a mountain of work standing before you, and it's hard to justify taking time off. Your life is more complicated than you would have believed ten years ago. "Is this all there is?" you ask.

You have learned very well all the skills necessary for success. You analyze, anticipate, compete, work toward future goals, perform up to expectations, and remain professionally objective in your work relationships. You have a good education and a strong internalized Success Ethic. In fact, you have all the Ingredients of Success. What is now becoming all too apparent to you is that you're trapped in a success-oriented way of relating, and you've carried it far beyond the boundaries of your work. Now you relate in a success-oriented way to your spouse and children, to leisure activities, in casual conversations with friends, even when you are making love. A vital part of you has been missing for some time. It's been buried beneath your "successful" exterior.

From time to time, you sit back and nostalgically remember how things used to be during the days of young adulthood. With a sad little smile, you recall how you . . .

• often took off at the drop of a hat for a movie or an outing with the gang;

- how you felt so good when friends dropped by, and you knew they would never be too busy to enjoy your company when you went to see them;
- were so expressive and spontaneous in your zest for living that everyone around you got caught up in it;
- were so close to a few Special People in your life and how you could talk for hours about anything and everything;
- enjoyed just sitting back and watching the clouds slip by or ducks swimming in a pond or the hustle-bustle of a busy street;
- worked hard, but you also made time for pleasant leisure activities because that was a priority.

Ah, those were the good old days full of dreams and schemes and the nature of things. But they're gone forever, aren't they? Not necessarily at all! In those days you felt really alive and the world was good. Although times have changed and you have changed, what really matters is that you have lost a vital something along your road to success that can be recovered. That something is Lifestyle Balance. It is your ability to creatively balance work with a quality Life After Work. Locked as you are into a success-oriented way of relating, you've lost some of your inner vitality, the ability to fully enjoy leisure and family and friends. Your first step in putting your over-learned success-orientation into perspective is to understand another mode of experience that will permit you to regularly "shift into enjoyment" once again.

The Nature of Natural Experiences

Put simply, Natural Experiences are spontaneous, creative, and very sensory-oriented experiences that are valued solely for themselves. You easily lose yourself in the pleasant process of whatever is happening. There are no goals, no products, and no success-failure ego-involvements in Natural Experiences. At one time, you related very well in this way. In fact, during your early childhood years, that's all you did from morning to night. That is, you did until the long period of parental and academic instruction on how to become responsible and successful began. From that moment, your capacity for Natural Experiences began to wane, being replaced by learning all the skills necessary for success. Striving to be successful was heavily reinforced and socially rewarded. Natural Experiences were not!

Ironically, you've come full circle. Now that you're successful, you are beginning to realize how necessary Natural Experiences are to make your success at work worthwhile. However, there's a snag. Natural Experiences are much more easily understood than put into practice. For Natural Experiences to occur, you must give up psychological control to "let it happen." When you are Naturally Experiencing, you are pleasantly and subjectively immersed in the experience and not attempting to control it. By contrast, your Success Ethic mandates that you focus and direct the experience so you can create a positive outcome to satisfy your strong ego needs to see yourself as a successful person.

Your success orientation and Natural Experiences represent two philosophies of experience that lie in direct opposition to one another. Here are spelled out some of the defining characteristics of Natural Experiences that will help you to distinguish them from your many success-oriented endeavors.

NATURAL CHARACTERISTIC #1: YOU ARE FLOWING IN THE EXPERIENCE. You've heard of "going with the flow." It's sound lay wisdom that advises you to move easily with the experience, not against it. As you become deeply and subjectively part of an experience, you begin to flow with it. It carries you, and you respond without either intellectual censorship or the need to control what is going on.

NATURAL CHARACTERISTIC #2: YOU ARE OPENLY AND EXPRESSIVELY YOU. In other words, when you are Naturally Experiencing, you have no image to protect, you don't hide behind facades, and you have no roles to play. You are comfortable in the experience and you relate in an easy, open, nondefensive way that reflects a deeper and more real you. And, it's almost effortless to do so.

NATURAL CHARACTERISTIC #3: YOU TRANSCEND TIME CONSCIOUSNESS. Part of being responsible is being aware of time and adhering to scheduled commitments. In a Natural Experience, you are so pleasantly and subjectively involved in whatever is going on that time is irrelevant. You are lost in the flow of the experience, and time doesn't really matter. After the fact, time seems to have passed very quickly.

NATURAL CHARACTERISTIC #4: YOU EXPERIENCE A DEEP CONTENTMENT. During a Natural Experience, you are free from worry, distractions, and the heavy burden of your many responsibilities. You are responding with a present-oriented subjective freedom that is experienced as an inner contentment. The reason is that Natural Experiences truly let you "get away from it all," if only for short periods.

NATURAL CHARACTERISTIC #5: YOU EMERGE EMO-TIONALLY REFRESHED AND STIMULATED. Natural Experiences are inherently energizing. In such activities, you may have expended considerable physical effort, but you have recovered emotional energy. You have freed yourself from constant mental "work" and, by so doing, dissipated some of the emotional fatigue that has built up from the daily grind of your work. You feel more refreshed, stimulated, and optimistic.

If you haven't been enjoying life lately, perhaps one major cause is that you've lost the ability to regularly shift into satisfying and rejuvenating Natural Experiences. Natural Experiences are valuable because they are true emotional breaks in your heavy load of responsibilities and the constant mental work that you do each day. When you lose the capacity for Natural Experiences (and it is so easy), you also lose the ability to relax deeply. And, when you lose the ability to relax deeply, the distressing signs of stress overload emerge, and the symptoms of Personal Burnout begin to exert their destructive influence on your health and happiness.

For contrast, here are summarized some of the major differences between Natural Experiences and a success-oriented mode of response.

NATURAL EXPERIENCES	SUCCESS-ORIENTATION
"Letting it happen"	"Making it happen"
process-oriented	product-oriented
sensory-based	intellectually-based
surrender to experience	direct the experience
subjective immersion	objective perspective
full participant	rational observer
ego needs absent	success required

Losing Richness in Pursuit of Riches

If you can't turn off your success-oriented "make it happen" way of relating, you are missing some of life's richest and most satisfying experiences. There are a number of human responses that operate solely on the "let it happen" philosophy of Natural Experiences. When you attempt to impose a success-orientation on any one of them, the Natural Experience is seriously compromised and often completely negated. In other words, the more you try to make Natural Experiences happen, the more you short-circuit the process and wind up frustrated.

If you have consistent difficulty "getting away from it all" and feel unnecessarily burdened by your responsibilities these days, you may have fallen into an easy trap. Because of the heavy emphasis placed on the "make it happen" orientation of success, you may be inadvertently using that philosophy on responses that require the "let it happen" posture of Natural Experience. Here are ten human responses that operate primarily on the "let it happen" way of relating. Make sure that you are not trying too hard to be successful in any one of them!

NATURAL EXPERIENCE #1: GOING TO SLEEP. Have you ever gone to bed and tried *so* hard to get to sleep? Trying hard to make sleep happen reflects the success-orientation and is an excellent prescription for insomnia. The more you focus on and direct your energy into going to sleep, the more you stay awake. The problem is that you are using the success-orientation in a response area where the "let it happen" philosophy of Natural Experiences is appropriate. The fact is that you can't *make* sleep happen because you are not in rational control of going to sleep. When you relax yourself and stop trying, sleep will come. You also easily teach your children these same counter-productive habits by constantly demanding that they go to sleep "right now" with accusations that they are "not trying." You are setting the stage for *their* later insomnia!

NATURAL EXPERIENCE #2: PERSONAL SPONTANEITY. Way back when, you were much more open and expressive in how you related. You laughed. You kidded around. You reached out to others in positive ways and drew them to you through your pleasant demeanor. At that time, you were comfortable enough to let others see that fun-loving expressive side of yourself. Now you're more careful, more "professional" if you will. Your Success Ethic demands personal control, and as a result you've lost personal spontaneity. The real issue is that you've become afraid of you. In your career, you have an image to protect. Uncensored remarks may cost you dearly. On the other hand, everyone loses because a warm and lively part of you has been buried under the need to "control yourself" at leisure, with your family, and with friends.

NATURAL EXPERIENCE #3: "LET'S DO IT" IMPUL-SIVITY. In the good old days of your youth, you acted on your impulses much more than you do now. On a moment's notice you took off for the beach . . . for a long walk . . . to visit friends . . . to see another city. As you became more successful, though, your responsibilities at work and at home mounted. Your delightful impulsivity dimmed. Everything had to be planned in advance. Your life slowly filled with routines and you became less comfortable with unstructured time and disruptions of your personal schedule. After all, efficient use of time is an important part of being successful. On the other hand, perhaps you've gone too far. Perhaps it's time to begin following those "get away" impulses once again, and you can do that without being irresponsible. It will give you a refreshing sense of freedom that you haven't felt for a long while.

NATURAL EXPERIENCE #4: SENSORY APPRECIATION.
Here's a pertinent question to ask yourself: "Do I stop to smell the roses — or do I stop to analyze the fragrance?" Each one of your senses has great potential to give you pleasure. However, as you become progressively locked into a success-oriented way of relating, sensory enjoyment begins to diminish. You substitute cognitive analysis for satisfying sensory experiences. No matter what the source, sensory stimulation is perceived merely as information to be processed. The end result is that you don't even see, much less enjoy, the beauty that surrounds you each day. You're too busy conceptualizing and thinking out the implications of the sensory information you've received. Experiencing and appreciating your senses is a Natural Experience. Why not take your senses to heart instead of to mind?

NATURAL EXPERIENCE #5: EMOTIONAL AWARENESS.
When how you relate becomes dominated by a success-orientation, a curious truncation of your feelings takes place. All of your negative feelings remain and gradually grow in strength. You constantly experience anger, nagging frustration, guilt, anxiety, depression, and a deepening cynicism. Simultaneously, those positive feelings you once enjoyed unobtrusively slip away. You don't have that feeling anymore that it's just great to be alive. That you've got the world by the tail. Moments of happiness and deep contentment. The joy in your life has disappeared. A good day is one when you don't feel quite as down as you did yesterday. Your cognitively dominated success-orientation acts as a lid to seal off positive feelings that you once enjoyed. Shifting into Natural

Experiences frees these wonderful feelings to become part of your life once again.

NATURAL EXPERIENCE #6: CREATIVE EXPRESSION. Every individual has an innate capacity for creativity. Some have more than others, but every person has some. In a young child, creativity is expressed in many and varied ways. However, with training to become successful, heavy emphasis is placed on convergent thinking. That is, to use logical processes to organize information and solve problems in such a way that everyone gets to the same end point the same way. Divergent thought processes, the ability to see and express things differently and the essence of creativity, are neglected or, worse, penalized. One result is that creative innovation and expression become buried beneath dull routines and the necessity for rational order that is part of being successful. When you lose awareness of your inner creativity, you lose one of the most personally satisfying Natural Experiences of all.

NATURAL EXPERIENCE #7: INTUITION. Intuition is knowing without the benefit of rational thought or the necessity for objective confirming information. Intuition is that little feeling you get now and then about something. It's your hunches. It's that sixth sense about people or events that you can't back up or justify. The reason is that intuitive knowledge rises from subconscious processes that are well beyond conscious control. The success-oriented man or woman often learns to distrust this kind of awareness *because* it is so subjective and unjustifiable. With time and neglect, intuition fades and the individual loses a valuable source of knowledge and a tool that can deepen self-awareness and interpersonal understanding. Needless to say, all children are naturally intuitive. They "know" without benefit of logic. You can again nurture this inner wellspring of knowledge to help you understand some of the more subtle dimensions of your world through Natural Experiences.

NATURAL EXPERIENCE #8: INTERPERSONAL INTI-MACY. Healthy emotional intimacy is an openness between two individuals who care about and deeply accept one another. Part of intimacy is expressing your feelings good and bad, revealing your fears and vulnerabilities, and learning to accept parts of yourself and your partner that aren't the most desirable. However, with success a distance develops where there used to be closeness.

Quality time spent together declines. It becomes harder to "really talk" to one another. Expressions of caring and non-sexual physical touching decrease. Two people live under the same roof, but don't emotionally share in positive ways anymore. You don't listen much and when you do, you give advice instead of empathic understanding. Intimacy is a Natural Experience that requires self-trust, and the price tag for success in terms of its toll on intimacy can be very high indeed.

NATURAL EXPERIENCE #9: MAKING LOVE TOGETHER. Having sex is easy, but making love is a flowing Natural Experience that you both "let happen" between you. It is not a one-sided, task-oriented achievement with specific goals and a success-failure ego involvement that concerns you. It is all too easy for your strong success-orientation to intrude even into your bedroom. When it does, you may be having good "technical sex," but you are probably not making love together anymore because you are trying to "make it happen" to meet your needs to be successful. Further, too much of your success-orientation may actually decrease your libido (sexual energy) over time and increase the possibility that an overt sexual dysfunction will develop. Giving up goals and your need for a successful outcome opens the way for the beauty and the deep mutual affirmation that only truly making love can bring to you both.

NATURAL EXPERIENCE #10: AWARENESS OF DEEPER MEANINGS. With the many responsibilities of success, life becomes very complicated because there is so much that needs to be done. The danger is that over time your attention becomes focused exclusively on strategies to get everything done today and how to prepare for tomorrow. As you succumb to this orientation to living, what is deeply important to you is overshadowed by daily details. Gradually you lose perspective on some of the most important and personally meaningful parts of living: doing things with your children, seeing friends, experiencing the beauty around you each day, enjoying life's small pleasures. Natural Experiences help you slow down and stay in touch with a deeper part of yourself and more meaningful priorities in your life. Too many successful men and women regain this perspective in a hospital bed recovering from stress-related diseases. For the first time in years they have been forced to slow down long enough to think out what is really important to them.

Healthy Lifestyle Balance

Take a look again at the ten kinds of Natural Experiences that must be preserved for healthy living and personal fulfillment. If you are successful, but have gradually lost the capacity for enjoying these kinds of experiences, it's no wonder that you're feeling far from your best these days and wondering if it's all worthwhile. You're stuck in a success-oriented way of relating that has diminished the quality of your life in general and the quality of your Life After Work in particular. THE HEALTHY INDIVIDUAL MAINTAINS THE CRUCIAL ABILITY TO EASILY AND REGULARLY SHIFT BACK AND FORTH BETWEEN THE ACHIEVEMENT-ORIENTED FUNCTIONING CHARACTERISTIC OF THE SUCCESS ETHIC AND THE RELAXED AND PLEASURABLE RELATING OF NATURAL EXPERIENCES.

As you move in the direction of healthy Lifestyle Balance, new skills will be required to make the shifts between these two modes of experience. Here are several points to keep in mind as you rebuild your ability to shift into Natural Experiences regularly and create once again that personally satisfying balance between work and Life After Work you used to enjoy.

POINT #1: YOUR SUCCESS-ORIENTED SKILLS ARE FUNCTIONAL AND VALUABLE. In Lifestyle Management, it is not hypocritical at all to further develop and refine all of your success-oriented skills. These skills are important to you, and with them you will become more competent, mature, and wiser in your chosen work. Maintaining the skills that have brought you success and the standard of living you enjoy today is crucial in your career and to your future satisfaction.

POINT #2: MAINTAINING HEALTHY LIFESTYLE BALANCE IS LIKE DIETING. The essence of sound dieting is to recognize that since you must eat well to stay healthy, you must eliminate bad eating habits. You must also eat in moderation. The same principle holds for learning to put your work into healthy perspective and for eliminating the personally destructive habits that have crept into your work over the years. Regular, healthy doses of Natural Experiences are a moderating must.

POINT #3: THE PROBLEM IS SHIFTING TO NATURAL EXPERIENCES. The major skill deficit found in highly success-oriented individuals is inability to shift into Natural Experiences, not the reverse. Shifting back to "work" from Natural Experiences is usually not a problem. In fact, it happens all too easily and prematurely. Transition skills to permit shifting to Natural Experiences more easily must be strengthened, as must tolerance for such experiences.

POINT #4: THE NECESSARY SHIFT IS PSYCHOLOGICAL IN NATURE. Maintaining Lifestyle Balance requires regular shifting between a success-oriented way of relating and Natural Experiences. It is not where your body is or what you are doing that is important. Natural Experiences require a psychological shift in the way you *relate* to a particular activity. It is entirely possible to "work" at leisure or to Naturally Experience at work!

POINT #5: YOU NEVER LOSE THE CAPACITY FOR NATURAL EXPERIENCES. The capacity for Natural Experiences is never lost although the ability to psychologically shift into them can easily be buried beneath a heavy cognitive layer of success-oriented functioning. You never have to learn how to Naturally Experience per se because this is an innate part of you. All you must do is to learn to turn off success-oriented functioning, and your Natural Experiences will gradually return.

Chemical Cop-Outs

Over the years, volumes have been written about the nature of alcoholism and the reasons for drug abuse. It's easy to label drug abusers as weak individuals who are unable to handle pressure, as individuals who don't cope well with life's problems, or as individuals who just don't care. What about very motivated and successful individuals, though? These individuals have worked hard to "make it"; they do care, and they have many personal and professional strengths. The easy labels don't fit well, if at all, for this sizable group. Yet, many of these highly educated and talented individuals do develop drug problems. There must be another motivating influence toward drug abuse in this select group that superficially seems to have everything going for them.

Typically, success-oriented individuals are highly responsible, over-worked, and under constant pressure to perform (much of it self-imposed). As you must suspect by now, many of these individuals have lost the psychological skills necessary to shift out of their success-oriented way of relating into Natural Experiences. The result is that they become trapped in this energy-consuming way of relating with no relief, no ability to "get away from it all."

As the capacity to make the PSYCHOLOGICAL shift into Natural Experiences is lost, many such individuals learn that they can make this critical transition CHEMICALLY. In fact, a CHEMICAL transition may literally become the only way such individuals can "let go" at all. But CHEMICAL transitions carry a subtle danger. Without doubt, CHEMICALS do work to help make the shift to Natural Experiences, at least initially. Alcohol, marijuana, cocaine, and many tranquilizing drugs are used (and abused) for this purpose by highly responsible people. Soon, however, a dependency on drugs to make these shifts grows. As it does, an overt drug problem emerges that quickly overshadows its original purpose in its destructive influence on personal health and happiness, family life, and ultimately, on career aspirations.

To put it bluntly, drugs used to make CHEMICAL transitions to Natural Experiences grow before you realize it into major dependencies that further deteriorate the quality of your Life After Work. It is a far better strategy to relearn the skills necessary to make PSYCHOLOGICAL shifts into Natural Experiences before all the negative consequences of a drug abuse problem develop. That's what Lifestyle Management is all about. Your ability to make PSYCHOLOGICAL transitions to enjoy Natural Experiences is undoubtedly one of the most critical skills you need to enjoy life and also to insure career longevity.

There are a number of danger signs that signal use of drugs to make CHEMICAL transitions. All of these signs have in common the use of a drug IN ANTICIPATION OF A DESIRED NATURAL EXPERIENCE. The drug is used to prepare for it. Examine yourself closely in this respect. Here are some signals to look for:

• You habitually have a drink or two before the party just to get in the mood.

• You make a daily stop after work to down a couple at a "happy hour" to unwind before going home or you have your own "happy hour" once you get there!

• You find that you must take something at bedtime to help you get to sleep.

• You use drugs before sex so that you can really relax and enjoy this kind of sensory experience.

• Drugs have become part of all your recreational activities to help you become more spontaneous and to have fun.

● The only time that you really feel things deeply is when you are under the influence of a drug.

● You tend to talk more and express your feelings only when you are high or "stoned."

Training Yourself to "Let Go"
Preliminary Exercises

Psychologically "letting go" of your success-orientation to enjoy Natural Experiences is easier said than done. To rebuild the necessary skills requires practice. It will also require time for which you have no tangible products to show, only your health and the satisfaction of enjoying life again. Interestingly, you will recognize that you have been pleasantly involved in a Natural Experience more easily after it's over because during the easy flow of a Natural Experience you're so deeply and subjectively involved in whatever you are doing. Here are some preliminary Practical Exercises designed to help you learn to "let go" once again. Keep firmly in mind the cardinal rule of Natural Experience: let it happen. Relax and be you. Don't try at all!

PRACTICAL EXERCISE #1: ACTIVITY IMMERSION. You're so busy these days that you've learned how to do two or three things at once. You also shift to what you've got to do next before you're done with what you're doing now. Begin to develop the positive habit of totally involving yourself in just one activity at a time. You can't fully "let go" into two or three activities, but you can into one!

PRACTICAL EXERCISE #2: SENSORY IMMERSION. Another helpful way to relearn to "let go" is to frequently turn your attention to your senses and to enjoy the stimulation that you receive from them. Practice your ability to stop analytical thoughts. Instead, experience sights, sounds, tastes, smells, and tactile sensations. As you learn to savor them, you increase your tolerance for suspending cognitive analysis.

PRACTICAL EXERCISE #3: TIME IMMERSION. To succeed, you structure your time according to a tight schedule. By so doing, you have also destroyed your ability to shift into Natural Experiences because you remain ever time conscious. It is helpful to learn to enjoy completely unstructured time again. Take a block of time (an evening a week, a day, a weekend), to get out of the house and do whatever strikes you moment by moment as you follow impulses, not a plan.

PRACTICAL EXERCISE #4: RHYTHM IMMERSION. Most individuals experience a powerful response to rhythms. Learn to "let go" by immersing yourself in rhythms. Let the rhythms carry you and flow with them with no attempt to control the experience. Jazzercise, aerobic exercise, the rhythm of dancing or jogging, fast walking, or even sexual rhythms all are helpful in this respect. Remember, no performances. Just surrender to the rhythmic flow.

PRACTICAL EXERCISE #5: PEOPLE IMMERSION. With success, you may have drifted away from enjoying people. To help you shift into Natural Experiences again, take regular time to spend with people for no purpose whatsoever other than enjoying them. Take the initiative to seek out people you care about. You'll feel less isolated as you reconnect with Special People, and those same people will soon be enjoying you once again, too!

Freeing the Prisoner of Success

As you have come to understand the differences between your heavily reinforced success-oriented way of relating and Natural Experiences, don't overlook one significant fact. There is nothing esoteric about Natural Experiences. Natural Experiences involve just being yourself fully and deeply and enjoying experiences for their inherent fulfillment. You have been taught for decades to use your head to get ahead. You analyze constantly. You anticipate and plan ahead. You compete to win. You're objective and professional in all that you do. You evaluate everything. As you have learned these skills, you have gradually lost your ability to "let go" to shift into the enjoyment of Natural Experiences. You have become a prisoner of success, and you suffer accordingly.

It is ironic that for many successful individuals, Natural Experiences are not only neglected, but subconsciously become emotionally threatening. Natural responses are viewed with apprehension because they represent loss of cognitive control. That's frightening to an individual who has strong needs to direct and control personal experience. "Letting go" to feel, to sense, to express emotions, to be impulsive and spontaneous, to "let" an orgasm or climax occur, even to go to sleep creates enough anxiety about loss of control to block the experience. It is a further irony that these same successful individuals who have learned so well to maintain personal control have actually lost control. They can no longer choose to "let go" and live a little. They remain prisoners of success.

As you look around and acknowledge what you've accomplished so far in life, there's little doubt that you're successful at being successful. The problem is that it doesn't feel as good as you thought it would. You simply aren't enjoying life enough to make it all seem worthwhile. While you've been so busy succeeding, at a personal level you've been involved in "wreck creation" and that's about how you feel. What is needed is energy turned in the direction of "recreating" your ability to shift into Natural Experiences so that you can enjoy a quality Life After Work again. Only then will you be able to gain the deep satisfaction of time spent in regular "recreation." The key to your freedom from the detrimental effects of success lies completely within you.

Chapter 6

The Lessons of Leisure: Learning to Relax and Live!

Relaxing. Taking it easy. Becoming more laid back. Living the good life. You dream about it all the time and it sounds so simple. You just go to the beach, the pier, the golf course, or the woods. You haven't done it much lately, though. You've been just too busy. You know that you need to relax more. You see the signs. But, somehow, something else always seems to get in the way.

If you step back and look at your behavior (behavior reveals the truth, you know), relaxing and living the good life just haven't been high on your list of priorities recently. You're aware of that. You also know that you could easily "get into'" enjoying life just given the chance. Or could you? Really relaxing is not as easy as it sounds. Witness these successful achievers.

• Jonathon takes the time quite regularly to go fly fishing in some of the beautiful mountain streams that abound near his home.

• Mary Ann loves to "get away from it all" on the golf course and does so every weekend that she can, and sometimes even during the week!

• Jody is a card aficionado and is part of a foursome that meets for a spirited game of bridge once a week.

• Jaime, who has taken to jogging, makes it an almost daily part of her lifestyle.

Each of these individuals is taking the *time* to relax. In that sense, they are a step ahead of colleagues who don't take time for themselves anymore. But are they really relaxing? Putting yourself in an environment where relaxation is possible is no guarantee whatsoever that relaxation and its rejuvenating effects will occur. Like stress, relaxation is "All in Your Head." Similarly, both stress and relaxation responses are determined by how you *relate* psychologically to an activity, not by the nature of the activity itself. In a nutshell, it's what goes on between your ears that really counts.

A basic problem with true relaxation is that it is a notoriously inefficient use of time in terms of the immediate tangible products that accrue from it. When you relax, you have little to show for the time spent save the experience itself. Because of this quality, relaxation is much harder to justify than working. Yet, the benefits of regular relaxation are strong — emotional survival, career longevity, intimacy, and enjoying the richness of life as you live it each day. Here is a framework for understanding relaxation and how to attain it for yourself, for your health, and for your future!

"Get Some R & R"

When an acquaintance is leaving for a vacation or a trip, you are likely to say something like, "Have a good time, now, and don't forget to get lots of R & R!" "R & R" stands for REST and RELAXATION. These are two different processes with separate biological and psychological functions. The confusion between these two processes is the root cause of much of the inability of individuals to get enough quality relaxation. Many believe they are relaxing when in fact they are merely resting!

The function of REST is to permit your physical being to rejuvenate. When you use your muscles to work they eventually tire. Then you need to REST so those muscles can recover and get ready to work again. Remember that REST is always passive and includes such activities as sitting in your easy chair, lying on the beach, spending time in your hammock, or sleeping. Your body needs a certain amount of REST each day to keep functioning well physically.

RELAXATION, however, is vastly different from REST. The function of RELAXATION is to *emotionally* rejuvenate because you are expending much mental energy coping with the pressures, challenges, and responsibilities of work each day. As a rejuvenating experience, RELAXATION can be either ACTIVE or PASSIVE. For example, RELAXATION can include such diverse activities as tennis, stamp collecting, lying on the beach, talking with a friend, taking a walk, or going on a picnic. The antidote for the emotional exhaustion of Personal Burnout is clearly more RELAXATION. However, because of the fatigue that stems from Personal Burnout, far too many individuals seek more REST instead. As a result, the problem either remains or worsens.

If you think about it, there are also striking differences between the experience of physical fatigue and emotional exhaustion. Remember that REST per se does little or nothing to relieve emotional fatigue. Only RELAXATION does that and it is most effective when you are awake. You just can't sleep emotional exhaustion away although many try. In fact, instead of sleeping more, it's a good idea to sleep no more than seven or eight hours each night and use the extra time for quality leisure to "get away from it all."

Without enough RELAXATION, stress symptoms remain or get worse as do a general pessimism, a diminished ability to cope, loss of enthusiasm, anger and irritability, a sense of personal isolation, and an awareness that you are using tremendous amounts of energy to get very little accomplished. A key question that you must confront is the issue of whether you are getting enough regular REST *and* RELAXATION to remain healthy, happy, and productive in the long run.

Are You Relaxing or Working?

In addition to enough rest, quality relaxation time is something that busy people everywhere wish they had more of to enjoy. To gain the benefits of relaxation, just spending time away from work is simply not enough. Let's go back to Jon, Mary Ann, Jody and Jaime. To the casual observer, each one is taking time regularly to "get away" from the pressures of work. Each one appears to have a pleasurable alternative to the stresses of a demanding career. However, the startling reality is that not one of them is really relaxing at all.

To understand why these four achievers aren't really relaxing, some of the prevalent mythology about relaxation must be addressed. Not only is there confusion about what is rest and what is relaxation, there is equal misunderstanding about the differences between true relaxation and psychological work! Here are some guiding principles to help you move in the direction of quality leisure time by helping you to understand the nature of the relaxation experience.

THE FIRST LAW OF RELAXATION: *True relaxation has nothing whatsoever to do with where your body is or what your body happens to be doing. Rather, the experience of relaxation is*

determined by how you psychologically relate to whatever ac-
tivity you are involved in at the time.

It follows, then, that if true relaxation is determined by a special way of experiencing an activity instead of by the activity itself, then perhaps a definition of the "relaxation" relationship is in order. Just how do you go about psychologically relating to an activity in this special way so that relaxation and its rejuvenating effects occur?

TRUE RELAXATION: *A deep and pleasant subjective involvement in any activity in which the primary reward is the experience itself. At every level, the process of the experience is valued above all else while products gained from the activity are of minor importance.*

It sounds so simple and it is simple to understand. However, many hard working and achievement-oriented men and women find it surprisingly difficult to relax in this way. This mode of responding directly contradicts all of the lessons of success. Compete and win! Pour energy into the task! Make it happen! Set goals and obtain them! Always produce! Only then will you succeed because you are in control of your own destiny. To really relax, you must be able to shift out of this success-oriented way of responding that has become a deeply ingrained habit over the years. Again, relaxation requires that you enjoy experiences primarily for the pleasant process involved rather than for the products produced. It's not as easy as it seems.

Just as relaxation is determined by your relationship to an experience, stress-producing psychological "work" is also defined by your approach to any given activity. As a result, what superficially appears to be a relaxing experience may actually be internally distorted into psychological "work." The benefits of quality relaxation simply do not occur when this subtle internal change takes place. When you are psychologically "working" at any activity (in contrast to truly relaxing), there are always four characteristics that are imposed on the experience.

WORK CHARACTERISTIC #1: YOU CREATE A STRONG GOAL-ORIENTATION FOR THE EXPERIENCE. In other words, you begin an activity with an already defined expectation for what you want out of it when it's all over. Your focus remains on your goal. And, during the course of the experience, you are working very hard to make sure that you reach your goal. That way, you'll feel that you accomplished something during the time spent.

WORK CHARACTERISTIC #2: YOU IMPOSE A WIN-LOSE EGO-INVOLVEMENT ONTO THE EXPERIENCE. You put your ego on the line when you're psychologically working. The result is that there's more at stake than pleasantly experiencing the process of the activity. Because of your ego-involvement, you can't enjoy yourself or have fun. It's a win-lose proposition, and it's serious business. You will feel very bad if you don't come out a winner so you make sure you do!

WORK CHARACTERISTIC #3: THERE IS ALWAYS A PRODUCT THAT RESULTS FROM THE EXPERIENCE. You've built your personal success on your ability to produce. You make sure that you always have a product to show for time spent because if you don't it's wasting time. The only problem is that during quality relaxation, the only product is the "process." This emotional product makes you very uncomfortable so you set up a more tangible one as your goal for the experience.

WORK CHARACTERISTIC #4: IN RETROSPECT, YOU IN-VARIABLY EVALUATE THE EXPERIENCE AS A PERSONAL SUCCESS OR FAILURE. Depending on goal attainment and the quality of the tangible products resulting from your experience, you can then label it as "worth it" or as a "waste of time," as a success or as a failure, as good or as bad. Your evaluation of the activity either supports your ego or negates it because your self-esteem is so closely tied to the success of the "work" that you do.

Now let's look at a couple of examples taken from our four professionals who *appear* to be regularly relaxing. You will see just how easy it is to subtly impose an internal work structure on a potentially relaxing experience.

EXAMPLE #1: JONATHAN'S FLY FISHING.

When Jon doesn't catch trout for whatever reason, he becomes irrationally angry and very disappointed. After all, what do you go fishing for, anyway? On several occasions, he's been ready to wrap his rod around the nearest tree. He gripes about the pollution in the streams these days and the fact that fishing just isn't worth it anymore. He feels like a failure when there are no fish in his creel that he can brag about when he gets home.

A RELAXING FISHING TRIP. Jon's friend Ted approaches trout fishing in a very different way. Coming home with no fish is irrelevant. In glowing terms he recounts how the sun was warm, how he enjoyed the quiet beauty of a mountain stream, and his delight at the wildlife observed during the day. During these times, he feels at peace within himself and returns home with a renewed sense of fulfillment. Fish or not, he can't wait to go again.

EXAMPLE #2: JAIME'S JOGGING EXPERIENCES.

Jaime took up jogging with a vengeance. She's in it to reach her own personal best. If she jogs three miles one day, she pushes herself to better that record the next day. She keeps the pressure on herself by constantly upping the ante. She is very concerned with the technical aspects of jogging and keeps careful records of her progress (or lack of it). When she doesn't do as well as she thinks she should, she becomes very frustrated and then works extra hard to find the reasons and to overcome them quickly.

JOGGING FOR RELAXATION. Bette also jogs regularly, but does it in a much more "laid back" way than her sometimes partner Jaime. Bette's style is to quickly relax into the rhythm of her body while jogging. Shortly she begins to experience primarily through her senses and soon loses herself in the beauty that surrounds her. When she tires, Bette stops. Over the past months, she has also increased her distance, but that's not the objective. She jogs solely to "get away from it all," and she does. It feels wonderful.

Take a moment now to guess how Mary Ann "works" at golfing as she cultivates business contacts on the course. Then, based on what you now know about quality relaxation, imagine how the experience of golfing would be different if "process" was Mary Ann's only product. As a further exercise do the same with Jody's vicious, competitive approach to bridge and how he could relax more easily and enjoy himself. As a third step, closely examine *your* leisure activities. Are you really relaxing or are you psychologically "working" at them? Imagine your leisure activities both ways. To the extent that you are "working" at relaxation, make a commitment to involve yourself more in the process of your leisure activities to maximize the health and happiness benefits that result from these kinds of experiences.

Level I:
Maintenance Relaxation

There are three interrelated levels of relaxation skills. Each is helpful in its own way to maintain health, relieve work pressure, and to enhance the quality of your Life After Work.

Maintenance Relaxation is the baseline level of relaxation that is most powerful in its effects on your ability to withstand the incessant demands of your work over the long term. Maintenance Relaxation consists of your regular pleasant diversions — *your* way of "getting away from it all" — that provide you with needed relief from daily frustrations. Without Maintenance Relaxation, the mental energy expended in your work is not recovered. Without Maintenance Relaxation, you become progressively more vulnerable to stress problems, to the Spread of Stress, and to Personal Burnout. Without Maintenance Relaxation, the quality of your Life After Work steadily diminishes.

There are two modes of Maintenance Relaxation: Active and Passive. Psychologically, Active Relaxation is really Play. As perhaps the major modality for relaxation, Play is active involvement in any activity that is enjoyed for the experience itself, rather than for any payoffs. Play is extremely important for adult well-being as well as for the health and happiness of children. It is stimulating and it is fun. Active Relaxation, or Play, has three other beneficial aspects as well.

1. PLAY keeps your muscles in healthy tone. A trim and fit body has a very positive effect on your self-esteem as well.

2. PLAY helps to limit your food intake. Mild exercise often cuts your appetite to help you keep your weight under control more easily.

3. PLAY tends to stimulate your ability to sleep soundly. You then awaken refreshed and energetic and ready to go in the morning.

Keep in mind that there is also a very helpful *bonus* for engaging in regular Active Relaxation or Play. Paradoxically, while Play may consume considerable physical energy, *more energy is created as the result of it!* Coming home mentally fatigued or emotionally exhausted after a long day's work, you frequently feel completely depleted of energy. You want to just sit down and do as little as possible. However, it is well known that lethargy only breeds more lethargy. You often feel worse if you give in to your tiredness and do nothing.

Instead of coming home and Resting, go out and Play for awhile. By being active and physical, you will more easily put the problems of the day aside and enjoy yourself. Soon you will feel yourself beginning to emotionally rejuvenate. Energy and optimism return. That dragging, tired feeling disappears. You're ready to meet the remainder of your day with a sense of renewal and in a more personally stimulating and positive way. Remember that Play is not only fun, but it's an essential survival skill to help you regularly diffuse the stresses of your work.

In contrast to Play, there is also Passive Relaxation. Passive Relaxation involves withdrawing into "inner space" to shut out the distractions and concerns of the world around you. Another term for Passive Relaxation is a Meditative Experience. Meditative techniques include self-hypnosis, Transcendental Meditation, autogenic training, the relaxation response, prayer, and many others. To gain maximum benefit from any Meditative technique, use it for about twenty minutes each day. However, you may need some formal training in the technique of your choice to use it well. Some of the major benefits of Passive Relaxation are the following.

1. MEDITATIVE EXPERIENCES keep you in touch with parts of yourself (your "center") that are often denied or buried beneath daily hassles and heavy responsibilities.

2. MEDITATIVE EXPERIENCES help you to slow down and maintain proper perspective on problems and frustrations so that you can cope better.

3. MEDITATIVE EXPERIENCES have strong energizing effects. After using one of these techniques, you are more refreshed and optimistic than before.

A Formula for Maintenance Relaxation

For continuing health and happiness, Maintenance Relaxation is clearly the foundation of Lifestyle Balance. However, you know how very busy you are these days. There is always so much to be done. As you add up the many responsibilities you are now shouldering, perhaps you are asking yourself this very important question: "Just how much Maintenance Relaxation is necessary to prevent stress problems and to enjoy life?"

This question is a most important one to address. If one hour of Maintenance Relaxation was needed to counter the stresses of one hour of work, then all would be lost. The reason is quite simple: very few career-oriented men and women could afford to spend that much time relaxing because of their busy schedules and ongoing responsibilities. Fortunately, the ratio of Maintenance Relaxation to work is nowhere near one to one. A solid rule of thumb is to consider the Maintenance Relaxation to Work ratio to be 1:10. That is, for every ten hours of work, you need one hour of quality relaxation time doing something pleasurable just for you. Here is a simple formula for calculating the minimum amount of Maintenance Relaxation time you need each week.

STEP #1: Figure the total time that you spend working *at work and at home* during an average seven day week (include evenings). *Example:* Consider Tony Tenacious to work a total of 60 hours during an average week (a ridiculously low total to be sure).

STEP #2: Because the ratio of Maintenance Relaxation to Work is 1:10, divide your total work hours by ten. *Example:* For Tony T., the result is a minimum of six hours of Maintenance Relaxation needed each week.

STEP #3: Next divide the number of relaxation hours you need by either two or three. Most individuals (particularly those out of practice) can't relax in just one hour. Two- or three-hour segments are necessary to "let go" to relax deeply, hence the division by a factor of two or three. The result is the number of two-or three-hour periods of relaxation time you need each week. *Example:* Our friend Tony T. needs either two three-hour segments or three two-hour periods of relaxation time weekly to maintain emotional and physical health.

Shift into Relaxation Using Transition Behaviors

Your ability to shift into a "relaxation mode" of experiencing is probably one of the skills that has deteriorated as you have become more successful and busier over the years. The absence of this skill also accounts for the work characteristics that show up in your leisure activities. The kinds of responses that facilitate these shifts out of the "work mode" of relating are called Transition Behaviors. Without them quality relaxation is more difficult and sometimes virtually impossible.

A critical aspect of bringing regular Maintenance Relaxation back into your lifestyle is to reestablish effective Transition Behaviors that work for you. Basically, Transition Behaviors are not difficult to understand. Essentially, they are "consistent patterned responses that permit a psychological shift from a success-oriented way of relating to the process-involvement experience of relaxation." It is when your transition responses are effective that relaxation occurs. Without them, you merely go through the motions of leisure. And, you often create more stress than is being diffused because you're either responding in a success-oriented fashion or you remain distracted by work-related worries.

Here are some of the most often asked questions about Transition Behaviors, along with answers to them to help you understand their important psychological function more clearly.

HOW MANY TRANSITION BEHAVIORS DOES A HEALTHY PERSON NEED? Most individuals who function well probably have several, each one used for a different purpose. It is also possible to have one highly developed Transition Behavior that can be effectively used for all the normal "shifts" required for daily living.

WHAT ARE THE MAJOR TRANSITIONS THAT ARE REQUIRED OF AN INDIVIDUAL EACH DAY? Basically, there are three. First, to "unwind" after a long day's work so Life After Work can be enjoyed. Second, to make the transition to a sound and refreshing sleep. Third, to shift into a relaxed mode of relating for your leisure activities.

ARE TRANSITION BEHAVIORS EASILY RECOGNIZED? Yes, if you know what to look for. These response patterns are well-developed in those individuals who relax easily, but are often ineffective or absent in those who have lost the ability to "let go" of work. Some individuals recognize their Transition Behaviors for what they are and others do not. These responses are often the innocuous little habits or rituals you use to help you unwind.

CAN SOME TRANSITION BEHAVIORS BE HARMFUL? Yes, one in particular. That one is use of chemicals (alcohol or drugs) to make a shift to a relaxed mode of experiencing. Use of drugs, even prescribed medications, for this purpose quickly becomes habit-forming. Often a resulting drug problem then compounds already-present stress overload and inability to relax. Further, consistent use of drugs to relax implies complete loss of ability to make the necessary transition any other way.

ARE MOST TRANSITION BEHAVIORS PRIMARILY PHYSICAL OR MOSTLY PSYCHOLOGICAL? Usually, effective Transition Behaviors are a combination of both. Involvement in a specific *physical* response pattern permits the *psychological* shift to take place. To put it another way, a consistently used behavioral response becomes the "carrier" that facilitates the emotional shift to a relaxed way of experiencing.

HOW MUCH TIME IS REQUIRED FOR A TRANSITION TO TAKE PLACE? Usually about fifteen to twenty minutes is necessary. In some individuals with highly developed Transitional Behaviors, the time may be somewhat shorter. If you are just learning new Transition Behaviors, however, it's wise to take a full twenty minutes or even more in the beginning.

WHY IS CONSISTENCY SO IMPORTANT IN USE OF TRANSITION BEHAVIORS? You know that your stress responses can be conditioned to specific stimuli (*i.e.*, the sound of the telephone, the sight of your office, certain kinds of interactions). Similarly, your ability to relax can be conditioned to a given Transition Behavior. The more often specific Transition Behaviors are repeated at specific times for specific purposes, the more likely they are to become effective "triggers" for you to relax both mentally and emotionally.

DO TRANSITION BEHAVIORS REQUIRE SPECIFIC KINDS OF RESPONSES? No, not really. The variety of Transition Behaviors that work for the individuals who use them is amazing. However, remember that all of these responses must be used consistently to work well.

WHAT ARE SOME EXAMPLES OF TRANSITION BEHAVIORS? Certain kinds of Transition Behaviors seem to be used more often than others. Here are just a few to give you some ideas. However, you can just as easily create your own. Perhaps you already have one or two, but just haven't recognized them!

- listening to relaxing music on the drive home from work
- taking a twenty-minute "catnap"
- taking off a uniform (nurses, police officers, and military men and women)
- putting on a uniform (getting into your tennis togs, readying your gear for fishing, preparing to go to the beach)
- sitting down to read the paper and enjoy a cup of coffee
- a short exercise regimen
- twenty minutes of meditation, quiet time, or prayer
- going through your "bedtime ritual"
- a daily chat with a friend or your spouse
- romping with the kids or a pet (or even walking the pet) after work

ARE THERE ANY OTHER BENEFITS THAT RESULT FROM USE OF TRANSITION BEHAVIORS? Yes, there definitely are. Not only do Transition Behaviors prepare you for quality leisure time, but they are relaxing by themselves. Further, these same Transition Behaviors help you to slow down from the fast pace of your lifestyle. One major result is that through their consistent use, you more easily maintain perspective on what is really important to you and what is not. Transition Behaviors also help you stay in touch with your deeper and more positive feelings.

Level II.
Attitudinal Interventions

A second crucial level of your relaxation skills consists of Attitudinal Interventions. Attitudinal Interventions are primarily intellectual shifts that help you keep the inevitable frustrations you encounter each day in reasonable perspective. By using well-developed attitudinal skills, you can avoid anger, frustration, and stress by learning to perceive events in a different way. These skills complement Maintenance Relaxation by preventing the buildup of destructive emotions. As a result, you are then able to "let go" of work-related pressures and concerns to shift into a relaxed way of relating more easily.

All well-developed Attitudinal Interventions reflect the internal control of your perspective on events that occur each day. The fact is that you *are* in control of your emotional responses. You can choose to remain calm and composed if you so desire. Your healthy perspective helps you to do just that. On the other hand, you can also implicitly choose to become upset over events that you cannot possibly control, prevent, nor eliminate from your life. In the great scheme of your life, most of these minor irritations make little difference one way or the other. To get upset about them is a waste of your emotional energy. Your highly-charged responses also create very negative feelings in you and in others.

It's a fact of life that anger consumes energy. Frustration takes energy. Anxiety or tension requires energy. Even depression uses up tremendous amounts of your valuable energy. As you have become more successful, you have more to do and your life has become very complex. One bad habit that has developed is your tendency to respond strongly and emotionally to minor events that hold you up or that get in the way of getting things done. You just react without thinking as your negative emotions override your objective perspective. You make mountains out of molehills. You say and do things that embarrass you. And, you are left with a sense that you are out of control.

All Attitudinal Interventions have in common a means to help you maintain perspective and preserve choice on how to respond to the many provocative situations you invariably encounter each day. As you learn these skills, you prevent negative emotions from overwhelming you. You also learn how to short-circuit negative responses. You feel better as a result. One pertinent saying epitomizes the central relaxation strategy of Attitudinal Interventions: "Life is really mind over matter. If you don't mind, it doesn't matter!" Here are five important Attitudinal Intervention skills for you to practice as a way to keep life and living in healthy perspective each day.

ATTITUDINAL INTERVENTION #1: IF IN DOUBT, WAIT UNTIL LATER TO RESPOND. As a first step to regain emotional control when you encounter a problem situation, start by physically or emotionally withdrawing from the situation for a time. This simple technique helps you to calm down and think about the issue more objectively. When you do, you find that the "problem" may not be as big as it initially seemed. In fact, it may not even be worth responding to at all. On the other hand, if the problem does need attention, you can then deal with it in an emotionally calmer way that will produce more positive results. You feel better because you have actively chosen how to respond to the situation. An added bonus is that you avoid the "egg on face" affliction and "foot in mouth" disease. Your ability to choose *not* to immediately respond to a situation is one of the basic foundations for short-circuiting negative emotions.

ATTITUDINAL INTERVENTION #2: USE THE SERENITY PRAYER FOR SORTING PROBLEMS: If you think about it, all problems are not the same. Some problems you can do something about and others you can't. Some problems are worth responding to and others aren't worth the effort. The Serenity Prayer, in use since the Middle Ages, helps put this wisdom into a practical context in a simple but eloquent way: "God grant me the serenity to accept the things I cannot change; the courage to change the things I can; and the wisdom to know the difference." Memorize this simple truth and use it daily. There are some problems you will encounter that you simply can't change or eliminate from your life. Human foibles, inevitable delays, mechanical breakdowns, forgetfulness, and the reality of error are but a few examples. Save yourself the frustration and the negative emotions that are aroused by taking these kinds of minor problems in stride. You know you have within you the capacity to choose how to respond, so save your energy for problems you *can* do something about.

ATTITUDINAL INTERVENTION #3: KEEP YOUR RESPONSES IN LINE WITH KNOWN FACTS. The absence of this fundamental skill is the root cause of much emotional upset, worry, and personal grief. And, most of it is entirely unwarranted. With obvious tongue-in-cheek, Mark Twain once commented, "My life has been full of misfortunes . . . most of which never happened." In other words, don't waste your time and emotional energy worrying or getting upset about something you don't know for a fact. Instead, trust in your ability to deal with problems as they arise. Avoid making assumptions about events. Don't jump to conclusions. When you do, you make the problem bigger, more emotionally threatening, and overwhelming in proportion to your resources. By dealing only with facts, you respond to a practical problem that is known. As you learn this skill, you will find your confidence increasing and your "worry factor" on the wane for sure!

ATTITUDINAL INTERVENTION #4: SEEK OUT ALTERNATIVE EXPLANATIONS FOR PROBLEM SITUATIONS. When you're feeling badly about yourself, it's quite easy to perceive even minor problems as a personal affront and then respond accordingly. You begin to assume the worst possible motives in others. When you're under stress and there's a problem, it easily becomes obvious to you that someone is deliberately trying to hurt your feelings, manipulate the situation, or reject you as a person. It's a wise and mature individual who is able to step back from a problem situation and examine it from several different perspectives including the other person's. As you develop this skill, you will find that there are viable and legitimate explanations for many events that you have taken far too personally in the past. The result is that you short-circuit all those unnecessary feelings of being unloved, unaccepted, and unworthy. And, then you can deal with the problem more effectively . . . if it's a problem at all!

ATTITUDINAL INTERVENTION #5: MODIFY YOUR INNER MONOLOGUE TO TALK YOURSELF UP, NOT DOWN. One of the recent major breakthroughs in mental health lies in the revelation that *emotions follow thoughts* rather than vice versa. Thus, healthy changes can be effected by modifying how you think about things. "What you think is what you get!" is a saying well worth considering in light of this discovery. Nowhere is this Attitudinal Intervention skill more important than in modifying your inner monologue of thoughts and perceptions of life events that go on around you constantly. From time to time, take a moment to listen to your inner stream of consciousness. If it is negative, cynical, angry, and pessimistic, it's little wonder that you feel down and depressed. Through your inner monologue, you are constantly reinforcing these feelings. By consciously modifying your thoughts in positive directions, even if it's a bit mechanical at first, you begin to break away from some of these "thought disorders" and help yourself feel better.

Level III:
Situational Relaxation Skills

The third level of relaxation skills is composed of a myriad of short-term techniques used to short-circuit situational stress, particularly at work. Much of the popular literature on relaxation emphasizes these skills. These techniques can be quite effective, but they are also somewhat limited. And, most of their effects are relatively short-term. However, Situational Relaxation techniques are helpful in two important ways.

First, Situational Relaxation skills do have a calming effect and help you to maintain personal control in situations where strong stress responses would otherwise be triggered. Before an important presentation, when you must discipline an employee, or when things just aren't going well, these techniques do work. They are most effective in helping you to calm down quickly so you can perform well in critical situations to get the job done effectively.

Second, you already know that your stress responses easily become conditioned to certain external stimuli (*i.e.,* a ringing telephone, criticism by someone else, a sudden change in plans, even the sight of your office). Thoughts or visual images of these stimuli then become capable of triggering global stress responses. At this point, your stress responses are independent of the work environment and the Spread of Stress occurs.

Situational Relaxation techniques help you to "decondition" these stimuli. It is a fact that you cannot be relaxed and stressed at the same time. By learning to relax in situations that typically induce stress at work, you are actually breaking down the conditioned stress responses that are triggered by thoughts or images of these situations that occur when you're *not* at work.

There are any number of Situational Relaxation techniques that you can learn. Their regular use is encouraged, as practice enhances their effectiveness. Here is a sampling of these techniques, most of which can be used within a time span of five to ten minutes.

SITUATIONAL RELAXATION TECHNIQUE #1: DEEP ABDOMINAL BREATHING. While lying down, begin to breathe so that your abdomen is pushed out when you exhale and your chest expands when you inhale. This technique helps to counter the rapid, shallow breathing characteristic of a strong stress response or even a panic reaction. Visualizing your breathing rhythm as a light that glows brighter when you inhale and dims as you exhale is also helpful.

SITUATIONAL RELAXATION TECHNIQUE #2: PROGRESSIVE MUSCLE RELAXATION. The essence of this technique is to tightly contract muscles in one body area for a slow count of five and then suddenly release them. Begin with the muscles in your feet and them move to your calves, thighs, abdomen, hands, lower and upper arms, back, neck (twice) and face. You relax your entire body very quickly in this manner.

SITUATIONAL RELAXATION TECHNIQUE #3: USE OF RELAXATION IMAGERY. Choose a beautiful outdoor setting where you have been very relaxed and happy in the past. As you lean back and close your eyes, produce in your mind's eye a picture of yourself in that place. Bring in all possible sensory experiences, the sights, sounds, smells, feelings, while you maintain a slow and steady breathing rhythm.

SITUATIONAL RELAXATION TECHNIQUE #4: TEMPLE AND SCALP MASSAGE. Lean back in your chair and become comfortable. As you establish a steady breathing rhythm, begin to massage your temples, forehead, face, and scalp in light circular motions with the fingertips of both hands. Focus on and enjoy the pleasant sensations you are producing.

SITUATIONAL RELAXATION TECHNIQUE #5: FOOT ELEVATION. Psychologically, a great deal of stress is centered in your feet. To use this technique, first remove your shoes and then lean back (or lie down) and elevate your feet approximately one foot above your head. Close your eyes and gently wiggle your toes for a few minutes. This technique helps you to redistribute much of the blood that has accumulated in the lower part of your body.

NOTE: In the beginning, avoid using these techniques when you are extremely tired or just after a heavy meal. You may easily fall asleep and that could be a problem at work!

Really Relaxing Is Really Living!

You owe it to yourself to recover your relaxation skills so that you can feel more in control and enjoy life each day. The best strategy is to relearn these skills at all three levels simultaneously. By all means, begin to make time available for regular Maintenance Relaxation each week. Bring your new Situational Relaxation skills into play to calm down in those tense situations where you need to perform well. Use the more positive perspective gained from your Attitudinal Interventions to remain objective and mature in your responses no matter what is going on around you. With these new skills, others will see you as a more upbeat and attractive person. More important, you will *feel* more optimistic and attractive within.

In another vein, a cartoon caption once pictured two obviously harried individuals talking. One is seen saying to the other: "I've tried relaxing. But, you know, I think I feel more comfortable tense!" This bit of humor has more than a little of psychological truth. Ironically, some people *do* feel more comfortable when they are tense and anxious. Emotionally, such individuals have learned not to trust being relaxed. It leaves them feeling vulnerable. For them, tension helps to anticipate problems they are sure will soon come. Conversely, learning to relax is actually learning to trust yourself to handle well any problems that come along. Seen in this way, your ability to relax is an assertion of your inner trust and sense of personal control. By learning to relax, you break down your needless and energy-consuming "defensive tension."

A final word about relaxation. Not only are your relaxation skills necessary for survival, but they are also an essential part of making life worthwhile and personally meaningful. If you can't relax and enjoy life, then what is all your success really worth? Further, when you lose your ability to relax, you also lose a vital part of your youth. Feeling young can't be defined in chronological terms. Rather, it is reflected in the positive quality of your outlook on life, in a contentment within, and in a joy of living that you experience each day. As you become more successful but also very busy, this important sense of youth may slowly begin to wither and die.

You *can* revive this essential quality within yourself by learning to enjoy regular relaxation time just for you. It's worth it. It returns an optimism to your thoughts. A lightness to your walk. A sense of being at peace with the world around you. Edna St. Vincent Millay lamented the passing of this life-giving feeling in one of her verses:

"I know that summer sang in me,

A little while that in me sings no more."

Think of relearning how to relax once again as some long-neglected singing lessons just for you!

Chapter 7

Decontaminating Your Leisure: Don't WORK at Play!

The driving force of the American Dream is success to the point where economic security is assured. Then it will be easier to relax and enjoy leisure time to the fullest. You sacrifice in so many ways now with that goal in mind. Unfortunately, however, for more talented individuals than can be counted, the End of the Rainbow keeps receding into the horizon of the future. In place of "the good life," work responsibilities increase, your career ladder becomes more difficult to climb, and financial security becomes an elusive phantom. The pessimistic thought that the End of the Rainbow may only be an illusion has been growing within you. It frightens you to think that how you're living now is what life after success is really like.

Enjoying regular leisure time is one of the primary casualties of your drive for success and security. However, adequate leisure time is not something that is given to you for working hard and doing all the right things. Nor is it a reward for being a "good person." Instead, leisure time is something that you take for yourself at all costs! There is an End of the Rainbow, but it's not in your future. And, you will not find it anywhere outside yourself. Not in your status, not in your power, not in your money in the bank. It is a quality that you define from within whenever you are confident enough to do so.

Contrary to popular belief, you can have both continuing success and a quality Life After Work. To enjoy both, though, you must take a good hard look at how you are living now and the values that underly your lifestyle. How you relate to leisure time at this point in your successful life is especially important. You may find that you have less leisure time than you need to be happy. It is also quite possible that the leisure time you do take is not as satisfying nor as emotionally rejuvenating as it once was. To allay the buildup of guilt and to get more work done, you may find that you have inadvertently learned to WORK at leisure in yet another way! Let's take a look at how this insidious process works. Take a moment to examine what these successful individuals have in common. Which leisure style is most familiar to you?

• Alan, a bright and innovative computer programmer, hasn't taken more than a handful of days off in more than six years because he has simply been too busy with his many work demands and responsibilities. He periodically takes a day or so off when he's totally exhausted, however.

• Audry takes vacations, but they are always associated with her real estate business. Her style is to attend sales or management meetings and then take a day or two extra to enjoy herself with family members who accompany her.

• Travis fancies himself an interested and involved family man. He regularly spends time with his spouse and children in leisure activities, but tends to be so distracted by work concerns that he never really relaxes and enjoys the time together.

These three career-oriented individuals, all going places, share a number of characteristics. Of course, they are all successful because of their motivation and intense dedication to their work. However, while all are fairly young, each is showing signs of growing distress. Alan suffers from constant insomnia. He tends to think too much when he goes to bed and can't get to sleep for hours. Also chronically tired, Audry has frequent tension headaches. She has also noticed that a nervous twitch around her right eye has become worse recently. Travis' stomach has begun to act up with frequent heartburn, and his already heavy smoking habit has picked up to further sap his stamina.

Related to these stress signals is another shared characteristic of these talented people who can be found in every community. In each case, leisure time has been contaminated — with work. As a result, although blessed with success in a career, each has experienced a slow decline in the quality of non-work life. Each believes that adequate time has been set aside for relaxation. The facts? Not one of the three is relaxing regularly, and it's beginning to show up in diminished productivity at work.

The solution to this unfortunately common problem is decontaminating your leisure time. It is only in the presence of uncontaminated leisure that emotional rejuvenation can take place. The process of decontaminating your leisure is really the practice of Lifestyle Management. Again, in a nutshell, Lifestyle Management is "the commitment to maintain a creative balance between achievement and success on one hand and satisfying involvements in family life, leisure activities, and friendships on the other."

As a busy achiever, Lifestyle Management requires a never-ending vigilance on your part. Maintaining the balance between your work and leisure activities is difficult because the rewards of work are so constant that adequate time for relaxation is continually in jeopardy. Effective Lifestyle Management is necessary for your personal survival in the long-term. Through Lifestyle Management, you maintain your health, remain professionally productive, and have your share of good times as you walk (not run) life's path. However, maintaining Lifestyle Balance means facing some key issues within yourself.

Three Types of Contaminated Leisure

Virtually all achievement oriented individuals suffering from significant stress problems and depressive states have problems with leisure. There are three major forms of contaminated leisure that negate the emotional rejuvenation you need for enjoying life and for career longevity.

A-TYPES: THE LEISURE AVOIDERS

Modus Operandi: Occasional lip service is given to the need for more relaxation combined with a pattern of consistently putting off time for leisure activities because of the pressing demands of work.

Alan is the epitome of a Leisure Avoider. He knows there has been a dearth of leisure time in his life for several years, but continues to rationalize working because he believes that only he can do the job that has to be done. He doesn't trust others to take over if he is away. Deep down, there's also another reason he avoids taking leisure time: he becomes absolutely miserable within a day or so when he is away from his work. He becomes worried and agitated and wonders what's going on back there. The result is that he hasn't had a true vacation in many years. He doesn't think he really needs it and knows from experience he couldn't stand it if he did take it.

Alan is only dimly aware that he is in a no-win situation. He can experience the pressure and stresses of work responsibilities, or he can be agitated and miserable when he's taking leisure time away. The net result is that he takes time off only when he feels he's about to go under and then only for a short time. Then he gets back to work. Time off for him is in response to an emotional emergency and after emergency intervention (read: *a day off*), he's back at his daily grind. For Alan, sadly, leisure has no other value than as an expedient when he feels so drained at work he can't take it any longer. He's been doing this for so long he thinks it's normal.

B-TYPES: THE LEISURE BLENDERS

Modus Operandi: Taking time quite regularly for relaxation, but doing so only within the context of ongoing, work-related responsibilities. Work responsibilities are dominant, while relaxation is clearly a secondary extra.

Audry has been spectacularly successful in developing a small commercial real estate firm into the largest in the region. She is also very devoted to her family and wants very much to spend more time with John, her husband, and with the kids. Over the years, she has become a Leisure Blender as a solution to her work-leisure dilemma. She and John regularly attend cookouts and cocktail parties, where she busily cultivates business contacts. The same is true on the golf course where she often plays as part of entertaining scouts looking for commercial building sites in the area.

The Leisure Blending style extends even into vacations. Audry loves to have the family with her when she goes to professional meetings or attends seminars at lovely resorts. While she is out fulfilling her work responsibilities, the rest of the family are enjoying themselves. She typically joins them — later. No wonder she is stressed! Although she ostensibly takes time off to relax and enjoy herself, she has subtly evolved a style of relaxation that is consistently contaminated with work. Current tight money and writing off the vacation become easy justifications for work-related leisure. Beneath the surface, she believes that she just has too much work to do and has no real choice in the matter.

R-TYPES: THE LEISURE RUMINATORS

Modus Operandi: At the behavioral level, there appears to be clear separation of work and leisure time. At an intellectual level, intrusive thoughts of work consistently lead to distraction, obsessive rumination, and worry that limit leisure involvement.

You may have guessed by now that Travis is a Leisure Ruminator, and it has become a constant source of irritation to his family. He does take plenty of time for relaxation, but his work still interferes because he can't get it out of his head. His capacity for relaxation can be measured in moments, not hours or days. He knows that for true relaxation to occur, he must leave worries and concerns behind and enjoy doing something pleasant. He also realizes that this rarely happens. His family appreciates the time spent with them, but they are also concerned that he is so distracted and "inside himself" so much of the time.

In fact, Travis is not relaxing in body nor in spirit and, so, is not really relaxing at all! His body just happens to be in a *potentially* relaxing place! Worried concerns about his work consistently intrude into his consciousness to disturb and distract him. He's noticed that these concerns plague him even when things are going extremely well. It is almost as if Travis has a need to remind himself that there is work to be done, lest he forget while relaxing. Brenda, his spouse, notices that at odd moments he mutters to himself about work, or that out of the blue he makes a comment about a work issue. She is aware that his intentions are to relax, but she also realizes how difficult it is for him. She knows that if he could just relax in his head, he could relax completely.

Irrational Beliefs About Relaxation

Beyond how you've managed to contaminate your time away from work over the years, a further block to quality leisure time lies in various Irrational Beliefs about relaxation that you've internalized. While it's true that you're very busy these days, realistically, after you've cut through all of your standard excuses, you *could* find time for regular relaxation if it were a priority. Intellectually, you know you need time away from work. At an emotional level, however, Irrational Beliefs about relaxation time prevent you from taking that time. These emotional barriers have slowly expanded their subtle power to become major blocks to living life to its fullest.

Most of the Irrational Beliefs about relaxation operate just beyond your conscious awareness. You may not even be aware of their insidious influence until you slow down and stop a few moments to conceptualize your *real* reasons for not taking regular time to enjoy pleasant diversions from your work. You're much more aware of the rationalizations you use to justify your heavy work schedule. It is a rare achievement-oriented individual who does not have lurking within at least one (and probably more than one) Irrational Belief about relaxation. The sooner you detect and resolve these unwarranted emotional barriers to relaxation, the sooner you will begin to enjoy Free Leisure uncontaminated by work.

IRRATIONAL BELIEF#1: ANY LEISURE TIME CAN BE JUSTIFIED ONLY THROUGH VERY HARD WORK. This is the commonly held "bonus belief" about relaxation that dovetails nicely with the work ethic. Its basic tenet is that leisure time and enjoying yourself is a form of reward for work well done. With this belief, relaxation becomes little more than a fringe benefit. Many fringe benefits are given to you by your employer. However, this one must be given to yourself, and that makes it more difficult to take regularly. You just don't know whether you really deserve it. The result is that the leisure time you do take — no matter how well justified — arouses uncomfortable feelings of anxiety and guilt.

CORRECTION: The fact is that leisure time, regularly taken, is a *health mandate and not a work bonus.* You need regular relaxation in order to survive in a demanding and pressure-packed work world. If you don't take time to regularly relax because you can't justify it, then you will find that Parkinson's Law will apply. Your work will expand to fill the time available for its completion and that might easily become 24 hours a day, seven days a week! You must learn to value leisure time equally with work time to insure your health, not to mention enjoying life along the way.

IRRATIONAL BELIEF#2: IT IS SINFUL TO SPEND TIME WITH NO PRODUCTS TO SHOW FOR YOUR EFFORTS. This Irrational Belief is encountered with surprising frequency. "Idle hands are the devil's playground" is the moral message that impedes your ability to relax and enjoy life. The core of this belief is that hard work is good, while leisure time spent with no tangible products to show for it represents something evil and thus is to be avoided. This belief in operation also quickly generates anxiety and guilt when you are relaxing. Why not? You're misbehaving, aren't you?

CORRECTION: You are in no way "bad" for enjoying leisure time. As a busy, responsible individual you work in a psychological environment that is chronically stressful. The only real antidote to stress is regular relaxation. The price of not relaxing is emotional fatigue that no amount of sleep will remedy, not to mention a myriad of other stress-related problems. You must resolve the no-win choice created by this Irrational Belief — that is, to be stressed and pressured at work or anxious and guilty when you're not. There is no sin in taking more than the Biblical seventh day for relaxation. You need at least that much just for emotional survival. Confront this Irrational Belief directly to take the "badness" out of enjoying the fruits of your labors. Emotionally, you need more leisure time than you're taking.

IRRATIONAL BELIEF#3: WORK IS TO PROVIDE YOUR FAMILY WITH ALL THE GOOD THINGS IN LIFE. This common "irrationalization" is really a red herring mouthed by workaholics who are busily climbing their career ladders. Outrageous work schedules and far too much time away from the family are justified by convincing yourself that you are working to provide those you love with comfortable living circumstances. There are usually promises that at some point in the future, when you've attained higher levels of success, then you can relax and the family can be together much more to really enjoy life. While there is consistent longing for that future time, it never comes because you keep putting it off in lieu of more work and getting to that next higher level of success and achievement.

CORRECTION: In all probability, your spouse and children aren't as interested in material things as you are. To you, these "things" are symbols that define you as successful. For your family, quality of life is gauged more by sharing life experiences with you. In short, what your family wants most from you is quality time spent with them. You also need time to be involved in your children's growth and development. If you think about it, you spend excessive time away from the family *for you*, not them! They are your excuses. Truly gratifying family involvement won't ever come unless you make the time to relax and be with them. Until you make that commitment, you will continue to isolate yourself, with family members becoming little more than housemates whom you support.

IRRATIONAL BELIEF #4: RELAXATION CAN'T BE JUS-TIFIED AS LONG AS THERE IS WORK TO BE DONE. When there is a comfortable end-point in your work, then you can relax without ongoing responsibilities hanging over your head. Conversely, when you relax "in the middle of things," then you tend to worry about what you've got to do, what's going on back at the office, and so on. The problem is that so much of your work is ongoing these days that true end-points may be virtually impossible to find. The net result is that really opportune times to relax never seem to come. One thing or another always gets in the way. (Note: This need for end-points dovetails nicely with Irrational Belief #1.) You have been taught all your life to work hard and get all of your work done before you go out to play. Way back when, you clearly knew when your work was done. That line is very blurred now and that is the trap!

CORRECTION: If you subscribe to this Irrational Belief, then the constancy of your work has probably eroded your ability to consistently enjoy your evenings, weekends, and mini-vacations away, much less longer vacation periods. After all, you are not supposed to relax as long as there is work to be done. You must learn to accept your work as an ongoing process with no clear starting or end-points. The process of your work can then more easily be broken by regular periods of relaxation and time spent in pleasant diversions. At the same time, you will be resolving that relentless drive to "get done" what has subtly plagued you for so long. However, overcoming this Irrational Belief will take more doing than saying.

IRRATIONAL BELIEF #5: IF YOU LET YOURSELF GO, YOU'LL ENJOY LEISURE SO MUCH YOU'LL NEVER BE EFFECTIVE IN YOUR CAREER AGAIN. What a frightening thought! It sounds absurd on the surface, but this belief is alive and well in the subconscious of many successful individuals who can't relax. This Irrational Belief stems from a perception of yourself as basically slothful and lazy. This belief about your basic nature is countered through strict self-discipline and dedication to your work along with limitations on relaxing. You never really "let go" because you fear that if you do so, your inherent laziness will overwhelm you. You fear becoming a professional dropout with family ruin as the consequence. It's far better to rigidly control that indolent part of yourself than risk relaxing too much.

CORRECTION: The fact is that you are not lazy at all, but you are very tired. You have developed the bad habit of demanding so much of yourself that when you slack off even the least bit you berate yourself unmercifully as your fear of laziness surfaces. Accept that you are not superhuman. Just like all mortals, you need regular time to relax and emotionally recharge so you can cope effectively over the long term with unyielding work pressures. Look at how irrational your fears of laziness are in light of your past accomplishments and the hours that you put in each week. Ironically, your fears of dropping out grow stronger when regular relaxation is lacking. If you are emotionally refreshed through pleasant leisure diversions, then work is stimulating and challenging. If you are chronically fatigued because you aren't relaxing, then the desire to run away and indulge in a life of "lazy leisure" grows ever stronger.

The Road to Free Leisure

Whether you are a Leisure Avoider, a Leisure Blender, or a Leisure Ruminator, you have significant issues to face on your road to Free (uncontaminated) Leisure. Free Leisure is a synonym for the relaxation time that your body requires to emotionally "get away from it all." Contaminated leisure does not provide the rejuvenating effects of Free Leisure which help you feel better about your work because you are enjoying pleasant diversions on a regular basis. Further, it is only when you have been successful in decontaminating your leisure that you retain perspective on the deeper emotional priorities that insure personal satisfaction and fulfillment in life.

At the risk of being a bit redundant, underscoring the definition of true relaxation might be helpful. As the most important of all the Natural Experiences, active relaxation (or true play) is becoming deeply and pleasantly involved in any experience where the primary reward is the experience itself. That is, you enjoy what you're doing as a process rather than for anything you might get out of it later. The relaxation "process" is diametrically opposed to the competitive, goal-oriented, success-failure, ego-involved experience of "psychological work."

After you understand and have confronted any of the Irrational Beliefs about relaxation that have been impeding you, the process of further decontaminating your leisure involves several steps. There are specific issues you must face as a Leisure Avoider, a Leisure Blender, or as a Leisure Ruminator. Here are the three basic steps necessary to move toward Free Leisure. Start wherever you are and move forward. Each step that you take will require you to face and resolve specific work-related issues that have so far effectively blocked the quality leisure time that you need not only to survive your work, but to enjoy a quality Life After Work.

IF YOU'RE A LEISURE AVOIDER, TAKE THE TIME. This shift involves carving from your busy schedule enough time to regularly involve yourself in pleasant leisure activities. As you closely look at your motivations for overworking, you may find that there are several issues that together have produced your Leisure Avoiding pattern. The result is that you don't take leisure time and find all kinds of excuses to justify working without regular breaks. Not one of them holds water! By facing these issues, you begin to grow personally and professionally.

AVOIDER ISSUE #1: YOU BELIEVE YOU ARE INDIS-PENSABLE. Being indispensable at work for most individuals is little more than an ego trip. Sound management requires training a protégé to take over when you are away and to relieve the burden on you. You are probably not indispensable. And, the only way to find out is to get away. If you don't have a capable assistant ready to take over now, begin immediately to train one.

AVOIDER ISSUE #2: YOU ARE RESERVED OR SHY. You may find it easier to relate to others through a structured work role than in unstructured social interaction. The result is that all your relationships are work-related as a way to reduce social anxiety caused by your reserve. As one way to begin breaking this pattern, take the time and the energy to develop a few friendships with people who have nothing to do with your work.

AVOIDER ISSUE #3: YOU HAVE NO LEISURE ACTIVITIES YOU ENJOY. The problem here is that you're out of practice. You've been working so long and so hard that your leisure skills are very rusty. Begin to experiment with new activities. You may have to be persistent and try several before you find one that "clicks" with you. Don't give up before you find a pleasant diversion that you enjoy.

IF YOU'RE A LEISURE BLENDER, TAKE THE WORK OUT OF THE TIME. Taking the time to "relax," but persistently combining leisure time with work seriously impairs the benefits of Free Leisure. Your second shift is to remove the "work" from your fun time. That's easier said than done because doing so necessitates that you face several other issues hidden within your Leisure Blending style.

BLENDER ISSUE #1: FACING YOUR GUILT. One important function of Leisure Blending is to remain connected to work to reduce the buildup of guilt for not always being "productive." As you disconnect from work, you will have to justify leisure time in other terms than "productivity." Take the time for Free Leisure to enjoy yourself for no other reason than you deserve it! If that doesn't work, justify your leisure time as a health mandate absolutely critical to your long term survival.

BLENDER ISSUE #2: SHIFTING OUT OF YOUR "WORK IDENTITY." In other words, if you're not an accountant, a manager, a military officer, an engineer, or a teacher, then just who are you? You've hidden behind your work identity to avoid defining yourself in nonwork terms. You as a person are important, and clarifying you at the person level is not only psychologically healthy, but also enables you to rediscover and enjoy many positive parts of yourself that you've long neglected.

BLENDER ISSUE #3: FULLY PARTICIPATING WITH YOUR FAMILY. One result of your habit of working at play is that you have missed out on full participation in leisure activities with your family. There's a fun-loving and upbeat part of you that they may not now know. Enjoyable family times together bond each of you emotionally to one another. Time passes quickly; if you don't do it now you may wake up one day to find the children gone and a stranger sitting across the breakfast table!

IF YOU'RE A LEISURE RUMINATOR, TAKE THE WORK OUT OF YOUR MIND. Once you've taken the work out of your leisure time, you are ready for your last and most difficult shift. Freeing your mind from work-related concerns is not easy, but it is necessary to enjoy Free Leisure. Thinking about work at leisure keeps you connected to it in a way that is subtle, yet effective in negating the positive effects of quality relaxation. Here are some issues that will confront you as you make this final step.

RUMINATOR ISSUE #1: YOU MUST LEARN TO TRUST YOURSELF. When you worry about work, it's a signal of personal distrust. Somehow, if you worry or think about it even while relaxing, you can make it come out all right. This habit is a subtle trap. When you do get away from work by freeing your mind to enjoy leisure, you can come back to your work refreshed to get more done more efficiently! Worrying does nothing but feed the negativity that is already too much a part of you.

RUMINATOR ISSUE #2: LEARNING A POSITIVE ATTITUDE. Think for a moment. Your thoughts about work are almost all negative. They reflect a larger pessimism that pervades every part of your life. Learning to "let go" of work frees you to see, to feel, to experience, the good parts of life and living. It is only when you are psychologically free from work that you can enjoy moments of happiness, deep contentment, and the feeling that you've really "got it made."

RUMINATOR ISSUE #3: CONFRONTING YOUR FEEL-INGS. If you're thinking all the time, you don't stay in touch with some of your feelings. They're there, but covered by the cognitive lid of your constant analytical thoughts. Through your years of striving for success, you have become uncomfortable with your feelings and with expressing them. The price is that you're incomplete. A vital part of you is locked up inside yourself. As you relax into Free Leisure, positive feelings of love, compassion, and joy will be your reward.

Some Rules of Thumb

As you confront the issues that lie behind your contaminated leisure, you will probably not have an easy time resolving them. Your focus on work has been part of your success and in that respect, many of the ways you relate have been quite functional. On the other hand, you've clearly but inadvertently carried them too far. These work-related ways of responding, helpful in proper context, now prevent you from enjoying life. You've slowly fallen into working day in and day out without thinking about why you're doing it or defining what you need to emotionally feel good about yourself.

As you move in the direction of regular Free Leisure, you will begin to gain all of the health and happiness benefits of Lifestyle Balance. In the process of facing parts of yourself necessary to enjoy Free Leisure, here are some Rules of Thumb that have proven helpful to many before you.

RULE OF THUMB #1: PUT YOUR INITIAL EMPHASIS ON ACTIVE RELAXATION. In the beginning, you will find active forms of relaxation or true play an easier way to "let go" into Free Leisure than passive or meditative relaxation exercises. There are also other benefits. Active relaxation not only helps you keep your muscles in tone, but also helps cut your appetite, and you sleep better as well. It also breaks your sedentary life-style by getting you away from your television set and those too frequent snoozes!

RULE OF THUMB #2: RELAX BY CREATING SOMETHING WITH YOUR HANDS. In general, the more mental work that you do, the more you need an avocational interest that is very concrete. As an alternative to the abstract nature of your work, do something with your hands through which you can create, control, feel, and see what you're doing all the way to the end. Such activities are a counterpoint to the highly intellectual work that you do each day. Working with your hands provides a needed outlet for pent-up needs to manipulate and directly control what you are doing that is often missing in your life's work.

RULE OF THUMB #3: PRACTICE DOING JUST ONE THING AT A TIME. Because of strong social emphasis on productivity and because you have so many responsibilities these days, you can keep up by learning to do two or three things at once. Doing more than one thing at a time easily becomes a habit. The result is that it becomes difficult to involve yourself in just *one* activity and to enjoy it deeply. In other words, you can't possibly relax doing two or three things at once. Practice enjoying just one activity at a time when you can. You'll be learning to relax in the process.

RULE OF THUMB #4: REMEMBER THAT SOCIALIZING IS NOT ALWAYS RELAXING. Partying, bar-hopping, or the cocktail circuit are poor ways to learn how to relax. Often the social atmosphere is permeated not only by discussions of work, but also by work-related attitudes. Competition, goal-orientation, evaluations, and "success-failure" attitudes are all part of many social activities, and they are mixed frequently with alcohol and perhaps other drugs. A better way to learn to experience Free Leisure is to spend at least some relaxation time by yourself or in the company of a few close and compatible friends.

RULE OF THUMB #5: BEWARE OF YOUR SUBVERSIVE WORK ORIENTATION. Once you have succeeded in decontaminating your leisure, you are not out of the woods. The fact is that you spend much more time at work than at leisure even under the best of circumstances. Work attitudes easily creep back into your leisure time to contaminate it once again. Intensely competing or trying to make money from newfound avocational interests are both extremely bad signs. Make it a point to periodically give yourself a "check up from the neck up" to make sure you are not again subtly contaminating the Free Leisure you now enjoy.

Work: Enough Is Enough!

Aristotle wisely noted centuries ago that "the end of labor is to gain leisure." A lifestyle with more leisure and less responsibility is a vision that most achievement-oriented individuals hold dear. For far too many, however, it remains a dream that never becomes reality. Over decades, your work attitudes have become a pervasive and deeply ingrained part of your orientation to living. There's a powerful part of yourself that keeps saying: "If you have a few minutes, use them to get something done!" The result is contaminated leisure. You have learned to work at play . . . if you play at all!

As you decontaminate your relaxation time and learn to experience Free Leisure once again, you also gain awareness of a deeper part of yourself that has been buried under work-related concerns and pressures for years. As you gain in your ability to leave your cognitively-dominated, goal-focused, success-oriented work world periodically, a new part of yourself begins to emerge from long dormancy. With your strategic retreat from your destructive over-involvement in work, you also gain three other benefits that are important to your feeling of completeness as a person. These Bonuses accruing from Free Leisure are also important to maturity and wisdom in your work.

BONUS #1: A DEEPER REFLECTIVE ABILITY. In your overwork, you've lost awareness of your center. That is, your ability to decide what is really important to you for personal fulfillment and life satisfaction. With more Free Leisure, you slow down long enough to ponder and reflect on some deeper questions that are ultimately far more important than, "What I've got to get done today."

BONUS #2: A DEEPER COMPASSION FOR OTHERS. As you have experienced constant frustrations and pressures in your life, your sensitivity to others' feelings has suffered. As you psychologically free yourself from too much involvement in work, interpersonal understanding combined with sensitive responsiveness to others' needs begins to emerge once again.

BONUS #3: A DEEPER PERSPECTIVE ON SUCCESS. With a strong competitive, goal-oriented perspective in your work, success has been defined in terms of a destination you are striving to reach. As you begin to slow down, you find that real success is actually a journey. Success is defined not only by reaching goals, but by enjoying what you do each day at work and at home.

As you enjoy Free Leisure and get more in touch with the real you, you will find that Free Leisure also has a definite spiritual quality. It gives meaning and depth to your life and to the will to go on. Free Leisure is your time for you to discover, to play, to contemplate, to grow within. The more that you do it, the more you realize that there is much more to life than figuring out how you're going to get through the next twenty-four hours. With a thought-provoking message to all of us, Henry David Thoreau (1817–1862) commented: "Time is but the stream I go a-fishing in." Take a moment to ponder just what *you've* been catching from the stream of time recently!

Chapter 8

The Gladiator Complex: When Winning Is a Losing Proposition!

You've been thrust into the arena once again. The stakes are high. You have no choice but to compete and win because losers don't count. You give it everything you have and more. The consequences of being second-best are just too terrible to contemplate. It's not just once. You know that you've got to do it over and over again. You can't escape the fear that drives you. In your gut you know that someday you must fail. You compete so intensely that it's as if your life depended on it. You're always vigilant. You know better than to ever relax. You're a Gladiator. Life is your arena. You're out to win and you are winning, but it doesn't feel good anymore. The Gladiator is tiring.

Let's face it. Competition is as American as Mom, the Flag, and Apple Pie. And, there are Gladiators all around. The culturally reinforced drive to be the best is the basis for tremendous motivational energy directed to achieving academic, athletic, and career development goals. In fact, competing and winning is the major highway to the good life, free of economic worries and personal hardship. Despite looming obstacles and mountainous barriers, you persevere in the competitive world of your chosen life's work. You're already way up there on the mountain of success, and you can see the top. You want to reach your personal pinnacle, and you've been pushing hard all your life to do just that.

It's certainly not bad to learn to compete even more effectively. In fact, competitive skills are a sound investment in your future. Millions upon millions of dollars each year are gladly (and wisely) budgeted by individuals and corporations to enhance personal skills vis-à-vis "the competition." The object? To provide key personnel with the psychological and technical weaponry to get ahead. To compete and win. To be Numero Uno. The fact that the professional training and development industry is alive and well and growing by leaps and bounds attests to the voracious appetite of motivated individuals to gain the competitive edge needed to survive in the cutthroat corporate or business world that must be faced each day.

There is no question that you live in the land of opportunity. Only you can hold yourself back. The American Dream is rather straightforward. You compete and win and get ahead. But now let's look at Joe and Lucy and Amy and Mike. Each is a successful competitor. Each has gone far in a chosen profession. Their collective skills and motivation and the savvy born of experience are unquestioned. Those in the know also realize that each one has a problem. All are Gladiators driven incessantly by a competition compulsion.

• Joe has difficulty constructively resolving any kind of conflict. He is easily threatened and makes even minor differences of opinion into no-holds-barred, win-lose confrontations. In all the emotionalism, the real issues aren't addressed.

• Lucy can't handle even little setbacks these days. She becomes extremely upset and takes it as a personal failure if she isn't Number One in situations where it doesn't matter at all. She gets down in the dumps, and it takes her days to regain her confidence.

• Amy never stops worrying. Amy's husband, whose patience is wearing thin, kids her that she is close to being paranoid about "the competition." Evenings, weekends, and vacations find Amy busily working or checking out her rivals. She is obsessed with the need to beat them.

• Mike, though competent and accomplished, has garnered a reputation as an insecure egotist. He constantly seeks praise from others and makes himself the center of attention wherever he is. He uses a bagful of clever ways to let you know all about his achievements.

Each of these successful individuals has developed an intense need to compete that has gotten totally out of hand. Their competition has extended into areas of life where it is at best socially inappropriate and at worst emotionally dysfunctional. Not one knows how to stop competing. Each is a Gladiator fighting an ongoing battle for supremacy in a world where second-best is just not good enough. As each has become locked into compulsively competitive ways of relating, a critical component of inner control has been lost as the ability to relax, to take it easy, and to enjoy life has slipped away.

Basically, the competition compulsion characteristic of all Gladiators can be defined as "an irresistible, consistent, and unquestioned need to aggressively compete and win in personally created win-lose contests with others no matter what the situation and without regard for the appropriateness of the competitive interactions." As you can easily surmise, it's most difficult to really enjoy casual relationships, fun games, and an easy give-and-take with others when you are driven by the competition compulsion. As many former Gladiators now know, when you compete compulsively and must win to feel good about yourself, winning clearly becomes a losing proposition!

Competitive Needs Are Created

There is no single cause for the compulsive competitiveness that is the hallmark of the Gladiator. Instead, a number of powerful psychosocial influences and reinforcements converge over a lifetime to create this personal and professional liability. Talented, achievement-oriented, and success-motivated individuals are especially vulnerable. It is ironic that while successful competition is of immense help in building a career, carried too far, it backfires because it interferes with enjoying the fruits of success once you get there. Here are the major determinant factors that together create the destructive and compulsive need to compete.

FACTOR #1: THE INFLUENCE OF INNATE DOMINANCE NEEDS. There is evidence of a biologically determined, but socially manifested drive to become the dominant individual in a group. This deep need produces the motivation to compete to become the "leader of the pack." Culturally, this "survival of the fittest" competition is channeled into socially acceptable outlets for dominance combat. Beyond sports, the major arena for cultural competition is professional excellence, where the payoffs are economic rewards and power.

FACTOR #2: THE REINFORCING EFFECT OF PARENTAL AND PEER MODELING. Parents are extremely important in shaping their children's perceptions of the world and their ways of interacting with it. Highly competitive parents often model a style of living and working characterized by constant comparisons, win-at-all costs performance expectations, and evaluative re-marks that are not lost on the children. Peer groups in academia and in the work world parallel these parental values to reinforce an intensely competitive mode of interacting that creates the compe-tition compulsion.

FACTOR #3: THE CONSTANCY OF EXTERNAL EVALU-ATION. Individuals are evaluated on their performance through-out their entire life span. Judgments by parents, grades in school, and performance evaluations at work all provide you with positive or negative feedback on how well you met the expectations of others. Immersed since early childhood in an unremittingly eval-uative environment that is highly performance-oriented, indi-viduals develop an awareness of personal potential and high expectations for self that are internalized. The need to demon-strate competence is the result and competition is the way to do it.

FACTOR #4: THE POWERFUL PERFORMANCE-ADEQUACY LINK. An inadvertent, but negative consequence of an evaluative performance environment is the development of a causal relationship between personal performance and self-esteem. In other words, the individual is only as personally ade-quate as performance. If performance is up-to-par or beyond, then the individual feels personally adequate and acceptable. If per-formance is down, however, self-esteem drops correspondingly because it is perceived to be a direct negation of the self. Mo-tivation is therefore directed to being a consistent winner.

FACTOR #5: YOUR CONSTANTLY NARROWING SUCCESS PYRAMID. With every year that you have advanced academically or in your career, there has been attrition. Some of your peers are left behind with every new rung on your career ladder that you climb. The inevitable consequence is that with each step forward, you must compete with a much more select and competent group of contemporaries to get to the next level. In your now rarified atmosphere of competition with savvy contemporaries, your skills are always on the line and you are being constantly tested.

The Gladiator's Scale of Competitiveness

There are a number of clear behavioral signs that characterize the Gladiator mindlessly caught up in compulsive competitive-ness. These signals should be considered not only an index of your personal vulnerability to failure, but also as a way to gauge your ability to relax and enjoy life. The more of these signals you see in yourself, the more likely it is that you have lost control of healthy competition and the less likely it is that you are as happy as you could be. Check yourself with these dirty dozen signals on the Gladiator's Scale of Competitiveness.

_____ **1. FOR YOU, THERE IS NO SUCH THING AS A "FRIENDLY" GAME.** There is a difference between doing your best and pulling out all the stops to win no matter what. The difference is lost on you, however. In a card game, tennis, or golf, your fragile ego doesn't let you relax and enjoy the process of friendly gamesmanship and rejuvenating play. Because your ego is so tied to being Number One, you simply can't play anything for fun anymore. Your pushy kind of competition ruins the fun for everyone else, too.

_____ **2. YOU CREATE COMPETITION WHERE THERE IS NONE.** You are quite skilled at creating competitive situations because you are not comfortable in any other mode of interacting. Socially, you play "one up" games. When fishing, you make a contest of it. Instead of walking, you want to race. In this way, you manage to contaminate your own leisure activities and that of others who innocently fall prey to your competitive suggestions. You work at play and create stress in the process.

_____ **3. THERE IS OBVIOUS AGGRESSION IN YOUR COMPETITIVENESS.** It is evident to everyone that you compete with an angry intensity. For you, competition has become a socially acceptable cover to act out your need for power, control, and dominance. It's also a major avenue for you to express the hostility you carry within you. The aggressiveness of your competitive actions sometimes surprises even you. Behind it all, however, you are insecure, and you've got to win to reassure yourself that you are okay.

_____ **4. YOU HAVE SEVERE PROBLEMS RESOLVING CONFLICTS.** With your competition compulsion in full operation, it is very difficult for you to resolve differences of opinion in ways that are satisfying to all. The problem is that any conflict triggers the win-lose drive of the Gladiator. The conflict quickly becomes nasty and ends only when one of you "loses" to the other. With your overriding need to win, creative solutions to problems are neglected in lieu of dominance combat.

_____ 5. YOU CONSTANTLY STRETCH THE BOUNDARIES OF FAIR PLAY. When you're competing, anything goes. You don't mind pushing the rules to the limit. Ethical considerations aren't much of a problem if going beyond them gives you a competitive edge. The social graces don't get in your way much any more either. Your need to compete and win is so dominant that nothing else matters. Others see your kind of competitiveness with its questionable ethical boundaries as a character flaw. In reality, it reflects your immaturity.

_____ 6. YOU SEE A "DOG EAT DOG" WORLD AROUND YOU. Your view of the world and the people in it has crystallized into pure jade. You are on your guard at all times because you believe that everyone is out to beat you or to take something from you. The struggle for dominance and power is the central theme of your perception of others. Take or be taken, win or you'll lose, control or be controlled, dominate or be dominated. These are the bases of your distorted way of relating. No wonder you can't relax.

_____ 7. YOU HANDLE EVEN MINOR SETBACKS MISERABLY. You just can't stand losing in any way, shape, or form. That's because, for you losing is self-negation. When you do lose, you regress to temper tantrums, personal attacks, accusations of unfairness, sullen disappointment, or even depression. Sportsmanship is just not one of your strong suits. After you lose, it may take you days to regain your confidence. And, because you're so emotional about losing, you also miss opportunities to learn from your mistakes and thus better yourself.

_____ 8. FOR YOU, FAILURE IS EXTREMELY SUBJECTIVE. Objectively speaking, you have been and are successful judging by external measures. Internally, however, it's a different story. You use standards so high for your performance that they diverge from reality. Although you may do extremely well, by your internal standards you may be an outright failure. Because of your perfectionistic streak, you have a remarkable proclivity to focus on what needs improving instead of what you've done well. Daily, you feed your own insecurity.

_____ 9. YOUR EVALUATIVE WAY OF RELATING PRECLUDES HAVING TRUE PEERS. Because of your bad habit of ranking everyone in relation to you, no one is ever your equal. You compartmentalize each person on specific dimensions as either one-up or one-down from your position. That way, you keep track of others as either more capable or less capable than you (mostly less capable). Those you define as less skilled, you don't respect and you write them off. Those who are more skilled threaten you, and you want to topple them.

_____ **10. YOU NEED CONSTANT PRAISE AND REASSURANCE.** Although winning is required for maintaining your self-esteem, the need to be recognized for your accomplishments is also necessary. You talk about yourself a great deal and find ways to let others know how important you are and what you have done. Relating in a quietly competent way is just too much for your vulnerable ego. You need a steady diet of recognition and praise to feed it. No matter how much of it you get, though, it's never enough.

_____ **11. YOU SENSE THAT OTHERS ARE NOT COMFORTABLE WITH YOU.** Your style of competitive relating generates discomfort in others. You are perceived as aggressive, opinionated, and rigid, and you have received overt negative feedback about it. You tend to create tension wherever you are and no matter who you're with. Others respond by politely keeping their distance or avoiding you completely. Your friends wonder why you can't lighten up a bit and "go with the flow" because deep down they like you.

_____ **12. YOU ARE CHRONICALLY INSECURE AND TENSE.** Because of your insatiable need to constantly demonstrate your superiority, you can never relax. There is always a competitor around. If there isn't, you'll create a competition. You constantly worry about how well you are doing and how long you will be able to keep it up. Your successes never "stick" to your self-esteem so you can't be comfortably adequate enough to enjoy life. Inside you're a bundle of tension and you're definitely not very happy.

"Slump Panic"

Despite your fragile sense of self and your vulnerability to failure, you function well as long as you keep winning. However, within there is a nagging worry that you can't get rid of. What if you aren't promoted? What if your ratings drop or your sales record declines? What happens if you don't get an "A" in that course you're taking? You know that there are always bright and eager youngsters coming up fast with an eye on *your* position. Everything is fine as long as you keep up the pace. The terrible insecurity of Slump Panic is held at bay until you falter.

Slump Panic may be triggered by one major setback or a series of small ones. The problem is not failure or a decline in your performance per se. All successful individuals fail on their way to the top. The telling question, as you now know, is how you handle failure and what failure means to you personally. When you're a Gladiator caught up too much in the competition compulsion as a way to validate your self-esteem, it is almost axiomatic that any significant decline in your performance will have such an ego-negating impact that Slump Panic may very likely result.

Whenever you encounter failure, you know that you must go back "on the firing line" to win again and reassure yourself that you are still tops. This is the only avenue to recovery from your negative feelings that you can see. And, it makes sense if your self-esteem is excessively tied to a winning performance. Yet, to put yourself on the line again is risky business. Your confidence is already shaken. What if *IT* happens again? A second failure would be an even more crippling blow to your self-esteem. You have to do it. You fear failure, but you are also driven by the need to demonstrate that you're a winner to reassure yourself. This fear-drive conflict is the psychodynamic core of Slump Panic. Avoiding performance situations altogether and living with your self-negating failure is the only other option (see Figure 1).

The intensity of the fear-drive conflict characteristic of Slump Panic often sets into motion a vicious cycle of performance anxiety that leads to even more failure. As a Gladiator, your need to be Number One is very intense because so much of your self-esteem is at stake. The result is a paralyzing anxiety that actually impairs your performance in critical situations. You have no "failure resources." With each subsequent failure, your confidence is more deeply eroded, your need to demonstrate your competence more intense, your desire to avoid performing stronger. You've been on a roll in a success cycle for a long time. Now you've encountered the devastating failure cycle that has been your hidden Achilles heel for years. It didn't emerge until a personal failure set it in motion!

Add a Tad of Hypocrisy

Winning is fine. Where winning stands in the overall picture of success is a much more meaningful question. To Gladiators, winning isn't everything. It's the only thing! The way Gladiators relate to performance is definitely a vulnerability. While such individuals win a lot, when they fail they go down hard. In our

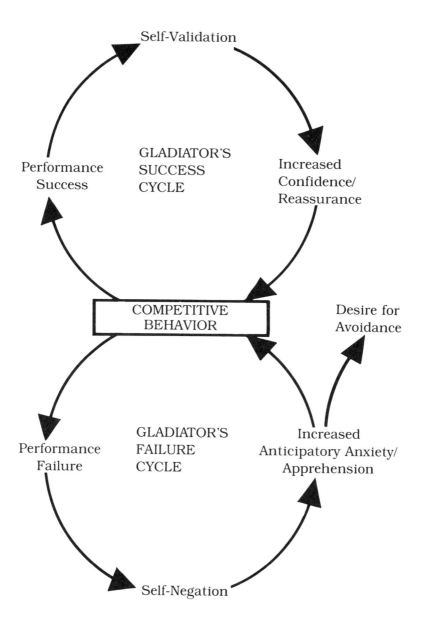

Figure 1: The Emotionally Entwined Success and Failure Cycles Characteristic of the Gladiator.

society, it is evident that there is deep conflict inherent in what is taught about success and winning. While tremendous lip service is given to sportsmanship and fair play, at another level the emphasis is clearly on winning and being the best. Period. No excuses. For many, the deeper message takes. Gladiators are one result.

As one way to illustrate the cultural mixed messages about winning, take a close look at some of the proverbs that are often quoted during contests and competitions. Many of these are quite familiar and sound just fine on the surface. Examined more closely, however, the psychological messages in some of these sayings are highly questionable and even unhealthy. These sayings are just one more way that those already vulnerable to the competition compulsion are reinforced for their socially inappropriate behaviors. Without belaboring the point, here are several proverbs that reflect cultural hypocrisy about winning.

"IT'S NOT WHETHER YOU WIN OR LOSE, BUT HOW YOU PLAY THE GAME THAT COUNTS." An emphasis on how you play the game is clearly healthier and more important overall than winning. In fact, playing to do your best without tying the outcome excessively to your self-esteem is the antithesis of the Gladiator's posture. On the other hand, how many times have you heard this proverb related to the *winners* of a competition? You probably haven't. It's usually stated as a sop to the losers. Compliments for playing well are your consolation prize if you didn't win. The message is not lost on *any* of the players!

"LET THE BEST MAN (OR WOMAN) WIN!" Again, superficially, this statement sounds fine. At a subtle psychological level, however, the message is highly questionable. The "winner" is definitely not the *best* man or woman. Rather, the winner is the *most skilled* individual in the competition. You are not a good person because you win nor are you a bad person if you lose, but this is the implied message. Reinforcing this direct link between performance and self-esteem brings with it the vulnerability and the interpersonally obnoxious behaviors of the Gladiator.

"TO THE VICTOR BELONG THE SPOILS." Historically, victors in war gained the prerogative to plunder and ravage the cities they captured. They thus received the spoils of war. In the modern competitive realm, the Gladiator takes the same spoils of war psychologically. Once a rival is vanquished, the loser is no longer respected and often that person's self-esteem is "plundered" with putdowns and tactless remarks. While the winners in any competition deserve recognition for their skill, the prize should not be the self-esteem of the losers. As emotionally punitive winners and poor losers, most Gladiators haven't learned how to be supportive to their competitors.

Preventive Maintenance: Taking the Ego Out

Up until now, you've been a Gladiator locked into a compulsively competitive way of relating. In the past, you didn't see that as necessarily bad, but you didn't examine the consequences in any depth either. At this point, you have begun to separate competition that is functional in your work from areas where it interferes with your health, happiness, and your ability to relax and enjoy life. And, you've begun to realize that the way you compete has some unhealthy qualities. You're getting ready to tackle your competition compulsion head-on because you want more out of life.

The essence of healthy achieving and functional competition is to "take the ego out" of these endeavors. To do so requires making several psychological shifts that are certainly more easily said than done. These shifts, once made, expand your capacity to enjoy experiences rather than to make everything you do into intense win-lose competitions. As with everything else in the practice of Lifestyle Management, *It's All in Your Head!* The object is to choose when to compete and when to relate in a more relaxed way. And, in those instances when competition is functional, to do so in ways that make you less vulnerable. Make these Psychological Shifts in sequence.

PSYCHOLOGICAL SHIFT #1: COMPETE WITH YOUR-SELF, NOT WITH OTHERS. In the past, your frame of reference for competing has been with specific others or with a group of your peers. You started to compete early in life and you've never stopped. As you've climbed the ladder of success, you are now competing with a highly select group of individuals who are just as motivated to make it as you are. You've learned over a lifetime to monitor your status by ranking yourself within a group. This monitoring process tells you that you're more vulnerable to failure all the time because the competition is tougher. Your first step in taking the ego out of your competition is to shift from an inter-personal to an internal frame of reference.

To put this shift into practice, train yourself to compete only with your own track record instead of with others. When you make this shift, you have already initiated the process of reducing your vulnerability to failure. You're more in control, and you're content to let others do what they may. It is your personal best that matters now even if others do better. Part of making this shift is to resist others who are compulsively competitive and who want you to compete with them. Now you see in them a very questionable part of you!

PSYCHOLOGICAL SHIFT #2: STRIVE FOR SELF-IMPROVEMENT, NOT WINNING. After you've made the first shift, your next step is to learn to perceive what you are doing in a different way. With the first shift, you have learned to evaluate your present performance in terms of your past record. With the second, you focus on what you've accomplished in terms of improvement, rather than on a win-lose comparison with the past. With this change, surpassing a previous record becomes much less important than whether you are progressing toward new learning and higher levels of personal competence. Your ego is becoming much stronger with your internal frame of reference and because winning (or losing) is now secondary to a desire to improve yourself.

Each day, you learn more. With every passing day you move just a bit further toward your vision of you in the future. You've become like the student who goes to class to learn instead of to make a grade. Your work has now become one way of expressing who you are and your healthy life priorities. You have reduced your need to compulsively compete to reassure yourself that you're adequate anymore. Because of this shift, you're more comfortable with yourself, and your ability to relax and enjoy what you are doing is growing considerably. You also notice that the quality of your work is improving because of the comfortable shifts in how you go about it!

PSYCHOLOGICAL SHIFT #3: LEARN TO BE YOURSELF INSTEAD OF PERFORMING. You have now positioned yourself to make an important third shift, and it's as necessary as it is emotionally risky. To further reduce your vulnerability and to increase your internal sense of adequacy, you must put to the test the fact that you are acceptable whether you are Number One or not. Over the years, you've been constantly reinforced for performing well. As a consequence, you've never been sure whether you can be accepted if you aren't performing. In fact, competing to win has become your defense against finding out. You're so intent on competing and performing that you don't really let others know you.

The essence of this shift is to learn to relax with others. Casual, easygoing, give-and-take interactions are the key. You will find that others will respond to you in positive and deeply affirmative ways. As part of this transition, you are also building your capacity to stop competing when you choose to do so. This inner control further strengthens your sense of self. And, in the competitive world of your work, you draw strength from the acceptance of Special People who care about you as a person, not because of what you do. In retrospect, you find that in the past *you've* also accepted yourself conditionally on the basis of your performance. You've assumed that others have done the same. It's a relief to find out that this conditional premise has no validity.

PSYCHOLOGICAL SHIFT #4: LEARN TO PLAY FOR THE FUN OF IT. The fact that you have learned to compete well and to win in your career to date can't be questioned. These skills have definitely been an asset. On the other hand, you now realize that you compete far too much and that your style of competing is not particularly healthy. You're aggressive and you're pushy, you're defensive and you're offensive, you're arrogant when you win but you fall apart when you lose. There's no doubt that you must compete in order to continue to progress toward your personal and career goals. There's also no doubt that you need to learn to play just for the fun of it. It is only when you can play that you can relax, and it is only when you relax that you can emotionally rejuvenate.

Playing for the fun of it is the fourth shift required to take the ego out of your competition. This means stifling your need to create competition where there is none. It also means learning to play a "friendly" game when that's what's going on. You learn to do that by doing your best, but enjoying the process. Remember, active relaxation (or true play) is letting yourself become deeply and pleasantly involved in any experience in which you value the experience above anything you might get out of it. You're now strong enough to give up your intense need to win and because you can do that you can play for fun and enjoy yourself. Others will enjoy you, too!

PSYCHOLOGICAL SHIFT #5: DEVELOP YOUR "FAILURE RESOURCES." Learning to lose gracefully is a sure sign of personal maturity, and it's certainly a career asset as well. It's also the core of your fifth shift. As the saying goes, "You can't win them all!" Your personal vulnerability to failure hasn't let you emotionally accept the validity of this fact until now. In the past, any setback or failure has been taken in a highly personal, intensely negative way. If you examine many of your failure experiences, two truths stand out. First, many of them could not have been prevented no matter how good you were. Second, the negation that these failures have represented to you has fed your insecurity and exacerbated even more your fear of failure.

Accepting failure as part of success is one aspect of this final shift. Accepting that you are a fine and adequate person even when you fail is the other. Accomplishing this requires practice, perspective, and deep self-acceptance. But when you do, you have strength because you have failure resources. Paradoxically, you can compete more effectively because you no longer fear failure. You learn from your mistakes and you get better for you. The more consistently you shift in this direction, the more resilient you become in coping well with life's disappointments. And, you will also be able to enjoy life's highs in a more satisfying and personally fulfilling way.

Winning at Life

As you make the suggested shifts to move beyond your competition compulsion, your self-esteem rises. You have developed a new sense of yourself as a well-rounded man or woman. And, you're less vulnerable because you are not dependent on your performance alone to feel good about yourself. You're aware that your "successful" status is but one part of you as a total person. In retrospect, you realize how completely you've put all of your self-esteem eggs in just this one basket. Now you know who you are and like who you are regardless how you perform. Further, because you draw positive feelings from many different kinds of experiences, your lifestyle has become more balanced and satisfying. You've begun to win at life.

Moving beyond the Gladiator in you is an important part of the process of coming to terms with yourself. It matures you as a healthier and more solid achiever, and it creates more depth within you as a person. Most motivated individuals are touched to one degree or another by the competition compulsion. Your strong competitive skills have worked to make you successful, but you've taken them too far. As you look around, you will see Gladiators everywhere. Sadly, many of your colleagues will never move beyond this way of relating to the full and rich and balanced way of living that you've attained. In the process of intensely competing and succeeding most of the time, they are also losing out on some of the most satisfying experiences life can offer.

Recently, a newspaper advertisement appeared with this banner headline: "In the beginning we are all created equal. Then you're on your own!" There's a basic truth in this catchy bit of media humor. You *are* on your own to make out of your life what you will. Your chosen path can lead you to on-going satisfaction and contentment at home and in your chosen life's work. Or, these rich experiences can be sacrificed to meet insatiable needs for recognition, reassurance, and the quest for ever bigger successes that declare you to be Number One. Top Dog. The Winner. As you shed the Gladiator's shell, you choose the path of fulfillment. Winning is fine in its place. But you also know from personal experience that when you can't do anything else, winning is clearly a losing proposition!

Chapter 9

Dimensions of Hurry Sickness: Consequences of Life on the Fast Track

In the well-known story of the tortoise and the hare, the tortoise eventually wins the race by taking a somewhat slower and steadier pace. It is easy to draw from this tale analogies to the achievement-oriented individual. It is your choice to race on the fast track or to slow down and last longer to emerge a winner in the end. Moving too rapidly from one career position to the next while climbing the ladder of success is one dimension of the fast track. Another important dimension is exemplified by Fred.

Fred is quite competent in his position as Executive Director of a large trade association. However, his professional image is becoming a bit tarnished these days. He is chronically tired and feels overwhelmed by the sheer volume of the demands made on him. At home, he is well aware that the quality of his Life After Work has suffered. Around the house, nothing gives him the satisfaction he once knew. He's not quite sure what has happened, but he is sure that it isn't the way he wants to live.

Fred is suffering from a virulent form of Hurry Sickness. Although he has paced his career moves very well, in each position (and especially the current one) life has become one big hurry — to get to the next meeting, to make all those calls, to get the budget done, to arrange the next conference, and on and on. While these responsibilities clearly go with his position, Fred has definitely changed.

At home and at the office, with people and while alone, when working or when at leisure, Fred finds himself in a tremendous hurry no matter where he is or what he is doing. He just can't slow down anymore. Twenty-four hours a day he lives by the code of the White Rabbit in *Alice in Wonderland:* "I'm late! I'm late for a very important date!" Fred has lost control.

The central element of Lifestyle Management is the skill to creatively balance achievement and work success with leisure activities, family life, and satisfying social involvements. However, another critical aspect of Lifestyle Management is the ability to feel comfortable enough at work and especially at home *to enjoy the experience* of whatever is being done at the time. Fred does take some time for the family and for leisure, but he's been living on the fast track so long that he's unable to enjoy these experiences. His mind constantly races. At times, his sense of urgency is almost overwhelming. His mind is always on what he's got to do next. Hurry Sickness has Fred in its clutches.

The Roots of Hurry Sickness

Hurry Sickness, defined from a psychological perspective is "a pervasive and progressively urgent need to complete tasks in order to obtain rewards at completion without regard for other aspects of the experience and to do so using maladaptive time strategies." With this definition in mind, let's examine the component parts of this common lifestyle problem.

The key casual factor in Hurry Sickness is the progressive need for TASK COMPLETION. Enjoying what you are doing is neglected in lieu of getting done as quickly as possible no matter what the activity. The need for TASK COMPLETION definitely extends to non-work involvements (*i.e.*, fishing, making love, a leisurely drive) and interferes with the enjoyment of these experiences because of your persistent need to "hurry up and get done."

Getting done has become such a strong need because the PAYOFFS at completion have assumed primary importance. Your work experience has taught you that rewards always come at the end — after you've put forth great energy to reach a goal. Not only do you feel a sense of personal satisfaction from your achievements, but you receive tangible rewards such as raises and career advancements as well. Over time, these PAYOFFS have become clearly linked to your self-esteem. Each time you succeed, it's a message to you: "You've done well. You're a good person because you've succeeded again." Your need for this kind of reassurance has become stronger than you'd care to admit.

TIME URGENCY quickly becomes a strong internal driving force toward TASK COMPLETION. Your life becomes a frenzy of completing one task after another. You are obsessed with time, and wasting any of it becomes almost a mortal sin. You strive to maximize your productivity by using your time ever more efficiently, but you also have a sense that you are controlled by time and you don't like it. Time is your challenge and your enemy. A telling sign of Hurry Sickness is that when you're relaxing, you have to constantly fight the TIME URGENCY that keeps distracting you.

Another method you use to increase your output is to adopt MALADAPTIVE TIME STRATEGIES. These questionable tactics do help you get more done over the short run, but you pay a high emotional price. You now do everything faster, you have learned to "double up" to do two or more things at once, and you are constantly preparing for what's coming next before you're done with what you're doing now. The insidious trap is that you get done quickly even when there's no reason to get anything done at all!

Because of your emphasis on TASK COMPLETION, you focus on finishing WITHOUT REGARD FOR OTHER ASPECTS OF THE EXPERIENCE. In short, you have lost the ability to enjoy yourself while doing anything because of your incessant drive to get to the finish line. "Letting go" to really find relaxing satisfaction in any activity has become more difficult. Because of this change, you have lost the ability to emotionally rejuvenate. Your chronic fatigue and pessimism are the symptoms of this loss.

The Components of Urgency

As the years have passed, you now see that the pace of your life has accelerated into overdrive. Now it's difficult, if not virtually impossible, for you to slow down. Many of your hurried responses have become so deeply ingrained that they are almost second nature. It's no wonder you're tired! Beyond the psychological factors already discussed, the convergence of other emotional needs and inescapable external realities have clearly exacerbated your urgent "rat-race" lifestyle.

You realize now that the primary motivating force in Hurry Sickness is that constant sense of urgency that drives you to keep moving toward task completion. For the purposes of self-awareness, it's a good idea to separate the various components of your urgency. While "insight is not the therapy" by any means, it does provide definition of pertinent issues involved and directions for implementing positive change. Here are outlined the five major components of urgency, each of which has probably had a part in producing your Hurry Sickness.

URGENCY FACTOR #1: YOU HAVE MUCH MORE TO DO THESE DAYS. With success, you inherit many more responsibilities at work. That's what you're being paid for. With a home, cars, appliances, and recreational devices that need upkeep, there's much more to do after work as well. Daily getting the children where they need to be adds to your burden of responsibilities. By the time that you've become successful, you probably have more to do each week than you can possibly get done. You just didn't realize that with success, the details of maintaining your middle-class lifestyle would be so overwhelming.

URGENCY FACTOR #2. YOU ONLY SEE "WHAT NEEDS TO BE DONE." Because there always seems to be a million and one things that need doing, you now focus exclusively on them. Your trained eye is constantly selecting the next task to tackle and the one after that. You've put your blinders on as your orientation has become completely externalized. Your emotional well-being is neglected. You take your relationships for granted. You're so locked into the endless stream of tasks that are undone that you can't take time for such "luxuries." You just keep accelerating in your narrow, task-dominated way of living each day.

URGENCY FACTOR #3: YOU HAVE A STRONG NEED TO "BE ON TOP OF THINGS." As a successful person, you have a well-developed ability to "make things happen." Along with this achieving orientation to living, you also have a strong need to be in control. You don't like feeling overwhelmed and not being able to get everything done that needs doing each day. The uncomfortable knowledge that you are constantly playing a game of "catch-up" with your responsibilities drives you to work longer and harder. It also creates additional stress because of the sense of failure that you feel when you don't get everything done.

URGENCY FACTOR #4: YOU "PRODUCE" TO AVOID THE BUILDUP OF GUILT. Over the years, your self-esteem has become closely linked to successfully producing. However, the converse is also true. You're not a particularly good person when you're *not* producing. You feel guilty and somewhat irresponsible and bad if you're not working all the time. Every time you slow down, that nagging guilt begins to build to drive you back to work. The busier you keep yourself, the less guilt you feel. Now you work longer and more quickly to avoid these uncomfortable feelings, but you also know that you can't stop to enjoy life either.

URGENCY FACTOR #5: YOU ARE BASICALLY AN ACHIEVER, A "DOER." You are definitely not a passive person. You enjoy activity and doing interesting things. There's nothing wrong with that. On the other hand, there's a significant difference between being active on one hand and orienting your life exclusively toward "getting things done" on the other. Over the years, your achievement motivation has slowly become distorted in this way. By confusing an active lifestyle with a "get it done" orientation, you miss out on the benefits of leisure activities. The consequence is that you may be getting lots done these days, but you're probably not very happy doing it.

The Efficiency Factor Effect (or, Frustrations, Frustrations, Everywhere)

It's a fact that every day you have lots to do just to keep up, much less get ahead. You push hard to do just that. Now take a moment to think about these kinds of events. They are an inevitable part of every person's life. Why? Because life is neither particularly efficient nor very predictable!

• Three times your child interrupts a critical conversation you are having with your spouse.

• Your tear your nylons on the way to an important meeting, and you must stop to get another pair on the way.

• One morning, your paper doesn't arrive before you leave for work so you can't check the stock market and the news.

• You misplace your wallet (handbag or keys) when you are trying to get out the door to get to work on time.

• You are unexpectedly held up on the road because of an accident ahead.

• A key memo that you need was inadvertently sent to another office.

• Just as you're hurriedly leaving for the airport to go on vacation, one of the kids suddenly discovers that a desperately needed toy has been left behind.

• You make a simple subtraction error in your checkbook and two checks bounce.

• Leaving the office to come home after a long day's work, you discover that your car has a flat tire.

• Your mortgage payment didn't get mailed because the envelope slipped down between the seats of the car and you didn't notice it.

Do these little frustrations of life sound familiar? Probably so, because they happen to everyone. You know that most of them are relatively minor. You also know that in the past, you were able to take most of them in stride. These are the inevitable delays, minor hassles, and accidental oversights that are part of living. The problem is that you can't keep them in true perspective these days. As you've become busier, you have much more to do, but much less time to get it done. And, you are plagued by details at every turn. One result is that you have placed a premium on efficiency. As long as everything runs smoothly, you can just manage to keep up.

There's only one problem with this strategy, but it's a big one. There's a flow of life around you, and it's *not* particularly efficient. Human fallibility, accidents, and interminable delays are all part of life. The difficulty you encounter is that for you to get everything done, everything must flow smoothly. In a nutshell, your extremely high need for efficiency (a very questionable by-product of Hurry Sickness), flies directly in the face of reality. You perceive every delay, accident, omission, and minor problem as just one more barrier to getting done what *you* need to get done. You become upset many times each day because life isn't the way you want it to be. You see everyone else as a problem, but in fact it's you who has totally lost perspective.

There's also another uncomfortable problem related to the Efficiency Factor and to your Hurry Sickness. That problem is that the more hurried you are, the *less* efficient you become! The more you have on your mind, the more apt you are to forget something. The faster you go, the higher the probability that you will make a mistake. The more pushed for time you are, the less likely it is that you will plan effectively. Then these problems compound the stress and frustration that you already intensely feel. In summary, one way to cope with all you have to do is to "hurry up" and become more efficient while you are doing it. However, beyond a certain point, just the opposite occurs: the more you hurry, the *less* efficient you become, and the more aggravated and frustrated you feel.

One final point is well worth making. Years ago, assessment of an individual's ability to handle stress focused on examining coping strategies used as responses to traumatic events or major life changes. That is no longer true. It has been found that a more accurate gauge of personal stress management skills lies in how minor day-to-day frustrations are handled. If you respond to these uncontrollable, inevitable, unpreventable, and unpredictable events by taking them in stride and keeping them in perspective, then the chances are that your coping skills are strong and healthy. On the other hand, if you have Hurry Sickness, these kinds of routine daily problems emotionally upset and overwhelm you with anger. You be the judge for you. As an overstressed wit who probably was suffering from Hurry Sickness remarked, there are only two rules to living: "Rule #1: Don't sweat the small stuff! Rule #2: It's *all* the small stuff!"

The Deadly Duo

It may now be dawning on you that the powerful emotional dimensions of Hurry Sickness also form the core of your growing relationship problems. The achieving individual who has also drifted onto the "hurry" fast track has also developed marked Impatience and strong Anger that further impair ability to enjoy leisure time, family life, and social outlets much less work experiences.

Impatience with anyone who is not rushing around like you builds slowly but surely. Your irritation mounts with time and with the increasing responsibilities that you assume. You consistently verbalize your displeasure in no uncertain terms to anyone who isn't as dedicated as you are. Looking back, you were very different some years ago. Then your pace was slower and you enjoyed life more. Now you become Impatient many times each day, and you tell everyone loudly and negatively how you feel about the situation.

The fraternal twin of your Impatience is Anger. Your pent-up Anger born of repeated frustrations now frequently explodes at any convenient target. The intensity of your Anger sometimes surprises even you. You have become unpredictable, emotionally volatile, and most difficult to live with these days. Those around you try not to rock the boat and to do everything just right to little avail. The hard reality is that most of your frustration is generated by how you view events, not by what has actually happened.

"The Attitude"

Along with your Impatience and Anger, "The Attitude" is also alive and well. The bottom line is that you have come to believe that the world is full of incompetent people and mechanical barriers put there just to get in YOUR way. Even minor setbacks are taken as personal affronts that trigger your anger and confirm your belief that people just don't care about anything anymore, that quality and dedication are a thing of the past, and that no one these days wants to take responsibility for meeting standards of excellence. Each day you fight your way to getting things done despite the odds. You end each day disappointed and angry.

You have changed. Your perceptions have become dangerously jaded in ways that are destructive to your emotional well-being, your relationships, your work, and ultimately, to your career. Those who care about you are well aware of these changes; they have taken the brunt of your cynicism, anger, and negativity. No one knows when even a minor event will set you off again. You don't think positively, you can't relax anymore, and you're not sure you even like people because they constantly let you down. "The Attitude" feeds itself because you see the confirming evidence everywhere.

Signs and Signals

There are many behavioral Signs and Signals that Hurry Sickness has set in if you take a close look at some of the ways you're doing things these days. The changes have probably occurred gradually over the years, but are presently affecting virtually every facet of your life. Now that you know something about the psychological underpinnings of Hurry Sickness, peruse this partial list of the behavioral manifestations of this most prevalent problem.

YOUR DRIVING PATTERN. It's amazing just how much of your Hurry Sickness emerges when you step behind the wheel. Here are some of the symptoms.

• You habitually drive faster than you used to.

• You have received tickets for speeding and other infractions recently.

• You are instantaneously angry at drivers who don't jackrabbit out of intersections when the light turns green.

- You speed through intersections on yellow lights.
- You change lanes and "jockey for position" constantly while driving.
- You rail frequently at the gross incompetence of other drivers.
- You can't stand drivers who insist on driving a bit slower than the speed limit.

YOUR EATING HABITS. As you have become busier, your eating habits have changed dramatically because you simply don't have the time to enjoy your meals any more.

- You frequently eat in the office while you continue to work.
- You prefer to eat alone and quickly unless it's a working lunch.
- At home, you finish meals well ahead of everyone else.
- You eat more food now and in bigger bites than previously.
- You've gained weight over the past year or so.
- Sharing pleasantries at the table is minimal because you can't sit still long enough.
- Your table manners have definitely deteriorated recently.

YOUR COMMUNICATION STYLE. Your way of communicating, even to those you care most about, has become a problem. One result is that your relationships aren't as solid and as close as they once were.

- Even when you don't mean to, a subtle sarcasm and put-down quality has crept into the way you respond to others.
- The emotional support and encouragement you used to give others is now absent.
- You don't take the time for pleasant easygoing chats with family members or friends anymore.
- You frequently catch yourself making demands on others rather than politely asking for what you want.
- You often carry on "conversations" while you are reading the paper, opening your mail, or watching TV.
- You frequently cut off family members or colleagues rather than really listening to what they have to say.
- When others hesitate, you habitually fill in words or sentences for them to speed up the conversation.

YOUR FAMILY INVOLVEMENT. There's no question that with Hurry Sickness, the quality of your Life After Work has deteriorated, and that definitely includes how you relate to your family.

- You're not at home as much now and when you are you're tired (or, you may be home more these days, but be very withdrawn and uncommunicative).
- Family members "report" events to you, but you share little of yourself.
- Your anger and impatience is just as strong at home as at the office.
- Relaxing family times together are much less frequent.
- You and your spouse bicker much more about little things that don't really matter.
- You do as little around the house as you can get away with.
- You nap or snooze or passively watch TV more than ever.

YOUR SEXUAL RELATIONSHIP. Along with other aspects of your family life, your sexual relationship is not as fulfilling as it once was. You pass it off as the age factor, but you know it isn't.

- Sex is quick these days because you don't seem to ever have the time it takes for romance.
- The frequency of your sexual relating is down these days, and it has taken on a routine quality that diminishes its meaning for you both.
- You're so tired these days that sometimes it seems that sex just isn't worth the effort.
- Non-sexual touching has been reduced to almost nothing.
- You don't feel sexual urges as much as in the past (or, you may need sex more as a way to reduce tension).
- Your tender and gentle caring has been replaced by a chronic sense of urgency to reach a climax.
- Your ability to stop thinking and "let go" sexually is impaired because you have so much on your mind.

YOUR LEISURE ACTIVITIES. Your fast-paced life is so filled with undone chores and responsibilities these days that truly relaxing is difficult, if not totally impossible anymore. The changes are apparent.

- You spend less time at leisure now than in the past.
- It seems that time off isn't worth it because work piles up so quickly.
- Many once-good friendships have died of neglect because you haven't taken the time to stay in touch.
- Vacation time has decreased, and you tend to take it in one big block once a year (if at all).

- When you sit still, you find yourself becoming uncomfortable quickly.
- In the leisure time you do take, you either sleep it away or spend the time in aggressively competitive activities.
- You once had interesting hobbies or diversions that you have given up as you became busier.

YOUR RELATIONSHIP TO THE PACE OF LIFE. You've got much to do and little time to do it. The pace of life around is frustrating because it's so slow. You do all you can to speed up.

- You consistently walk up "up" escalators and down "down" escalators.
- You can't stand waiting, even in a short line.
- You become irritated when elevators don't come immediately.
- People who aren't on time drive you right up the wall.
- You become extremely frustrated with anyone who is a beginner at anything.
- You perpetually carry on disjointed conversations while "on the run."
- You'd rather do most things yourself because no one else moves fast enough for you.

YOUR FEELINGS WITHIN. Your emotional life has changed considerably over the years. It's easy to see the changes as the result of the loss of your innocence and youth, but that's not really the case.

- You feel perennially out of control of your life and all you have to do.
- Your dominant feelings these days are anger and a nagging low-level depression.
- A good day these days is one when you don't feel as pessimistic as usual.
- You are chronically tired and fight fatigue all the time.
- Your once delightful sense of humor has disappeared (or, a marked cynicism has become quite evident in your attempts at humor).
- The occasional feelings of happiness or joy you used to have are long gone.
- You sense within that your spiritual self is withering away.

Reversing Hurry Sickness

Diagnosing Hurry Sickness is not difficult. Reversing it is also quite possible. To do so requires both understanding and persistence. It also necessitates your commitment to "bite the bullet" and take some steps that initially won't be comfortable. You are now ready to begin, one step at a time.

STEP I: ACCEPT PERSONAL RESPONSIBILITY. It is easy to blame Hurry Sickness on the pressures of the job, what you "have to do to survive," and on the insensitivity of the organization. While each of these perceptions undoubtedly has a grain of truth in it, the fact remains that most of the responsibility for Hurry Sickness lies within you. Your drive to get ahead is the real root of the problem and in the process you have lost perspective. Until you accept personal responsibility for your present status, you will not be in a position of strength to confront and reverse the real issues of Hurry Sickness.

STEP II: CONFRONT THE INITIAL PARADOX. Because you have Hurry Sickness, your initial tendency is to effect your "cure" in a hurry, too. However, the fact is that your "hurry up and get it done" attitude will actually sabotage your recovery. What is required is patience, perspective, and ability to deal with setbacks in healthier ways. Learning these behaviors is the process of recovery. If you accept that it will not be easy, that it will take time, and that you can do it only by learning to relate in other than the "hurry" mode, then you're well on your way. By slowing down, you also begin to recover the capacity to enjoy experiences that will improve your relationships and enhance your productivity.

STEP III: DON'T FALL INTO THE "TIME MANAGEMENT" TRAP. Achievement-oriented men and women love time management strategies to become more organized and efficient. However, such individuals often subvert the real purpose of time management by carrying the "organization-efficiency" philosophy too far. The goal of time management is to become reasonably well-organized so that you then have time to enjoy life. Those with Hurry Sickness tend to use the extra time purchased through effective time management to accept more tasks or to get more done. This trap increases your stress and builds more frustration when anything goes awry (as they are prone to do). From this misuse of time management skills, you have gained nothing but more pressure and aggravation. A much better plan is to become more organized and use the extra time to slow down so you can keep your life and your responsibilities in true perspective.

STEP IV: ACCEPT THE FLOW OF LIFE AND THE "SMALL STUFF." If you pause a moment to look, there's a flow of life around you. People talk in a set rhythm, walk at a consistent pace, drive close to the legal limits, and work at their own speed. Add to this that people make mistakes, unexpected problems develop, and miscommunication often occurs. To overcome Hurry Sickness, you must accept the flow of life around you. You must also come to terms with the inevitable problems and delays that are part of life and simply can't be eliminated. Because you're in a hurry, you want everyone else to adjust to your fast track, and it can't be done. It's far better for you to slow down and accept the pace of life around you as the norm that probably won't change no matter what you do.

STEP V: CONFRONT YOUR IRRATIONAL IMPATIENCE AND ANGER. Your constant impatience and flareups of anger have at their root your inability to accept inevitable problems and the somewhat slower pace of life of others around you. On the other hand, you have within you the capacity to choose *not* to become angry and impatient. Part of this important aspect of internal emotional control stems from accepting realities, such as the fact that mistakes will be made and that others move a bit slower than you. Another part of your control will stem from consciously choosing not to become upset when problems or delays do occur. This will be most difficult at first because your anger and impatience are long-standing bad habits. As you consciously slow yourself down and choose to remain calm, it soon becomes much easier and you will feel much better. And, you'll have more energy because you won't be wasting it in useless tantrums.

STEP VI: ENJOY EXPERIENCES, NOT REWARDS. The trap of Hurry Sickness is rushing to "get done" to obtain a sense of satisfaction or a reward at the end to the point where it has become your only mode of experience. However, breaking this response pattern requires that you learn to enjoy experiences for their inherent pleasures. When you gain pleasure from an experience, there is no need to get done faster. In fact, you will find yourself wanting to prolong the process because you are having such a good time! While difficult at first, with practice you will find it easier to become pleasantly involved in experiences without worrying about what is coming next or becoming distracted by your irrational need to "get done" with what you're doing now.

STEP VII: DECELERATION TECHNIQUES. Here are a number of strategies to help you get started in the difficult process of psychologically slowing down. You may think of other techniques as you become more involved in reversing your Hurry Sickness.

a. Catch Yourself. Fix your hurrying tendencies so well in mind that you are aware of them every time you begin to rush around. At first you won't always catch yourself, but you will soon get better with practice. You will also learn how to slow down quickly when you find yourself in high gear.

b. Remind Yourself. Many times each day remind yourself of the futility of hurrying and the negative impact it is having on you. Remind yourself that you have more than enough control to stop it and how good you feel about the gains you are making each day.

c. Rescheduling. Avoid scheduling appointments back to back. Give yourself a breather between each one. Use that time to sit back and relax for a moment. Leave home a few minutes earlier to enjoy a leisurely and pleasant drive to work.

d. Get Away. Your workplace *and* your home may contribute to your rapid pace. ("There are so many things that need to be done.") Get out of the house with the family regularly on weekend excursions, day trips, or evenings out, in lieu of big blocks of time once or twice a year.

e. Focus on the Positive. Begin to build cooperation and a team spirit by consciously dropping your negativity and cynicism. Focus on the positive in yourself, your subordinates, and your family. Respond to problems with encouragement and support, not the impatient, explosive anger that is so personally rejecting of others.

f. Small talk. Take time for pleasant chats with colleagues, family members, and your support staff each day. A lunch with your spouse, an easygoing chat in the car, and playing with the kids are all opportunities to build relationships, relax yourself, and get to know people you care about once again. Take care not to talk about work.

g. Quiet Times. Get back in touch with some of your deeper feelings and maintain perspective by spending thirty-minute quiet times by yourself several times a week. Leisurely walks, sitting in a quiet chapel, or watching the sun go down are helpful to get comfortable with yourself and gain the perspective you need to slow down.

Life is For Living

When you get caught up in the throes of Hurry Sickness, you rush through life vainly trying your best to get everything done. In the never-ending process of trying to get caught up, you don't really live life fully. An insightful individual who may have been speaking from personal experience with Hurry Sickness once remarked that, "Life is what happens to you while you're busy making other plans!" Now you know that you can slow down if you choose to, and you have a workable strategy to go about it. To do so, however, will require commitment on your part and perspective on how you want to live your life and why. If you keep on going the way you are now, one day you may look in the mirror and find yourself considerably older (where did the time go?) and look back with regret on years that you didn't really live for you.

As you know, the essence of relaxation is to slow down and experience the *process* of whatever you are doing. That is nearly impossible when you are living each day with Hurry Sickness. You are rushing hither and yon constantly, so you never have the time to psychologically remove yourself from the worries and concerns of the day to emotionally rejuvenate. Your leisure skills soon become rusty, so you can't relax even when you do have the time. Slowly and very subtly, your world becomes a very superficial one devoid of the self-awareness and the deeper meanings that make life worthwhile. With Hurry Sickness, your relationships suffer. You don't feel good. And, life loses its zest as you focus exclusively on what needs to get done. It's time to put a stop to it. Now.

One final point is well worth making. Often one of the driving forces behind Hurry Sickness lies in linking feelings of personal failure to not keeping up or getting everything done. You're a good person and you try to do your best. However, there's a time to just stop, get away from it all for a while, and do something nice for you — for no reason other than it's fun and pleasurable and for you. Abraham Lincoln, a great president and a very wise man, once commented, "The best thing about the future is that it comes only one day at a time." The future is great if you live it fully and richly, one day at a time. That's vastly different than just trying to get through each twenty-four hour segment of your life driven by Hurry Sickness. Hurry Sickness speeds up the pace of your life so you can get more things done. It's up to you to slow it down so you can live a little too!

Chapter 10

Living in the Lion's Den Learning to Work Smarter, Not Harder!

You probably spend more working time in your office than any other single room. In that office lurk pressure and tension. Demands are made on you there day after day, week after week, month after month. It's a grind, and you're not sure that you want to be doing it anymore. The hassles at the office are beginning to get to you. You're becoming more cynical and jaded and hardened by the day. But what can you do? Running away isn't the answer and you're too young to retire.

During the Second World War, "battle fatigue" was a very common malady. It resulted from the prolonged stress of being on the front lines without relief. Some forty years later, Personal Burnout is used to describe a very similar syndrome. If you feel that you are going into battle each day, you may be burning out! And, you're frustrated because life just isn't much fun anymore. You drag yourself home each evening emotionally depleted and physically exhausted. You've been living in the Lion's Den too long. The handwriting is on the wall. Something has got to give. . .and soon!

The essence of Lifestyle Management is balancing work success and achievement with family life, leisure activities, and solid friendships. This strategy insures that the emotionally draining responsibilities and pressures of work are at least partially neutralized by rejuvenating experiences away from the job. In a nutshell, good Lifestyle Management is having enough time to enjoy some of the finer things in life — watching the sun go down, relaxing small talk with a friend, holding hands with a loved one, enjoying a good novel, or just puttering around.

However, to practice Lifestyle Management well, keep several points in mind. First, make a distinction between "Standard of

Living" and "Quality of Life." Your Standard of Living reflects your success in the work world. It is measured by your material possessions, power, status, and your financial assets. On the other hand, Quality of Life is more subjective. It is measured in terms of personal contentment, a sense of inner control and acceptance of self, and an ability to enjoy the emotional richness of life as you live it each day. For motivated professionals, it is far easier to reach a high Standard of Living than to maintain Quality of Life while you are doing so!

Second, it is likely that you have more control over what you do at home than what you do at the office. In your workplace, you are subjected to many pressures and responsibilities that are not of your making. They come with the job and you have no choice but to deal with them. At home, it is easier to make the needed changes to practice Lifestyle Management. If you don't, stress from work spills into home life and the quality of Life After Work deteriorates while you maintain an ever higher Standard of Living. At this point, your success and the personal happiness that should go with it begin to diverge.

Third, while the primary interventions for Lifestyle Management lie in enhancing the quality of Life After Work, there are certain skills that can be used at the office, the Lion's Den, to make your life a bit easier. Thus, the overall strategy for Lifestyle Management is twofold. First, to improve the quality of your Life After Work so that you can emotionally rejuvenate each day from the stresses and pressures of work. Second, to examine life at work closely and make specific changes that will prevent the same pressures and stresses from building to intolerable levels in the first place.

The Backside of Time Management

Before delving into stress-reducing skills that can be used at work, a word of caution. Time Management training is much in vogue these days, but it may also be an indirect cause of Personal Burnout. You are exposed to these helpful organizational skills in the professional literature you read, in in-house training programs, and in the seminars you attend. As a rule, Time Management training seems to have three major thrusts.

1) Reorganizing Your Work. Through better organization and setting your priorities, you gain better control over your many responsibilities and thereby become more efficient. Another way to improve your effectiveness is to be sure that you are . . .

2) Making Every Moment Count. There is great emphasis in Time Management to be engaged in some productive activity every moment. Otherwise you are wasting valuable time. By searching out and eliminating these wasted moments during the day, you are . . .

3) Increasing Your Productivity. As you learn Time Management skills, your output during a given period of time (your workday) increases. As your productivity goes up, you feel better because you are more in control, and the work is getting done.

Now where are you? It all sounds so well and good. However, from a health standpoint, there are some reasons to be cautious about Time Management and not carry these skills too far. In your training, you have been warned about the Dreaded Time Wasters, the Terrible Trauma of Lost Moments, and the Heartbreak of Disorganization. You have been implicitly threatened with the Galloping Guilties if you don't correct these glaring problems right away and make every minute count from now on! The savvy professional keeps Time Management in perspective. Here are three potential problems to keep in mind.

CAUTION #1: BEWARE OF "PRODUCTIVITY COMPRESSION." In other words, recognize and accept your limits. You can get only so much out of a given amount of time. To be reasonably efficient is one thing. To push yourself into becoming a machine that runs faster and faster to get more and more done is quite another. Machines that run continually a high speeds wear out quickly. So will you!

CAUTION #2: BEWARE OF LEISURE TIME SPILLAGE. From a health standpoint, there is only one justification for Time Management — to become reasonably more efficient at work so that you have more time to relax and enjoy life. It is easy to carry Time Management skills home and make them work for you there. At the same time, your ability to enjoy leisure time erodes away. One part of being in control is letting go of Time Management needs so you can enjoy the freedom and spontaneity of leisure activities.

CAUTION #3: BEWARE OF GUILT. Guilt can easily become a subtle driving force behind Time Management. Most professionals have within them a bit of the Puritan ethic that says it is an abomination to waste time. And, leisure time is quite non-productive in terms of tangible products to show for it. You must justify your leisure time in different terms — your health, your happiness, and your career longevity. Confront and break the insidious guilt habit that drives you to work when you should be enjoying some well-deserved leisure activities!

Eliminating "Neurotic" Overtime

A major step in establishing control of your life and working smarter instead of harder lies in examining your relationship to work for any personal vulnerabilities that may lead to unnecessary overtime. It is not uncommon at all to find dedicated and highly skilled individuals working many more hours a week than required because of a personality quirk that has not been resolved. That result is that you work overtime because of *your needs*, not because the organization demands it. In the end everyone loses. You experience all the symptoms of stress overload and Personal Burnout. The organization is scapegoated. Productivity declines. "Neurotic" overtime is a bargain for no one!

By recognizing and taking the necessary steps to resolve any personal vulnerability that leads you to inappropriate overtime work, you are also freeing more time to involve yourself in leisure activities, family life, and friendships. In short, you will be removing a major barrier to the practice of Lifestyle Management. Here are a number of the most frequently encountered personal vulnerabilities that lead to "neurotic" overtime and some directions for resolving each one. Remember, each one of these is "All in Your Head," and that's where each one must be resolved.

OVERTIME VULNERABILITY #1: YOU ARE A PERENNIAL LIFE GUARD. The Life Guard is a too nurturant man or woman who has a high need to rescue other people from their distress whether they actually ask for help or not. John, a very sensitive man, was an otherwise excellent Executive Assistant in a busy city manager's office. However, he directly and indirectly fostered the image of a caretaking parent for everyone in his office as well as in other departments. However, his need to be needed by people in trouble eventually took a heavy toll on his performance, and he worked unnecessarily hard to keep up.

John couldn't help taking other people's problems home with him. To ease their distress, he often took over some of their responsibilities at work. Much of his energy went into helping several colleagues or staff members at a time with after-hours contacts, long discussions, and deep sharing of his obvious concern. He justified his efforts by telling himself that he was helping the office run more smoothly. In fact, he was meeting his own needs to have others depend on him emotionally.

It was true that John was needed by many other people, but how many he was actually helping in a positive way is highly questionable. His attitude was, "Here, here, let me take care of you." He subtly fostered dependency on himself in other people, rather than encouraging competence and independence. Perhaps you have observed parents who supportively express their concern when a child comes running home with a scraped knee. Shortly, the child stops crying and goes out to play again. Other overprotective parents focus entirely on the child's pain and try to take it away with too much sympathy. They attempt to shelter the child from "that big bad world out there." The result? The child clings, cries harder and longer, and becomes more dependent as fears grow. Life Guards like John do the same thing to other adults!

With a helping style like John's, it's no wonder he feels overworked and emotionally exhausted. He needs to be needed in unhealthy ways, but then resents those same people for needing him so much! He sets himself up. No matter where he finds himself, John will continue to experience the inevitable results of his particular kind of neurotic overtime until he breaks the habit of being a too nurturant parent bent on rescuing others from life situations that they must ultimately face themselves.

OVERTIME VULNERABILITY #2: YOU ARE AN APPROVAL SEEKER. Approval Seekers are plentiful everywhere. Their vulnerability is the inability to say "no" and mean it. The result of this deficiency is a destructive overinvolvement in work that the Approval Seeker has accepted, but may not want at all. These unfortunates become office doormats. Everyone steps on them because they always say "yes." They feel like victims and they are right!

What accounts for this common problem? Two factors show up consistently. First, many of these individuals can't deal with conflict so they say "yes" as a way to avoid the possibility that anyone may get mad or upset with them. Second, the fear of rejection or of being left alone (abandoned) is strong in others. For this kind of Approval Seeker to say "no" means to risk that perhaps others will go away and leave them permanently. All too often, these fears stem directly and realistically from childhood experiences. However, they bear no relevance to adult functioning.

Tracy, a bright and articulate securities analyst, couldn't say "no" for both of the above reasons. When no one else wanted to work on a particular project or research difficult data, someone inevitably turned to her. It was well-known that "good old Tracy" would do it even if it wasn't her job. Colleagues learned they could slough considerable work off on her because she wouldn't complain. Later, Tracy became resentfully aware that she had done it again by saying "yes" for the wrong reasons. By then it was too late.

Tracy badly needed some assertiveness training focused on helping her to accept anger and to deal with the typical day-to-day conflicts that are inherent in most relationships. She had to face the fact that conflicts are not necessarily bad and to learn how to handle them constructively. Second, she needed to find out that others can accept conflict too and that everyone didn't have to totally approve of her to get along. Third, she would have to break her perceived link between someone else's anger and *ipso facto* rejection or abandonment of her. Until she faced these issues, she would continue to be victimized by other people. She would remain an exhausted doormat who was depressed and angry to boot!

OVERTIME VULNERABILITY #3: YOU ARE A SUPERMAN/ SUPERWOMAN. If you are not a Superman or Superwoman yourself, you have undoubtedly known one or two along the way. These are individuals who attempt to be everything to everybody. They fulfill multiple roles and juggle their many responsibilities like an acrobat. Their problem, however, is that they accept much more than they can possibly do. They simply don't have the time or the energy to meet all of their commitments. Their problem is that they say "yes" too often, also, but for a different reason than the Approval Seeker. Supermen and Superwomen are competent, but insecure, and haven't yet developed a realistic perspective of what they can comfortably accomplish and still have time left for themselves.

Jack is a classic example of a Superman. As senior personnel officer for a large company, he is also involved in several civic organizations, serves on town government committees, is an officer at the country club, and is a leader in his church. Jack feels chronically overwhelmed by his commitments. His family is angry that he spends so much of his nonwork time away from them. They are being shut out because Jack can't say "no" when asked to chair one more committee or manage one more fund raiser.

Obviously, Jack is a capable and competent administrator. Within limits, he handles stress well. His vulnerability is that he's insecure enough to fall for flattery every time. He's a goner when someone else says, "We need you, Jack. You're the only one who can get us through on this project. You're the best there is." He quickly succumbs to the flattery and gets caught up in the excitement of one more challenge — until he has some time to think about all the other things he has to do. Then he gets depressed. He constantly feels overwhelmed by his responsibilities, but that is because he creates these situations for himself.

Jack must reduce his susceptibility to flattery, an ego trip, and the contagious excitement of a new project. He must learn to back off and examine with real perspective whether he wants to add one more responsibility to his already overloaded schedule. If he could train himself to wait twenty-four hours to think over any new request before impulsively saying "yes" for the wrong reasons, he would find himself saying "no" more often for the right reasons. His family would appreciate the time he would then have to spend with them. And, Jack wouldn't always be on the verge of serious Personal Burnout. Lately, he's been wondering if anything's worthwhile anymore. A bad sign.

OVERTIME VULNERABILITY #4: YOU ARE A PERFECTIONIST. Perfectionists strive to live in a perfect world and they are always disappointed. Unrealistically high personal standards are the hallmark of the Perfectionist, but these standards are also the source of personal discontent and interpersonal difficulty. The fact is that perfection is simply not required for most organizational work. Yet, for the Perfectionist, not being perfect or not producing perfect work brings pervasive feelings of failure, guilt, and inadequacy. Perfectionists are prime candidates for neurotic overtime because of these needs.

Jan was every bit the Perfectionist. She was hard driving, and, as production manager for a mid-sized garment factory, paid attention to details. She saw herself on her way to a satisfying and productive career with the firm. Her perfectionism was her downfall, however. She wasn't able to delegate responsibility at all because no one could do a job as well as she could. "If you want it done right, do it yourself!" was her motto. This was fine if the work needed to be letter perfect. Most of it wasn't. She turned quite acceptable work back to subordinates or personally redid their work to bring it "up to par." She alienated many of her office staff because nothing anyone did was right, and she consistently told them so. Her perfectionism led Jan to work long into the night many weekdays, and of course her work spilled into her weekends. The constant turnover of secretaries in her office was a sad commentary on her perfectionistic style.

There was no question that Jan was dedicated to her work. It was her unrealistically high standards that eventually got her into trouble. Everyone knew that any work Jan was entrusted with would always be of very high calibre. Also observed by her superiors were her interpersonal problems with her staff, the generally low morale, and her virtual inability to delegate responsibility. Jan didn't advance far in the company. She was talented, but her perfectionism stopped her cold.

Jan, and all who are like her, carry a double-edged sword in their perfectionism. She definitely has some learning to do if she is ever to reach her career goals. Her first difficult task is to adjust her standards to the level required by the firm. Second, it would help office morale if she began responding to the positive in her staff in lieu of her constant critical barrage. It's a fact that Perfectionists are some of the most unhappy people in the world, and Jan is no exception. All she sees around her is failure. To beat her career problem and to experience more personal satisfaction, Jan must accept herself as fallible and human; she must cease defining her adequacy using the impossible criterion of perfection.

OVERTIME VULNERABILITY #5: YOU ARE A WORK-AHOLIC. Workaholics are success junkies. They are addicted to achievement, and achieve they do but for all the wrong reasons. Their vulnerability is that they directly link achievements to their self-esteem. If they succeed, they feel good. If success isn't forthcoming, the resultant feeling of failure is tantamount to a negation of the self. Further, a Workaholic can't stop because there is a constant need for reassurance about personal adequacy that comes only through repetitive successful achievements or winning. Conversely, true relaxation brings anxiety, guilt, and with time, depression.

Karen was the epitome of a Workaholic. An aggressive and well-known young attorney, she had long experience with the symptoms of Personal Burnout. She had little time for relationships and even in occasional recreational activities (tennis), she demonstrated a competitive edge that was close to vicious. As with most Workaholics, Karen was very product-oriented. She couldn't slow down to enjoy the *process* of anything. Her total being was geared to reaching goals successfully at all costs.

Karen expected things to change when she left law school and was disappointed when they didn't. Instead, her career picked up speed with more work involvement, more achieving, and less time to relax and enjoy herself. Karen was on the fast track and was quickly burning out — again! To relieve work pressure, she was drinking more after leaving the office. She was also drinking before social engagements to "relax," but even her social outlets were always work-related. Karen was skating on very thin ice and she knew it.

Karen, the ambitious young attorney, had serious issues to face. Chief among them was her inability to separate who she was as a person and as a woman from what she did at work. She had no way of defining herself except through her achievements. Her high need to achieve was actually her way to reassure herself that she was adequate. It is ironic how many star achievers, like Karen, drive themselves for such questionable emotional reasons. As Karen knows, the Workaholic fast track consistently leads directly to unhappiness. The only way to beat it is to define yourself as personally adequate regardless of your work. Then you can enjoy life and people and fun things *and* produce successfully. Karen may back off and find this solution. On the other hand, she may just keep unhappily achieving *ad infinitum*.

Surviving in the Lion's Den

Given that you have little control over your responsibilities at the office, there are a number of survival skills that you can learn to reduce the stress in that environment. These suggestions are common sense, but examining each one carefully will help you become aware of the roots of the stress and the loss of control that you are experiencing these days.

FRONT LINE SKILL #1: MAINTAIN CLEAR WORK BOUNDARIES. A major cause of the deterioration of Life After Work is diffusion of work boundaries. Way back when, your work was confined to specific hours each day. As you've become more successful, the division between work and home life has blurred considerably. Work has invaded evenings, weekends, and even vacations. If you're not actually working, you're thinking about it constantly. The more you work in your head, the more trouble you have "getting away from it all." You may be in a relaxed setting, but you're there more in body than in spirit.

SUGGESTIONS: Set specific times to arrive at work and leave no matter what happens. Take your full lunch break. When working at home (if you have to), do it in a room away from the living area. Go in at a specific time and come out at a specific time. Leave your briefcase at home when you are relaxing or on vacation. Refrain from calling the office so much.

FRONT LINE SKILL #2: LEARN HOW TO DELEGATE. Frequently, inability to delegate is a cause of Personal Burnout. Perfectionists don't trust others to do anything as well as they can. "Stars" don't want to share the limelight (except when things go wrong). Sometimes there is a futile struggle to remain involved in all facets of a business that has grown too large. Whatever the reason, when you don't use your staff well, everyone suffers. Support staff members don't learn needed skills or actualize their potential. A true team doesn't have the opportunity to develop under these conditions. And, you go down the tube trying to meet some highly questionable internal needs.

SUGGESTIONS: Examine your job description or create one for yourself. Do the same for your support staff. Assign duties to staff commensurate with their capabilities. Provide staff members with opportunities to learn and to make mistakes. Give clear directions to staff with deadlines in writing if necessary. Examine carefully your motives for not delegating and the price you are paying.

FRONT LINE SKILL #3: DO ONLY YOUR OWN WORK. Ask yourself this question; "Am I doing only my own work these days?" If the answer is no, then ask yourself why. Maybe you're covering up the incompetence of others. Perhaps colleagues are shifting their work to your desk because you're knowledgeable and willing. You may be conned into extra work through flattery ("Only you can do it"). Or, you may be singlehandedly trying to maintain high quality services in an organization with low productivity norms. No matter what the reason, picking up the slack for slackers is a thankless job, and you suffer as a result. Unless you love martyrdom, here are some things that you can do.

SUGGESTIONS: Choose quality over quantity by concentrating only on your responsibilities. Take an assertiveness training course so you can say "no" to slick buck passers. Don't protect incompetence, and let the chips fall where they may. Examine your vulnerability to flattery. Never say "yes" until you've had a chance to think the proposition over.

FRONT LINE SKILL #4: LEAVE YOUR WORK AREA PERIODICALLY. With more responsibilities, perhaps you've drifted into sitting at your desk for long hours without moving. Psychologists know that lethargy breeds lethargy. The more sedentary you are, the less pep you have and the more you want to sit around. Further, concentrating on close paperwork (or a computer terminal) tires you because of the mental energy required for such activity as well as from eye fatigue. These days, you may habitually eat at your desk and work right through the breaks you used to take. The result is that you are more tired, out of shape, and listless than you can ever remember.

SUGGESTIONS: Always leave your office to eat. Preferably leave the building. Eat lightly at noon and follow it with a short brisk walk in the fresh air outside. At work, take mini-breaks every ninety minutes or so and leave your desk to move around and chat. A regular exercise routine at noon or after work helps. Cut out those long, three-martini lunches.

FRONT LINE SKILL #5: BREAK OUT OF MONOTONOUS ROUTINES. Do you realize that part of your burned-out feeling may be due to nothing more than the deadening routines you've created for yourself? There is an element of boredom in any burnout syndrome. Routines are insidious and deceptive in their influence. They are antithetical to spontaneity and change. You need the new and the refreshing to generate interest and stimulate you. When you keep doing the same things in the same order in the same way day after day, something inside you begins to die. You begin to function like a lifeless automaton trapped in a web of routine. No wonder you're tired of it. And, the more you let routines rule you at work, the more likely you will slip into a similar rut at home!

SUGGESTIONS: Vary your work routines periodically. Pursue a personal development project. Take advantage of professional training seminars. Look into a lateral transfer to broaden your skill base. Seek new and different friends. Don't talk about your work. Find a satisfying new avocation. Take off spontaneously for interesting diversions. Rediscover and savor simple life pleasures.

FRONT LINE SKILL #6: PERSONALIZE YOUR WORK AREA. Your office is like a second home except that it's not as roomy. Because you spend so much time in this small closed environment, it is beneficial to assess its psychological impact on you. It is not uncommon to find offices furnished in a very spartan fashion with uncomfortable chairs. Your office may be dim because of inadequate lighting and full of bland, unstimulating colors. In fact, some offices have a downright depressing effect. There may be little or nothing in that office that reflects you and what you need for comfort. You may have to personalize your office yourself, and it may cost a bit. However, a stimulating office environment may have a strong and positive effect on how you function during the long hours you spend there.

SUGGESTIONS: Keep your blinds open for plenty of sunshine. New and more adequate lighting is a must. Exotic plants will make your office feel alive. Stimulating pictures or posters give you interesting diversions during moments of relaxation. Get a new desk chair to prevent back strain and fatigue. Have favorite magazines and other nonwork reading material available for periodic "time outs."

FRONT LINE SKILL #7: PSYCHOLOGICALLY WORK FOR YOURSELF. A consistent characteristic of strong performers who last is that they work for themselves. Regardless who pays their salary, such individuals work to reach *their own* personal and professional goals. Those who practice Lifestyle Management well also share this orientation. It is very easy to hand over psychological control of your goals and actions to others as you become more and more a company man or woman. At the same time, you lose your center within and the perspective you need to clearly define what is good for you and what you want. By regaining your center, you reestablish control from within. Your priorities become clearer, and you are more productive because you are working for you. With your new center, enjoying life more will become a strong personal goal.

SUGGESTIONS: Carefully review your career to date. Decide what your work means to you personally. Define long term career goals. Admit your hopes and fears. Make major decisions based on *your* best interests. Remind yourself constantly that *you* are in control. Consciously work toward *your* goals each day. Review your progress periodically. Take time regularly to "get away from it all."

FRONT LINE SKILL #8: DON'T DISSIPATE EMOTIONAL ENERGY NEEDLESSLY. As you become more burned out, your sensitivity to small frustrations increases proportionately. Without thinking about it, you now emotionally overreact with frustration, impatience, and anger many times each day. It is now known that how you handle small, recurring hassles is a better predictor of stress-related problems than the big traumas you experience (such as loss of a job, divorce, or death in the family). You have only so much energy to get you through each day, and you are wasting it in these useless emotional responses. And, your reactions change virtually nothing! The very same frustrations will still be there tomorrow. Because you are in control from within, choose not to react. You'll feel better and so will others around you.

SUGGESTIONS: Accept the pace of life around you and gear yourself to it. Relax a moment when you're delayed. Decide to let little problems pass instead of nitpicking. Don't verbalize every critical thought you have. Focus on the positive side of things. Maintain your sense of humor by chuckling at the absurdities that you encounter each day.

FRONT LINE SKILL #9: DEVELOP A PROFESSIONAL BUFFER RELATIONSHIP. A sound psychological rule of thumb is that the stronger your emotions, the more difficult it is to maintain an objective view of yourself, of problem situations, and of the actions of others. It is precisely when you are emotionally reactive that you need an objective "second opinion." This kind of feedback comes best from a colleague who knows you well, who is familiar with the kind of work that you do, and who you trust. This kind of person can be invaluable in making difficult decisions, seeing all sides of a problem, and helping to identify your blind spots. It's up to you to create and use this kind of professional resource wisely. If you do, you will feel less alone and more able to deal with the "bumps" in your career than was possible before.

SUGGESTIONS: Make sure that your buffer will be objective and honest with you. Chat when there is a problem, but also keep in touch when things are going well. Keep your interactions upbeat, not gripe sessions. Avoid overusing your friend. Don't make your colleague into an unofficial therapist. Be willing to reciprocate in kind when your buffer person needs you.

FRONT LINE SKILL #10: BEWARE OF ESCALATION OF OUTPUT. If you are a highly motivated and involved person, it is likely that your sense of personal adequacy has become linked over the years to symbols of your success; that is, your income, your steady advancement, your possessions, your power, and your status in the organization. Each year, you may feel that you must up your "adequacy ante" to continue feeling good about yourself. You have to keep moving upward and onward, and it's a trap. You have inadvertently begun to define yourself as adequate or not through external symbols of success. Conversely, as this process has occurred, you have given up the perception of yourself as a good person based on internal beliefs about yourself. The result is your drive to accomplish more and more and a corresponding difficulty in handling setbacks and failures because your self-esteem is so highly linked to what you do.

SUGGESTIONS: Spend thirty minutes three times weekly alone in contemplation. Separate you as a person from your professional identity. Define your personal strengths. Keep failure in perspective. Rediscover your inner, spiritual self. Reveal yourself to loved ones. Get rid of your "performance fronts." Relax and let others accept you. Ask for emotional support when you need it.

Create Inner Direction

Without question, you live in a highly complex technological world. Less obvious is that you must function continually in a work-oriented society where considerable psychological sophistication is necessary to emotionally survive. For your emotional well-being, it is important for you to have a sense that you retain some modicum of control. That growing trapped feeling that plagues you is really your perception that you have no choice but to continue day after day in the same job with the same continuing frustrations.

It's true that in your office, you must continue to direct your part of the organization's operation. And, you will continue to deal with most of the same hassles that you have always faced. Some things never change. However, to rid yourself of that trapped feeling, you must redevelop inner direction. The fact is that true control lies within. It is your ability to make choices about how to respond to events around you. You can choose to become angry about little frustrations that you can't possibly predict or control.

Or, you can choose to remain calm no matter what happens. All of the Front Line Skills are geared to helping you to regain this type of inner control, but no one will hand it to you on a silver platter. You must realize that your emotional overreactions aren't automatic and that you can choose not to indulge yourself in these emotionally destructive ways.

It is also clear that there is a readiness factor in your ability to once again seize inner control. You're not ready until you perceive yourself as worthy of the good things in life beyond the externals of success. You're not ready until you've concluded that you've paid your dues. You're not ready until you've decided that you are adequate and skilled from within and don't have to constantly demonstrate it to yourself and to others. You're not ready until you see the validity in enhancing your Quality of Life instead of your Standard of Living. When you reach this important crossroads in your life, and it can come at any time, only then are you ready to practice Lifestyle Management and make it stick.

As you begin to take care of yourself emotionally, you not only feel more in control, but your interest and energy return with your productivity. You've made some important decisions within, and you're beginning to enjoy some of the good things in life. And, you're beginning to feel better about yourself in a whole new way that is deep and good. It was Ralph Waldo Emerson who noted that "the only true gift is giving of yourself." You're giving that gift more than ever these days. The fact is that you've regained your center. As you continue to make a good living, you know that you will also be experiencing good living! Not everyone makes it through this difficult turning point in career development. You have . . . and you're glad.

Chapter 11

Softening Up Some: Tactical Communication for the Inadvertent Autocrat

As you climb the ladder of success, your ability to communicate clearly and effectively is a powerful and positive asset. It is virtually impossible to make it to the top without well-developed communication skills. On the other hand, your communication style may be changing. Lack of awareness of the impact of your communication on people may be a significant liability to your continued success and in maintaining healthy marital and family relationships.

Tim is the epitome of a go-getter. An up-and-coming financial services officer, he is hard-driving and intelligent, but is noted for his well-organized and effective presentations to staff and clients. Further, his memoranda are thorough, to-the-point, and compact. His standards are high, and colleagues know that when they are dealing with Tim, they must be on their toes. Over the past two years, Tim has lured several large accounts away from competitors largely through his persuasive communication skills. He is valued at work and is being groomed for a top management slot.

Joanna is Tim's spouse, and she has quite a different story to tell. She sees a Dr. Jekyll and Mr. Hyde in her husband. Well aware of his effectiveness at work, she doesn't understand the dramatic changes in how he communicates with the family. In fact, she is fearful that their marriage is in serious trouble. Tim talks much less these days, and it is impossible to get him to converse pleasantly. He is demanding and sharp with the children and hardly ever smiles at anyone. He distracts himself with the newspaper and television and is annoyed when anyone wants to chat with him. There are frequent arguments with Joanna over little things that shouldn't matter, and a subtle hostility pervades their relationship. Talking to one another these days centers on how to handle the kids or the mechanics of the family finances. Joanna is scared and unhappy. Deep down she suspects that Tim feels the same way.

Tim is, unfortunately, an all-too-common victim of an autocratic communication style that has been growing from the pressure of his steadily increasing responsibilities at work. It is now beginning to show up as a morale problem with his staff although he doesn't realize the seriousness yet. However, its primary impact has been on relationships within the family and especially with Joanna. When he thinks about it, he senses a deep estrangement. The little satisfactions of home life aren't there anymore. He's worried and apprehensive, but doesn't know what to do about it.

Relearning some of the techniques of Tactical Communication is one major avenue to regaining closeness within the family and the personal satisfactions of home life. Tim doesn't realize it yet, but he really needs to "soften up some."

"We Just Can't Talk Anymore"

In the business and corporate world, a high premium is placed on communication that is direct and to the point, that is persuasive, that reflects being in control, that closely adheres to the task at hand, and that is concise. In addition, there is a managerial quality to communication that represents hierarchical lines of authority. Direction is accepted from "upstairs." Direction is given to subordinates who are expected to follow through. Corporate communication is designed to achieve the goals of the organization ever more efficiently with a minimum of wasted effort.

At home, however, such communication expectations don't necessarily apply and in fact may be counterproductive to healthy family relationships. In a marriage, two spouses occupy equal positions of influence with sometimes quite different spheres of expertise and responsibility. These two individuals must negotiate not only the day-to-day activities of the "family organization," but must also nurture a deep, personal relationship at the same time.

In a marriage, "getting things done" must be accomplished within the context of an emotionally-based relationship. Extreme rationality, competitiveness, and the managerial mandate to "do as you're told" must give way to negotiation, compromise, and open discussion of alternatives to preserve the essence of a viable relationship at home. The feeling that "we can't talk anymore" is a symptom of neglected communication skills.

Tactical Communication is "expressing through your verbal responses to another person an essential respect, an acceptance of that person's competencies, a willingness to listen and learn, and an involvement that nurtures growth and development for both." Here are some of the indicators that these qualities have been lost and that an autocratic communication style is now determining your responses. The more of the following statements that you answer "true," the more likely it is that your communication has serious problems that need to be addressed.

T   F

_____ _____   1. It angers you when family members question your judgment or don't immediately accept your solutions to problems.

_____ _____   2. You consider yourself to be more logical and realistic in dealing with family issues than your spouse.

_____ _____   3. You rarely give spontaneous compliments anymore, but you do continue to make critical comments frequently.

_____ _____   4. You tend to be curt and demanding in your responses without taking the time to say "please" or "thank you" anymore.

_____ _____   5. You rarely sit down just to talk with your spouse and children unless it is a crisis situation.

_____ _____   6. You ask many and very direct questions when you communicate with family members.

_____ _____   7. You often "talk" with family members while you are focusing on something else, and you respond without eye contact.

_____ _____   8. You attach evaluative labels like good-bad, right-wrong, OK-not OK, to many more of your responses than in the past.

_____ _____   9. More likely than not, even casual conversations somehow turn into arguments or a fight these days.

T   F

——— ——— 10. You have a bad habit of interrupting other people so they never get a chance to finish what they started to say.

The Techniques of Tactical Communication

Tactical Communication helps you to "soften up some" and become once again that easy-to-talk-to man or woman you were years ago. Remarkable changes will surprise and delight you when you employ the techniques of Tactical Communication at home and at work. Your image will change. Communication will become easier as it becomes more open. You'll feel better about yourself. Here are some tips to start this process.

TIP #1: SYSTEMATICALLY REMOVE JUDGMENTAL STATEMENTS. At work, you are constantly evaluating and being evaluated. However, it is easy to begin to see your world in terms of evaluative dichotomies — success-failure, good-bad, OK-not OK, right-wrong. When you constantly relate in this way, you begin to close the doors of open communication. Other people particularly resent being constantly and negatively judged. You probably have developed the habit of making too many evaluative statements in general. This communicates that you think you're better than anyone else. Reducing the number of negative statements you make and replacing them with positive feedback (or saying nothing at all) will be an important first step in eroding the negative and autocratic image you have created.

Autocratic Style: "You were wrong to stay out late, John. You know that's not OK."

Tactical Style: "We missed you when you didn't get here on time, John. Hope there wasn't a problem."

TIP #2: USE THE SUBTRACTION METHOD. If a judgmental statement is absolutely necessary, the subtraction method will soften it and increase the chance it will be accepted. Instead of making a statement of the negative, subtract from the optimal. When you use the subtraction method, you communicate to the receiver that you see the norm as positive and that you care. Straight negative feedback communicates the opposite, that the norm is negative and that you are confirming it — again!

Autocratic Style: "What's *your* problem? You look just terrible today."

Tactical Style: "Gee, you don't seem to be your usual bright self today."

TIP #3: MAKE POLITE REQUESTS, NOT DEMANDS. In a hectic work environment, it is easy to turn what should be polite requests into cold and autocratic demands. Begin immediately to use the magic words "please" and "thank you" again with everyone. Not only are these words part of common courtesy, but they also communicate your respect and consideration of other people. Cold and demanding and unfeeling are psychological attributes that tend to be perceived together. With more polite requests, you will generate much good will and cooperation from those around you at work and at home.

Autocratic Style: "Get me another tablet when you go out again."

Tactical Style: "Jan, I'd appreciate it if you could pick up a tablet for me next time you get to the store. Thanks."

TIP #4: ELIMINATE THE ACCUSATIVE "YOU." When you are responding to any kind of problem situation, beginning a statement with "you did" or "you didn't" almost invariably creates a defensive reaction in the receiver. Your comment comes across as a blaming accusation. This habit, over time, generates a divisive "me" versus "you" attitude that sparks resentment and conflict. To eliminate this problem, substitute team pronouns like "we" or "us." These togetherness words imply (correctly) a shared responsibility and a shared motivation for a positive outcome.

Autocratic Style: "You didn't get the house cleaned up again. It looks like a wreck."

Tactical Style: "Let's all try to keep the house picked up as much as possible."

TIP #5: REDUCE YOUR USE OF QUESTIONS. In your work world, a prerequisite for efficiency and success is obtaining relevant information as rapidly and as effectively as possible. To get information quickly, you learn to ask questions—Who? What? Where? When? Why? These are the "W" questions that when overused, place you in the role of interrogator. Again, defensiveness and withholding are often the result. This is particularly true if your questions have a rapid-fire quality. To create more open communication, drastically reduce your use of "W" questions or the closed questions that require only a "yes" or "no" answer. Instead, use leading statements like, "Tell me more," "Uh-huh," "That's interesting," and so on.

Autocratic Style: "What happened here? Why did Billy do that?

What's the matter with him? Why didn't you try to stop him?"
Tactical Style: "Let's sit down and talk about the situation to find out what happened and what we can do about it."

TIP #6: STATE WHAT YOU WANT, NOT WHAT YOU DON'T WANT. A habit of highly dubious value is continuing to make negative statements that could easily be phrased in positive ways. In practical terms, you tend to state what you don't want instead of what you desire. We all seem to have a sensitivity to words like "no," "can't," and "don't," just to name a few. These overused words trigger emotional and rebellious reactions in other people that are entirely unnecessary because when you state what you want, then these words won't be used. Further, you will be perceived as much less critical and as easier to talk with as well.
Autocratic Style: "You can't go out Saturday night, Andrea."
Tactical Style: "Andrea, we'd like you to stay around Saturday evening, please."

TIP #7: OFFER HELPFUL INVOLVEMENT INSTEAD OF NEGATIVE LABELS. Purely and simply, negative labels are put-downs that inhibit communication and damage self-esteem. Labeling others (name-calling) as stupid, impulsive, crazy, or careless, isn't a constructive response because you sit aloof in judgment in lieu of helping to create new learning. Many problem situations are actually "teachable moments" where you can be most helpful in guiding the development of someone else. It is also by far the best way to prevent similar problems from occurring again. You will be seen as caring and concerned, and your help will be appreciated. Getting mad and putting someone else down is just an easy copout.
Autocratic Style: "What's the matter with you? That was the stupidest move I've ever seen."
Tactical Style: "Dave, I know that that situation didn't work out well for you. Let's talk a bit about what you could do differently in a similar circumstance."

TIP #8: ACCEPT OTHERS' VIEWPOINTS AND LEARN FROM THEM. The philosophy of the autocrat is that there are just two ways to do anything, your way and the wrong way. The fact is that you are not wiser than everyone else, only more insecure. Encouraging others to state their views and accepting these perspectives as valid, even though different from yours, is most helpful in opening channels of communication. When you do this,

you convey respect for the wisdom and experience of other people, and you make fewer mistakes because you have additional relevant information. It is a tactical plus to pool wisdom and learn from others rather than letting your insecurity turn every difference of opinion into a "me" versus "you" struggle for dominance.
Autocratic Style: "I don't care what you think; do it the way I told you to."
Tactical Style: "You have a good point there. I don't totally agree, but I can see your rationale. Let's talk about it some more."

TIP #9: ADMIT YOUR FALLIBILITY. You are not superhuman and you *do* make mistakes from time to time. Too often when it is abundantly clear to everyone that you goofed, and you know it deep down, you can't admit it and open communication is dealt a severe blow. Your inability to admit mistakes and apologize for them directly and sincerely is an index of the insecurity that creates your false pride. Accepting your fallibility is really the process of accepting your humanness, and everyone will respect you for it. It's an unnecessary burden for you to maintain the facade of perfection. It wastes your valuable energy and distances you from other people.
Autocratic Style: "I did that because I'm right and you know it" or stony silence.
Tactical Style: "Jeff, I know what I said hurt you, and I want to say I'm sorry. I hope you will forgive me. I made a mistake."

TIP #10: GIVE DIRECT ATTENTION AND LISTEN THOUGHTFULLY. One of the surest signs of a communication breakdown in the family is avoiding a spouse or children who want to talk with you. Giving perfunctory reponses while watching TV or reading the paper doesn't cut the mustard for a good relationship. Without eye contact and your full attention, communication becomes frustrating to others. Your message is: "I don't care. Go away, you're bothering me." If it's not an opportune time to talk, suggest a later time when you can give your full attention to that other person. Don't say "later," though, just as a way to avoid discussion at all! Just a few moments of your full attention works wonders. Remember, you may be producing many "nagging" responses through your lack of willingness to take a few minutes to talk now and then.
Autocratic Style: (while watching TV) "OK, OK, I heard you. Talk to me about it later."

Tactical Style: "Let's go into the living room where we can sit and talk. It will take me just a few minutes to wind this up."

Giving Compliments (and Making Them Stick)

Not nearly enough complimentary remarks are made these days. The standard fare in both organizations and families is swift, sure, and specific critical responses when something goes wrong or when a mistake is made. On the other hand, verbal support for what is done well is a sorely neglected skill and motivational tool. It's also a sad reality that many compliments that are given simply aren't effective. That is, they are communicated in such a way that the potentially positive impact on the recipient is virtually eliminated. Far too many compliments are absolutely *incredible.* That is, they are without any credibility at all to the person who receives them!

There are several advantages gained by learning to give quality compliments. By responding to the positive in other people, you communicate that you really "see" their strengths and appreciate them as individuals. By so doing, you enhance your own image as a positive and supportive person as well. An equally important reason for giving clear positive feedback is that it increases the chances that negative feedback will be heard and accepted as constructively intended by the recipient. In other words, when you give consistent positive feedback, your perceptions are more likely to be trusted when corrective feedback becomes necessary. Your motives will more likely be perceived as helpful.

Compliments can easily be made more effective in producing a positive impact on the self-esteem of the recipient by following a few simple guidelines. These suggestions will help you to eliminate the factors in compliments that negate the positive message you want to communicate. In some ways, it seems silly to talk about the guidelines for giving compliments. In truth, however, there are so many bad habits associated with compliments that it is well worth the time it takes to overview them with suggestions on the Complimentary Corrections necessary to make them pure and effective statements of positive regard.

POSITIVE NEGATION HABIT #1: YOU MAKE COMPLIMENTS VERY GENERAL. Examples: "You're such a nice person." "You're a great date." The problem with this kind of compliment is that there is very little useful information contained within it that can be attached to the recipient's self-concept. On the other hand, negative feedback is usually very specific. "Stop pushing your sister." "Get to work exactly on time tomorrow morning." If you have consistently received global positive feedback and highly specific criticism, then over time you have learned much more about your weaknesses and failings than about your personal strengths and assets.

COMPLIMENTARY CORRECTION. Make it a point to make your compliments behaviorally specific. That way, the recipient will know exactly what you are responding to in a positive way. It then becomes usable information that can be more easily integrated into and used as part of the self-image of the recipient.

POSITIVE NEGATION HABIT #2: YOU USE FLATTERY IN A MANIPULATIVE WAY. Examples (in rapid sequence): "You're the greatest. I don't know what I'd do without you. You're the best we've ever had around here." How do you feel when someone else begins to shower you with flattering remarks right out of the blue? In all probability, you become suspicious and defensive. The giver's motives are questioned because you sense you're being "buttered up" for some reason. If you're insecure enough, you melt under this barrage of manipulative support and give in to the request you know is coming. Whether you fall for this ploy or not, you resent the manipulation and distrust the manipulator.

COMPLIMENTARY CORRECTION. To build trust in your compliments, give positive feedback consistently. With regular supportive remarks, a strong and trusting relationship with the recipient will grow and cooperation will be enhanced in an open, nonmanipulative way of relating that will benefit you both.

POSITIVE NEGATION HABIT #3: YOU GIVE COMPLIMENTS IN THE FORM OF EXPECTATIONS. Examples: "You could be the best student in your class if you'd only study harder." "I know that you could have the top sales record in this region if you'd only make the effort." The essence of an expectation compliment is your statement of what someone else *could be* if they were only more motivated. In fact, this kind of compliment actually communicates your disappointment in the recipient's failure to measure up *now*. No wonder these kind of "compliments" hurt a bit. They are really failure statements that aren't complimentary at all!

COMPLIMENTARY CORRECTION. Instead of communicating your expectations of someone, find something positive to respond to in what that other person is already doing. In other words, consistently support and build on what is, not what could be (in your eyes).

POSITIVE NEGATION HABIT #4: YOU HAVE A "STROKE AND STINGER" PROBLEM. Examples: "The quality of your typing has really improved lately. Now if you'd only get here on time we'd be all set." "You look great in that suit, but you could stand to lose a bit more weight." Some individuals just can't bring themselves to make a positive statement and let it stand by itself. Instead, they inevitably follow a compliment with a stinging negative remark. Stroke and stinger responses seem to say: "You've made a start, but don't let it go to your head. Here's the next thing for you to work on to improve yourself." The recipient can never feel good in these circumstances because another weakness to correct is always being pointed out.

COMPLIMENTARY CORRECTION. Clean up these questionable compliments by letting your positive statements stand alone. Without the "stinger," the recipient will feel good about the compliment and about you. If you have something negative to say, do it later and privately in proper context.

POSITIVE NEGATION #5: YOU COMPLIMENT THROUGH COMPARISONS. Examples: "I know that you're much brighter than your brother will ever be!" "Why can't you be more like Andrea? She's a real go-getter." In all comparison compliments, you say something positive about one person by putting down another. Sometimes these kinds of "compliments" are a distorted attempt to motivate. In fact, everyone loses. The "winner" is not seen as a unique individual, but only as "better than" someone else. The "loser" is put down and indirectly shamed, sometimes publicly. Comparison compliments are an easy bad habit that not only hurt others, but also create deep ambivalence about you and your motives.

COMPLIMENTARY CORRECTION. Keep direct comparisons out of your compliments by training yourself to see an individual clearly. Then direct your comments specifically to that individual's personal strengths and unique attributes. You help build positive self-esteem in the recipient by taking pains not to create a "winner" at the expense of a "loser."

POSITIVE NEGATION #6: THE COMPLIMENT WITH A CUTTING EDGE. Examples: "I really love your home. It looks so 'lived in.'" (Translation: "Your house is really a mess.") "I really like that dress on you, now that after all these years you can wear size ten." (Translation: "I remember when you were really fat.") On the surface, these compliments sound fine. A bit deeper, though, there's a cutting edge that hurts. Because the putdown is usually so well hidden, it is difficult to confront directly either publicly or privately. Basically, cutting compliments are a way to express ill will without taking responsibility for it. These kind of responses are a passive-aggressive way to communicate your bad feelings and have been raised to nearly an art form by some men and women.

COMPLIMENTARY CORRECTION. Learn to work out issues with other people in direct and mature ways. Then clean up your "chocolate-covered, rotten-cherry compliments" by taking the putdowns out of them. Also listen carefully to what you say. You may not even be aware that your compliments cut!

POSITIVE NEGATION #7: YOU RESPOND WITH "COMPLIMENTARY" INSULTS. Examples: "Why, you no good s.o.b., why don't you stay home where you belong instead of coming over here to bother me!" (Translation: "Welcome. I'm really glad to see you!") "For someone as feeble-minded and lazy as you are, you must have paid someone off to get all those new accounts!" (Translation: "I'm really impressed by what you did!") This kind of compliment is disguised within an overt insult (the opposite of the "cutting compliment"). Used more by men than women, insulting compliments are designed to communicate positive feelings without expressing them openly. For some individuals, it's the only kind of positive comment used, and everyone receives complimentary insults. Too often, these kind of remarks are misunderstood by the recipient and result in hurt feelings and resentment.

COMPLIMENTARY CORRECTION. Reciprocal complimentary insults exchanged with another person who understands is fine. However, also learn to be more direct in your expressions of positive regard when the situation calls for it. That way, you can choose how to respond to particular individuals to prevent misunderstandings and consequent negative feelings.

How to Gracefully Receive Compliments

As much as we all crave positive feedback, it seems almost inconceivable that so many individuals can't gracefully accept a compliment when it is given! Lowered eyes, blushing, and obvious embarrassment are combined with statements intended to refute the positive message: "You don't mean that." "That's just not true and you know it." "You don't know what you're talking about." These kinds of negating responses reflect your personal insecurity and damage your image. Negating responses to compliments also communicate low self-esteem, immature humility, and distrust of anyone who could possibly say anything nice about you.

Accepting a compliment directly and sincerely is not difficult. In doing so, you interact with the positive self-esteem of a mature and competent person. It is to your benefit to learn not only how to *give* effective compliments, but how to *receive* them gracefully as well. When you do, more complimentary remarks will come your way. If you don't, you may inhibit others' positive responses to you because of your embarrassed denial.

The guidelines for receiving compliments are simple and easy. When a compliment is received, look the giver right in the eye and respond with a sincere acknowledgement and a simple thank you. Then go on with the conversation. Here are some sample responses to help you start receiving compliments in a more positive way. Train yourself to use them.

- "Thank you. It's so nice of you to notice."
- "I really appreciate you saying that. Thank you for mentioning it."
- "Hearing that really makes me feel good. Thank you so much."

Everything to Gain, Little to Lose

As you have become more autocratic in your communication, you are losing touch with people because safe and open relationships are compromised by your insensitivity. The consequences are serious. Your responses create defensive reactions and promote perception of you as a negative, unyielding, and uncaring person. That may not be you at all!

In addition, several other considerations are important if you have inadvertently adopted an autocratic communication style. First, be aware that in your visible roles at work and at home, you are a model for those around you. This is particularly true of your children. You are important to them and they will emulate you. You may not see the results for years, but be sure that you are influencing them each and every day right now. Not only are the seeds of later relationship problems now being sown for them, but it is quite possible they will use *your* tactics on you later!

Second, if you look closely you will find that people important to you are: 1) withdrawing from you completely or not relating to you unless absolutely necessary; 2) working around you in indirect ways without letting you know what's going on; or 3) engaging you with a combative expectation that produces arguments and conflict. You are progressively isolated because no one wants to deal with you. No wonder you feel estranged.

As you again create open communication using tactical responses, take note of three other important points.

1. Tactical Communication Requires More Words. "Softening up some" means taking a bit more time to say a few more words. This extra effort will pay handsome dividends in restoring openness in your relationships and that sense of togetherness that has been lost.

2. Watch Your Body Language. More often than not, autocratic communication brings with it a frowning face, aggressive gestures, and threatening postures that exacerbate the negative impact of what you say. Relax your body, and especially your face, when you talk to reduce this effect. Frequent smiles help, too.

3. Your Tone of Voice Is Important. Reasonable words said in an inappropriate tone of voice destroy your message. You may also have become very loud, so listening carefully to yourself is a plus. Remain calm and low key and completely remove subtle mockery, sneering undertones, facetiousness, or that sarcastic edge from what you say.

Restoring Tactical Communication as your natural style of relating will be difficult at first. Don't expect others to immediately open up with you because they don't trust you yet. However, with consistency and a sincere effort to change, soon enough the pleasant give and take that will make you (and everyone else) feel so much better will blossom. Someone has commented that charm "is an inner glow that casts everyone around you in a positive light." You can afford to be charming. For your ultimate success and quality in your relationships, you can't afford not to!

Chapter 12

Angry Interactions: Conflict and Compatibility in the Combat Zone

Without question anger is the most misunderstood and abused of all the human emotions. Anger is an emotional energy with great potential for spurring personal awareness and deepening relationships. More frequently, angry interactions play havoc with family life, with career, with relationships at work, and with self-esteem. Few of us have been properly trained to handle anger in constructive ways. Healthy role models are few and far between. No wonder so many relationships at work and at home are broken on the inability of the individuals involved to express anger and to resolve conflicts in healthy ways.

In examining the many people problems that result from maladaptive expressions of anger, several basic facts about this controversial emotion must be clarified. First and foremost, anger is a healthy emotion. Everyone experiences anger from time to time. Some individuals experience too much of it. Others suppress it as undesirable or immoral and go to great lengths to deny its presence. Your anger is an emotional message. It is a form of communication that indicates that something is not quite right in a relationship and that there is a problem that should be addressed.

Second, it is axiomatic that anger and conflict are highly related. The experience of anger is the impetus for conflict. Conflict is also normal in healthy relationships and is not anti-thethical to compatibility at all. No two individuals in a relationship are alike. Personal opinions, values, ways of doing things, and approaches to tasks are likely to be different. Conflict is the result. The critical element, however, is how the conflict is handled. Working out conflicts in adaptive ways can enhance your compatibility with another person and deepen trust between you. Or, anger and conflict can be a destructive wedge that keeps you apart.

Third, much of the problem with anger is that it results in aggressive responses rather than healthy conflict resolution. A conflict does not necessarily include hostile or aggressive (punitive) interactions. To put it simply, your angry feelings can be talked out or acted out. When you act them out, aggression is likely to be the driving force of your responses. Anger acted out leads to negative feelings in everyone involved, and the probability of more conflict later is increased. With aggressive responses, issues are not addressed in a constructive way because the intent is to overpower and hurt instead of to understand and find a workable solution to a problem.

Learning more about anger and conflict and how to handle these emotionally sensitive interactions has everything to do with your health and happiness. When you use your anger to find solutions to problems in ways that lead everyone to feel good, then you have made a long step toward personal maturity. You also become a more effective leader and a better manager. Without such skills, you compromise yourself at work *and* on the home front!

When Anger Is *YOUR* Problem!

Misused anger is a tremendous people problem. It is important to determine whether your anger is evoked by an actual difference of opinion with someone else or whether you are using anger for highly questionable emotional purposes. Misused anger is very common and in all such situations, the anger you express is unfair to others, interferes with positive relationships, and diminishes your self–esteem (not to mention the self–image of the recipient). At its core, misused anger is a personal problem, not an interpersonal one — until you make it so.

Misused anger always reflects an unresolved emotional issue within you. If you suspect you are misusing anger, then examine your anger responses carefully. You will discover a definite pattern. Your anger is triggered in certain kinds of situations to serve specific emotional needs of which you may or may not be aware. Here are the seven most common ways that anger is misused.

MISUSED ANGER #1: TO AVOID PERSONAL RESPONSI- BILITY. Angry blaming is your very immature tendency to *al-*

ways find a scapegoat for whatever goes wrong. Conversely, you are unable to accept personal responsibility for goofing up, making a mistake, or just not getting done what needs to be done. To hear you talk about it, you are perennially the victim of circumstances for which you cannot be held accountable. Because you feel victimized, you lash out with blaming anger. Deep down, you know that you are responsible, but you just can't bring yourself to admit it. It's easier to blame whatever happened on someone else. That's what children do, and in this way you've never grown up.

AN ANGER ALTERNATIVE. Begin to mature by admitting your failings and taking full responsibility for all of your actions. Learning to apologize sincerely and directly will help your image immensely. In the process, you will learn to separate your behavior from you as a person and drop your false pride. It's only human to be wrong now and then and to admit it. When you deny responsibility and blame other people, the only one you're fooling is you. Further others easily see your insecurity through the transparent image of infallibility you attempt to project.

MISUSED ANGER #2: TO "HURRY UP" THE WORLD. Your easily aroused impatience is nothing more than your angry response to what you see as a slowly moving and imperfect world. You have things to do, people to meet, and places to go. When things don't happen fast enough to suit you or, when little delays are encountered, you get mad. You used to be easygoing and patient, but now you're not only extremely busy, but continually frustrated as well. You find yourself angry many times each day about little things that you cannot possibly predict or control or prevent. You have completely lost objectivity, and you're very verbal about your irritation. Nothing moves fast enough for you as you angrily buck the normal flow of life around you.

AN ANGER ALTERNATIVE. It's a grave mistake to think that your anger will speed up everyone else and eliminate all the barriers to your progress. Instead, recognize that you have a choice in every one of these situations: to get angry and waste your energy with no results or to choose to maintain perspective and "roll with the flow" of life. By choosing the latter alternative, you are relearning patience by putting minor hassles in perspective. In the big scheme of things, these daily irritations make absolutely no difference at all!

MISUSED ANGER #3: PSYCHOLOGICAL DISPLACE-MENT. The dynamics of this destructive habit are that you become angry in one situation, but wait to express it later in another setting that is safer and less threatening. For example, you become angry at someone in the office, but suppress it there. Later, when you get home, your spouse, the children, and even the household pet are unfairly blasted. Displaced anger is extremely detrimental to relationships because those who bear the brunt of your angry outbursts don't deserve it. They are your chosen emotional victims because they're safe and vulnerable. Some of your anger may even be legitimate, but you don't deal with it at the source. Instead you cop out and let it destroy intimacy, family life, and ultimately, your health and happiness.

AN ANGER ALTERNATIVE. The solution to displacement is straightforward. Sure, you can't let your anger out in all circumstances. The consequences could be disastrous. But you *can* learn to talk out the major issues with the individual with whom you have a conflict. It's surprising how well things work out if issues are presented in a mature, calm, and tactful way. If that's not possible, *talk* it out at home or with a friend who can offer alternatives or help you to maintain perspective. Learning to *talk about* your feelings instead of *acting them out* is a most valuable skill.

MISUSED ANGER #4: TO REDUCE TENSION. Constant work pressure and chronic stress that isn't released through relaxation is quite frequently emotionally transformed into anger and irritability. With a stress overload, you have a short fuse that is easily set off by inconsequential events. Relating with a chip on your shoulder, you may even pick fights as a means to reduce stress through angry interactions. There is tension release in the short term, but in the long run, this bad habit backfires because you sow ill will wherever you go. People you were once close to become uncomfortable around you. They may even begin to attack you in return because of your irrational touchiness. More stress is then created. You lose!

AN ANGER ALTERNATIVE. Realizing that your anger is actually a symptom of stress overload, seek other more adaptive strategies for tension reduction. An exercise program, a daily walk, a pleasant avocation, or just sitting for a few moments by yourself to read the paper are all examples of effective decompression techniques. Experiment to find a technique that works best for you and then practice it regularly. By making this time a priority, your anger is reduced as you learn to relax and "get away from it all." You'll keep your center and your perspective!

MISUSED ANGER #5: TO CREATE INTERPERSONAL DISTANCE. A subtle misuse of anger is to reduce the vulnerability of emotional closeness through conflict. Every person maintains a "comfort zone" of interpersonal distance from those they love or care about. When there's too much closeness, one way to create distance is through angry interactions. Sometimes, constant petty bickering is used for the same emotional purpose. Often the individual does not recognize this pattern because it is subconsciously motivated. However, it is effective in reducing openness and trust in a relationship. Ongoing problems are created when one person wants closeness, and a partner constantly reduces it through anger and conflict. True intimacy is denied to all involved.

AN ANGER ALTERNATIVE. To break this pattern, recognize that you're using anger to sabotage intimacy. The second step is to figure out why emotional closeness is so threatening to you. Past hurt, fear of commitment, the dread of abandonment, or mixing up intimacy and dependency can all produce this destructive coping response. Enhance your tolerance for closeness by slowly increasing your openness with someone else. Choose *not* to use anger to create distance. Instead, simply say you need some time alone or that you are uncomfortable with so much closeness, and then work out a compromise.

MISUSED ANGER #6: TO DOMINATE AND CONTROL. In other words, you use anger as a destructive weapon to get *your* way. A sure sign of insecurity is use of temper tantrums or angry denunciations to dominate people or control situations. You're too immature for healthy give and take. In your mind, there are two ways to do anything: your way and the wrong way! You are not open to other viewpoints, change, or creative compromises because you fear being controlled yourself. You have developed a jungle mentality: control or be controlled, dominate or be dominated. Your ploy is to use attacking anger and personal put-downs to stifle any "opposition" to what you want. At the first hint of dissension, you wade in with both feet and ask questions later.

AN ANGER ALTERNATIVE. The bottom line of resolving this personal problem is to drop your distrustful "me" versus "you" attitude. When you feel threatened, stifle your angry offense and listen carefully instead. Not controlling someone else does not mean that you are being controlled or that you are out of control. Instead of attacking the other person, cooperatively attack the problem to find creative solutions that leave everyone (including you) satisfied. A whole new perspective on people will open to you as you learn to work *with* others, not *against* them.

MISUSED ANGER #7: TO MOTIVATE INTO ACTION. In this case, your view of motivation is sadly simple: intimidate and create fear to get something done. This is the KITSE Method (Kick In The South End) of motivation. Your only decisions are how hard to kick someone else and how often. It is inconceivable to you that anyone could be internally motivated to do well or to be externally motivated through positive incentives. With your blinders on, you never give anyone else a chance before you initiate swift KITSE motivation. Your style stems from your perception of people as basically lazy, unmotivated, and potential slackers unless *you* "motivate" them to do otherwise. Your angry attacks are your narrow-minded and unsophisticated way of doing just that.

AN ANGER ALTERNATIVE. A breakthrough for you will be learning the value of positive incentives. Direct support and back-up, encouraging words, and consistently responding to what is being done well works wonders. When you begin to put these kinds of responses into practice, it will also mean that you are changing your negative view of people and broadening your motivational skills. Others will soon perceive you in a more positive way and will work for you, not in spite of you as respect for your leadership grows.

Styles of Conflict to Avoid

In time, any two individuals in a given relationship evolve a particular style for dealing with anger and conflict. There are a number of commonly encountered modes of angry interaction that are clearly divisive and disruptive to healthy relationships whether at home or at work. All share aggressive and punitive motivation as the basis for the interaction. Little healthy discussion of issues is evident in any of them. Perhaps you will see yourself in one or another of the following scenarios. Now is the time to eliminate any of these patterns you see in your angry interactions. You will mature in your ability to constructively handle conflict as a result.

STYLE #1: THE FIRECRACKER: The fuse is lit and it's a short one. There's a quick, highly charged explosion of blaming anger and then it's all over. Calmness reigns and all is forgiven. These individuals would have you believe it's nothing personal. It is simply a way of blowing off steam, but it's hard to take repeatedly by the person who has been selected as the target. You're the target because you're convenient and vulnerable.

STYLE #2: THE VISIT TO ICELAND. This is the classic cold shoulder technique. You punish through silence and refusal to respond to that other person who made you angry. The freeze-out is sometimes used by both individuals in senseless contests to see who can last longest (and win) before one breaks and sues for peace. Tremendous energy is wasted when you use this style of conflict. Further, it rarely solves problems and only breeds resentment.

STYLE #3: THE MEMORY LANE REHASH. The idea here is to store choice hurts over the years and then bring them out as weapons when in conflict with another person. The angry interaction always moves quickly from the present to rehashing the past with no resolution. Present issues are lost as the battle rages over past wrongs that can never be forgiven. You keep hurts alive for the sole purpose of beating someone else with them.

STYLE #4: THE SOCIAL ZINGER CHAMPION. In this type of warfare, anger may never break out into the open. The motive here is to express your outrage through verbal darts thrown in social settings. Little cuts, perhaps some choice gossip or subtle put-down humor, all difficult to confront directly, are favorite tactics here. You know you're under attack, but you may have no idea why because the issues haven't been brought out into the open for discussion. This person would rather stab you in the back than talk to your face.

STYLE #5: TRIVIA FIGHTS. Repeated confrontations about little irritations are the hallmark of this mode of conflict. Forgetting to put the toothpaste cap on, being five minutes late, or the way you organize things are all cause for conflict. These brushfires don't represent the real issues which may be bigger than either party is willing to face. Instead there is constant picking at the little things about someone else that bother you.

STYLE #6: THE GUERILLA FIGHTER. The core strategy of guerilla war is harassment and sabotage while large-scale confrontations are avoided. The enemy is slowly worn down. You find that suddenly a myriad of little things begin to go wrong — a crucial memo is misplaced, the dog found its way to your bed and slept on it, no one told you about a particular important meeting. Once or twice is coincidental, but three times makes a pattern. Someone is using a passive-aggressive style to get you in little ways, and the Guerilla Fighter is a pro!

STYLE #7: GANG FIGHTS. When conflict breaks out, the first thing to do is to mobilize support for your side. Go immediately to your friends, your parents, your colleagues and tell them about it. Then they will know how oppressed you are by that certain person. You don't fight your own battle; you only talk about how victimized you are. Others see your immaturity in these responses. If they knew what was good for you, they would refuse to take sides and send you back to deal with the issues. The Gang Fighter is an expert at putting other people in the middle.

STYLE #8: THE "LAST WORD" SCENARIO. Here a conflict is never permitted to really end. These are drag-on, drag-out fights in which one person won't let go until he or she has the final word. Things go along well and then it erupts again a day or so later. One person follows the other from room to room instead of disengaging to calm down and then talk it out. Conflicts like these may go on for days or weeks at a time. This kind of conflict always signals lack of ability in one or both individuals to sit down and talk things out in reasonable ways.

STYLE #9: THE PROVOCATEUR. This person plays a potentially dangerous game. One individual knows exactly what to say and how to say it so that the other person totally loses control. A strong counterattack is provoked and it confirms a basic belief. "See, I knew you couldn't handle this problem. You just lose control." There is little possibility for healthy conflict resolution here because one person immediately strikes at the other person's vulnerabilities. The intent is to hurt that other person emotionally, not to solve a problem.

STYLE #10. THE SEMI-ANNUAL FREE-FOR-ALL. These all-out bouts tend to occur at regular six- to eight-month intervals. These explosive confrontations quickly escalate from a minor disagreement to total war. While it is not a prolonged conflict (a day or so), it is no-holds-barred while it is going on. Then it is over, and things go smoothly for another six or eight months. These periodic world wars feature a clear pattern in which things slowly build up to a flash point at which time everything is let loose at once. When that happens, it's not a healthy forum for any sort of decent dialogue!

Three Attitude Readjustments

If you have concluded that how you handle anger and conflict could stand some improvement, then you have made a big first step to better relationships that will improve family life and your career potential. As the basis for healthy conflict resolution, a proper attitude is a must. Here are three attitude readjustments that may be necessary for you to make. With them, you will create an atmosphere where differences can be discussed and creative solutions found that will benefit everyone involved.

ATTITUDE ADJUSTMENT #1: IN CONFLICT RESO-LUTION, THE ONLY HEALTHY OUTCOME IS TWO WINNERS. Almost everyone can use a refresher on this basic principle of conflict resolution. Your gut-level tendency is to fight to win. Fighting has become an extension of your competitive skills that you have used to succeed all your life. However, any time there is a clear "winner" in a conflict, there are actually two losers. The "winner" has become a powerful and punitive oppressor, and the "loser" is now a resentful victim. You learn to dread conflicts because aggression and hurt are the primary ingredients. With every new conflict, the self-esteem of both parties is damaged further and interpersonal trust is progressively diminished. To produce two winners, put your competitive urges and your pride aside in lieu of opening a genuine dialogue with that other person. Strive to protect the self-respect and self-esteem of that other person as well. When you do so, trust will build and you will feel better about yourself and your relationship with that person.

ATTITUDE ADJUSTMENT #2: ACCEPT ANGER AND CON-FLICT AS A HEALTHY FORM OF EMOTIONAL COMMUNICA-TION THAT PROMOTES PERSONAL GROWTH AND EN-HANCES RELATIONSHIPS. For mutually satisfying conflict resolution, it is necessary to view an angry interaction as a forum for learning about yourself and that other person. By making it an opportunity for sharing perceptions, opinions, or how to get things done, communication is opened. You may get some feedback that you may not particularly like. However, it may be necessary for your growth and development to accept it and make needed changes. If the sharing on each person's part is motivated by genuine caring and helpful intent, then it is much easier to "hear" what is being said. Remember, though, that this atmosphere is predicated on talking about your feelings and the issues involved instead of acting out your anger. When this happens, conflict is not dreaded, but instead becomes an accepted form of communication that accommodates both points of view and that promotes healthy change in each person.

ATTITUDE ADJUSTMENT #3: AGREE TO DISENGAGE FROM INTERACTING IF RESPONSES ON EITHER PART BECOME OVEREMOTIONAL AND/OR PUNITIVE IN NATURE. One of the major problems with conflict is that the interactions escalate to emotional diatribes that go well beyond the boundaries of healthy discourse. When the interchange becomes aggressive and punitive, then the stage is set for two losers to emerge from the conflict. Remember, you are particularly vulnerable (as is your partner) when you are attempting to change unhealthy angry interactions into healthy conflict resolution. One protection for you both is to agree mutually to disengage when things seem to be getting out of hand. By agreeing to "let go" and back away from one another for awhile, you are able to calm down and regain perspective on the issues. Then you can reengage to talk out your differences and find a solution to the problem that will be satisfying to you both. In the beginning, this is a difficult step, but it becomes easier (and less necessary) as your style of conflict resolution becomes healthier!

A Code of Ethics for the Combat Zone

With your new and better attitudes about conflict in place, it is time to consider specific guidelines for angry interactions that lead to a positive outcome for all parties involved. Both parties must understand and abide by these guidelines or healthy conflict resolution is compromised. Here is a Code of Ethics for conflict that, if followed, will help you both find satisfaction in the results.

THE ETHICS OF CONFLICT #1: PERMIT THE OTHER PERSON TO RELATE WITHOUT INTERRUPTION A PERSPECTIVE ON THE PROBLEM SITUATION. In other words, have the courtesy to listen before you say anything. The other person will then extend to you similar courtesy and respect. There are always two sides to every issue, and often both have merit. Too often, both sides aren't heard as the interaction deteriorates into a series of interruptions, denunciations, and defensive responses that serve little purpose. Try to see the other side of the issue and integrate that viewpoint with your perception of what happened. It is only when both parties have been adequately heard that any real problem solving can begin.

THE ETHICS OF CONFLICT #2: THE DISCUSSION IS LIM-ITED TO ONLY THE PRESENT ISSUE THAT IS ADVERSELY AFFECTING YOUR RELATIONSHIP RIGHT NOW. One of the fastest ways to get off to a bad start in resolving a problem is to begin rehashing the past. What is important is what is affecting you both right now and what you can do about making it better for each of you in the future. The past is water under the bridge and bringing up old hurts or bygone problems is just a way of striking at someone else and getting away from what needs to be discussed. Don't fall into this trap because it is a guarantee to leave you both feeling awful and the issue isn't usually resolved. It will just pop up again because you haven't really talked about it.

THE ETHICS OF CONFLICT #3: CHOOSE AN OPTIMAL TIME TO BRING UP AND DISCUSS PROBLEMS BETWEEN YOU. Many problems with conflict resolution can be prevented by carefully choosing the time to discuss a particular issue. Blowing up on the spot with angry put-downs or saving up your anger until you can't hold it in anymore are equally unsatisfactory. Instead, carefully think out the problem. Then approach the other individual at a time when you are both free to talk and when you are calm. When you react emotionally, you really haven't taken the time to see the issues. By thinking about it a bit and then choosing the right place and the right time to bring it up, the outcome has a better chance of being positive.

THE ETHICS OF CONFLICT #4: ENGAGE THE OTHER PERSON IN A DISCUSSION OF CREATIVE SOLUTIONS AND VIABLE ALTERNATIVES THAT MAY INVOLVE PERSONAL CHANGE. You are both changing and growing individuals. As you change, issues will emerge between you that will have to be discussed. Individuals unskilled in conflict resolution forget this fact. Attempts are made to impose a personal solution on an interpersonal problem. With open dialogue, look for ways that the problem can be solved. That may involve change for one of you or both of you. In fact, an excellent way to approach a problem is to begin by stating what *you* could do differently to make such situations better. Creativity, compromise, and personal change are all part of healthy conflict resolution.

THE ETHICS OF CONFLICT #5: WHEN YOU DISCUSS AN ISSUE, MAKE SURE YOU POINT OUT WHAT HAS BEEN DONE RIGHT ALONG WITH THE BEHAVIORS THAT HAVE CREATED A PROBLEM. It is very rare that a situation arises where everything has been done completely wrong. As you discuss the issue or problem situation, separate what has been right from what has created the difficulty. You will then be thinking in terms of specific behaviors instead of generalities that aren't adequately defined. The other person will hear your balanced perception and respect you for it. When everything is negative and global, the interaction already has two strikes against a positive outcome. This process will also train you to think things out before you approach a problem and to give that other person credit where credit is due. Emotional over-reactions are the antithesis of this Ethic of Conflict.

THE ETHICS OF CONFLICT #6: JUDICIOUSLY AVOID THE OTHER PERSON'S VULNERABILITIES OR EMOTIONAL SENSITIVITIES. Each one of us can be easily hurt in certain ways. When you have a relationship with another person, over time you become aware of their vulnerabilities. It is to your credit and an index of your maturity to avoid these areas when engaged in a conflict with another person. Deliberately striking at these areas of vulnerability only hurts that other person and invites a counterattack focusing on *your* areas of sensitivity. By that time, the interaction has become an emotional war, and the chances of working out the problem are lost. By respecting that other person's vulnerabilities, you invite respect for yours. Further, this is the one habit that does the most to destroy trust. Be aware that that other person will not trust you with emotionally sensitive information when you are not in conflict if you use it as a weapon when you are!

THE ETHICS OF CONFLICT #7: MAKE IT A POINT TO TOUCH BASE WITH THAT OTHER PERSON ON A REGULAR BASIS TO DISCUSS HOW THINGS ARE GOING. It is very easy not to take the time to talk when things seem to be going well. Problems may be brewing and neither of you may be aware of them. If you don't talk when things are going well, then angry interactions may be the only time when you really connect with that other person. Your relationship now has a significant skew. You talk only when things go wrong. This is not good for a relationship nor for either of you as individuals. Make it a point to take time to share on a regular basis how things are going with each of you. Sharing information in this way makes you feel part of a team whether at home or at work. It is also quite evident that an ongoing dialogue is the best way possible to prevent problems from developing between you! By catching them early, you can more easily head them off before they become serious.

Your Anger: Handle with Care

It's so true that you must handle your anger carefully to make sure that this powerful energy is channeled into constructive ways of relating. An unknown armchair philosopher has observed the following: "Speak when you're angry, and you'll make the best speech you'll ever regret!" Learning better ways to deal with anger and conflict is well within the reach of every one of us. And, most of us need a refresher course now and then. Anger is so intense at times that it is easy to forget all that you have learned about it. Then it becomes destructive to you and to others as well. Two winners become two losers in a relationship.

Mental health professionals are well aware of the hazards that go along with the inability to express anger in appropriate ways. Anger unacknowledged and denied (sometimes without the awareness of the individual doing it) is often found to be the root cause of depression. On the other hand, anger that is frequently acted out can easily produce most of the physical symptoms associated with stress. In fact, it is not uncommon to find that stress is transformed into anger that is expressed in situations far removed from its source. When this happens, the person on the receiving end of your anger is truly an innocent victim. Your inability to handle *stress* is the problem, and that's *your* responsibility.

With a healthy perspective on anger and basic conflict resolution skills, a creative energy is mobilized that can be used to deepen relationships and enhance self-awareness. No longer will your anger cause you to slip out of control and into embarrassing immaturity at home and at work. Dealing with conflict in ways that produce two winners is a very powerful way to earn the respect of others and to build trust in your leadership capabilities. Your path through life will be easier and personal satisfaction will be yours because you live by a healthy Code of Ethics in the Combat Zone!

Chapter 13

Staying Alive Inside:
Choosing Intimacy Over
Emptiness for REAL Success!

As the years have passed, you have grown in your career. You have accomplished many of your goals. You have paid your dues at the bottom. Now you're a seasoned professional. The house, car, adequate salary, employment stability, and the bit of money left over for extras all attest to your success. Not as obvious as what you have gained is what you have lost. Life just doesn't seem to be as much fun anymore. You're doing all the right things, but there's a nagging emptiness inside that you can't seem to kick.

We all desire emotional intimacy and closeness to others. Lurking beneath crusty and hardened exteriors there lie deep needs to be known, accepted, and loved. Looking back, the emotional openness and joy you once shared with loved ones has slowly but surely disappeared. You don't feel that wonderful exhilaration of just being alive these days. Your warmth and caring have diminished, and you feel more alone than you should at this point in your life. Intimacy has been fading for some time. You've just begun to realize it. So have these others.

- Art has become very rational in his approach to everything. Lately, there seems to be an invisible barrier that he just can't break through to really express his caring to family members. He analyzes everything instead.

- Helena knows that she's defensive and easily hurt and that she has a quick temper. What she doesn't know is that people she cares about don't open up to her because she strikes angrily at their vulnerabilities whenever she gets mad.

- Pete and Amy sense they've been growing apart for several years. They live in the same house, but they don't really "connect" anymore with their separate careers, friends, and leisure interests.

● Joanna and Jeff know something's awry because they don't laugh together anymore and seem to bicker much more these days. They still make time for sex, but it's more a physical release than anything else.

All of these relationships have growing problems with intimacy. Defined, intimacy is "a state of mutual trust and acceptance between two individuals that permits open communication, emotional sharing, and a willingness to be deeply known by another person." Basically, intimacy is a vulnerable openness between two individuals who are also good friends. Intimacy can deepen or disappear with time. When it grows, you become more self-accepting with a base of strength in a special friendship with a loved one. When intimacy disappears, a vital quality necessary to live life fully fades away.

Perhaps the richest gift you can give in a relationship is sharing your inner self with someone you love. Perhaps the greatest gift you can receive is the knowledge that you are deeply loved and fully accepted for who you are as a person. When intimacy has been lost, rebuilding closeness with a Special Person is a most important avenue to personal fulfillment, without which career success is a hollow victory.

Signs of Emotional Distance

Here are some questions about how you relate to the Special Person in your life to determine if intimacy is alive and well. The more questions you answer "true" the less intimacy there is likely to be in that relationship. Your answers may surprise you. Deep down, you may already know the outcome!

T   F

1. Those occasional, spontaneous little things you used to do just to show that you care have virtually disappeared.

2. These days, touch seems to be primarily a sexual signal except for a perfunctory peck on the cheek now and then.

3. You now spend very little time alone away from the house relaxing with your Special Person.

4. Your relationship has become much more serious with little of the kidding or humorous horsing around there used to be.

T   F

_____   _____   5. You don't make a big thing of birthdays or an-
                niversaries anymore and often forget them com-
                pletely unless reminded.

_____   _____   6. When your Special Person has a problem, you
                quickly jump in with logical solutions and much
                advice.

_____   _____   7. Your physical relationship is much less fulfilling
                because you are having sex, but not making
                romantic love anymore.

_____   _____   8. You are very uncomfortable when someone else
                cries or expresses heartfelt emotion, and you
                either avoid the situation or try to shut off the
                feelings.

_____   _____   9. You and your Special Person "hit below the belt"
                when you're angry, although you both may regret
                it later.

_____   _____ 10. You don't say "I love you" or "I really care" these
                days and instead assume that your Special Per-
                son knows it by your actions.

Three Prerequisites for Intimacy

Three basic qualities in a relationship are the building blocks of intimacy. While none of the three guarantees that intimacy will grow, each in its own way is important. If any of these qualities are absent in your relationship with a Special Person, begin to build intimacy by building them in!

QUALITY #1: TIME TOGETHER. There are two important kinds of togetherness. Psychologically, it is a most positive sign if you perceive you and your Special Person as a couple or team sharing the good and the bad in the present and the future. At a physical level, sheer volume of time spent relating to one another is necessary to create this perception. The time you spend with that Special Person must be quality time, however, in which your attention is focused on experiencing together. Sharing mutual interests, completing a project together, or just playing silly games are all examples. It is far too easy to take that Special Person for granted and turn your attention to more pressing needs. It's an easy mistake that quickly becomes a habit.

QUALITY #2: TALKING TOGETHER. To really get to know another person, you must learn to talk comfortably together.

Talking together doesn't have to be emotionally heavy or involve critical issues. Instead, it can easily be light and fun and interesting. The important thing is to give your partner your undivided attention with good eye contact and a willingness to share your thoughts and perceptions (but not particularly to give advice). When you overcome initial discomfort and awkwardness, you will likely find a whole new dimension of relating opening up again. Be careful to keep your sense of humor in these conversations, and sarcasm, subtle put-downs, or cynicism out of them.

QUALITY #3: TOUCHING ONE ANOTHER. One of the most powerful forms of communication is physical touch; nowhere is this more important than in building intimacy. It is distressing to find how often touch (except sexual touching) disappears from once good relationships. Maintaining nonsexual touching seems to be more a problem for men than for women. It can easily become a problem for both, however, when HE doesn't touch except sexually and SHE doesn't touch because it is *interpreted* by HIM as a sexual signal! Holding hands, massage, hugging and snuggling, sitting close together, and gentle touches in passing are all extremely important to intimacy. To touch again may be somewhat uncomfortable at first, but you will soon learn to like it. (SPECIAL MESSAGE FOR MEN: One of the very best ways ever discovered to improve your sex life is to begin to consistently touch your Special Partner nonsexually *with feeling* again!)

Beware of Your Antitrust Acts!

Along with Time Together, Talking, and Touch, Trust is also a critical ingredient in rebuilding intimacy. Without Trust, your relationship will likely remain emotionally safe and quite superficial. Intimacy requires that you permit your Special Person to know you deeply and to understand you "where you live." It requires removing that polished and professional exterior armor that you find safety behind. It means giving up rationality and logic for emotional openness. It means revealing your weaknesses, fears, and imperfections. That requires Trust!

Betrayal is perhaps the most frequent reason why intimacy disappears in a relationship. When you are betrayed, you hesitate to continue being open because you know it will hurt you later. It will be helpful to you and your Special Person to remove any and all of these betrayal patterns in your relationship. If there has been betrayal, you BOTH may have to work very hard to rebuild the trust necessary for intimacy to bloom once again.

ANTITRUST ACT #1: BETRAYAL IN ANGER. The most common and least pretty form of betrayal occurs during conflict. In anger, you strike directly at your Special Person's sensitivities. What is shared during moments of closeness becomes a cruel weapon to be used to batter during conflict. When you betray in this way, you make a statement that you cannot be trusted. Further, the issues that provoked the conflict are lost in a morass of hurt and resulting anger. Nobody wins under such circumstances. It is far better to bite your tongue and resist this temptation. With every betrayal in anger, trust is diminished and intimacy is dealt a blow.

ANTITRUST ACT #2: BETRAYAL BY TELLING. Another betrayal pattern to eliminate is your tendency to "spill the beans" to others. Disclosing intimate information to parents, friends, or acquaintances is a very questionable practice at best. What is shared during intimate moments is precious and if you don't respect it, then you have not earned the right to be trusted. Regardless of your intentions, your betrayal in private or (too often) in public may embarrass, hurt, or cause deep resentments in your Special Person. And, your betrayal is usually found out. Unless you have express permission to share sensitive information, keep it to yourself.

ANTITRUST ACT #3: BETRAYAL BY TEASING. Many regard teasing as innocent and playful, and indeed it can be. It can also be a very painful form of betrayal. Teasing someone else about parts of themselves about which they are sensitive and vulnerable can easily negate intimacy. This is *not* innocent fun. There is almost always hostility and rejection embedded in this kind of teasing. It may also represent a twisted and distorted attempt to motivate change though humiliation. This kind of betrayal is especially destructive when done in public. Why should anyone trust you if you poke fun at them in this cruel way. Instead, offer gentle support and encouragement and you'll be far ahead of the game. This kind of teasing just isn't funny and isn't worth the price in intimacy you pay for it either!

Breaking The Clam Cycle

Albert and Abby live in a nice home in a pleasant neighborhood. They are well-liked and have plenty of friends. As parents, they are devoted to their two children and try to spend as much time with them as they can. Albert is sales manager for a large book wholesaler and has been quite successful over the years. He is respected by his colleagues for his quiet competence and dry wit. Abby is a bookkeeper and has also done well in her career. Since the children have come along, she works at the firm only part time.

Few suspect that there are growing problems between Albert and Abby. Over the years, their once-close relationship has gradually grown more distant. They don't talk much anymore. It seems that there is more tension between them every year. Both are unsure of the other's love and deep caring. This is not a new problem for them, but it has certainly been worse lately. The obvious issue is intimacy. They just don't have that special closeness any more. The root of the problem lies in their very different emotional styles and how they each deal with stress.

ABBY'S EMOTIONAL STYLE: When she has a problem, Abby needs to talk it out. And, she especially likes to talk to Albert about how she feels and the things that bother or are important to her. She also likes to hear from him that he loves and cares about her no matter what and that he still finds her attractive. Without this reassurance, she grows uneasy and insecure. The fact is that she hasn't been getting much supportive feedback from Albert lately.

ALBERT'S EMOTIONAL STYLE: Albert is somewhat reserved and self-contained. When there is a problem, he thinks it out for himself and then deals with it. Although his feelings for Abby run deep, it is difficult for him to express them openly. He loves Abby, but he doesn't see why he has to tell her over and over again. He also doesn't understand why she always wants to talk to him and why she especially likes to hear about *his* feelings.

Albert and Abby have divergent emotional styles that have created a problem in their relationship. This difference has always been there, but it has gotten worse over the last year or so because they have both been under pressure. Albert's constant overtime at the office and Abby also working hard at the firm and caring for the youngsters most of the day has done it. Not only have they not been talking much lately, but each has developed dangerous misperceptions about the other. These misperceptions are erroneous, but they do get consistently confirmed through the responses of each partner to the other.

ABBY'S MISCONCEPTION: She is insecure because she has become unsure that Albert really cares anymore. He doesn't tell her he loves her, and when she wants to talk about anything, he withdraws into silence or monosyllabic responses with a cutting edge. Since he doesn't volunteer anything, she feels that he is emotionally avoiding her.

ALBERT'S MISCONCEPTION: Deep down, he is resentful because he feels that Abby has become a nag. She never lets him alone. When he has a problem, he solves it. All she ever wants to do is talk. He especially dislikes her probing at his feelings all the time. Pushing him this way only makes him want to withdraw further.

These two different styles of dealing with emotions are frequently encountered differences between men and women. Combined with the misconceptions that grow from these differences over time, the CLAM CYCLE evolves. The CLAM CYCLE further erodes intimacy as actions and reactions serve to confirm the negative perceptions of a partner. Resentment and insecurity grow and closeness wanes. Soon two competent and talented individuals like Albert and Abby are living together, but not emotionally connecting anymore.

Once the CLAM CYCLE begins, a very destructive sequence of events is initiated. In this case, Abby wants to talk but every time she tries, Albert withdraws more and more blatantly. The more stress he is under, the worse his withdrawal, and the less spontaneous affection he gives. This makes Abby, needing reassurance and someone to talk to, more insecure. Her response is to seek an outlet by pushing Albert to talk more and respond to her. This prompts an even stronger withdrawal response, and the vicious CLAM CYCLE shifts into high gear.

In all too many relationships, the CLAM CYCLE gradually evolves toward a very negative end stage where Albert and Abby now find themselves. Abby has found that the only way that she can get Albert to really talk to her is to become angry. When he becomes angry enough in return, he responds. It's certainly not a very positive interaction, but it is better than none at all. At least Albert is responding to issues between them, albeit in a negative way. He is also expressing his feelings which he doesn't do much anymore. The problem is that this mode of emotionally connecting only confirms even more dramatically the already negative perceptions Albert and Abby have of one another.

The CLAM CYCLE can be broken with understanding, persistent effort, and acceptance of one another's emotional style. It takes time and patience, however, for this to occur, and *one person cannot do it alone.* However, with joint commitment, the CLAM CYCLE dissipates and intimate closeness returns to the relationship. While working out the CLAM CYCLE is difficult, the benefits are that it relieves the characteristic loneliness, resentment, and insecurity that this vicious cycle produces. To aid in breaking the CLAM CYCLE, there are definite changes for each partner to make.

SUGGESTIONS FOR ABBY:

1. to talk to Albert about the positive things that occur during the day, not only her problems;

2. to avoid presenting problems as if she is overwhelmed or out of control and wanting Albert to "take over";

3. to make conversations about feelings brief when talking to Albert;

4. to avoid constant probing of Albert's feelings about things, especially in the beginning;

5. to accept Albert's reserve as a part of his personality, and not as a sign of dislike or lack of love for her;

6. to initiate discussions while they are doing something together, not sitting face-to-face with heavy eye contact.

SUGGESTIONS FOR ALBERT:

1. to accept Abby's emotional expressiveness as healthy and not as a sign of weakness or dependency;

2. to take the initiative to tell her on a regular basis he loves her and that he cares about her deeply;

3. to relate his thoughts and/or feelings about his experiences so that Abby will have an ongoing sense of "where he is" these days;

4. to respond to Abby in ways that communicate that what she is saying is important and valued;

5. to suggest a later time to talk if he is unable to do so at the present time, and *then to make it a point* to bring the subject up again;

6. to give feedback to Abby about what he needs from her and exactly what she does that causes him to withdraw.

The CLAM CYCLE is a vicious circle that destroys the intimacy in all too many relationships. When this cycle is resolved, not only does closeness return, but self-esteem of both partners is enhanced. The relationship grows deeper and stronger as a result. However, an unwavering commitment by each partner to work on these changes together is necessary because there is constant vulnerability to backsliding in the beginning. Anyone knows that a clam will open up only when it feels safe in doing so. It's up to the two of you to make your relationship safe for intimacy to blossom again. The only other way to open a clam is to get all steamed up, and you already know that's not healthy for either of you!

Stepping Stones to Intimacy

Once the three foundations of intimacy are in place and you have removed betrayal patterns, you will begin to notice positive changes already. Breaking the Clam Cycle will bring even more openness between you. Here are some additional changes to consider as you renew your relationship and restore intimacy. When you try these new ways of relating, that Special Person of yours will soon begin to reciprocate in kind. Everyone wins!

STEPPING STONE #1: SEND REGULAR "CARE CAPSULES." Care Capsules are those thoughtful little things you do just because you care about your Special Person. They shouldn't be expensive gifts. Rather, try a phone call just to say, "Hi, I'm thinking about you," an invitation to lunch, a flower, or a cup of coffee brought without being asked. All these things say that "you are in my thoughts" to that Special Person. You're never too old to begin sending Care Capsules. Remember, these thoughtful little considerations when it's not a birthday or anniversary are what make them so special. Besides, they're lots of fun and you may get some interesting Care Capsules in return!

STEPPING STONE #2: GIVE A COMPLIMENT A DAY. Don't be bashful at all about commenting on the positive. Through your sincere compliments, you say to your Special Person that you are sensitive and notice even little things. It's just possible that you have slipped into the nasty pattern of consistently verbalizing negative thoughts, but skipping the positive. A compliment a day helps you to break this habit and become more upbeat. You'll being to come alive again, and you'll feel better about yourself. Don't just think it. Say it out loud. While you're at it, a few compliments at the office wouldn't hurt either!

STEPPING STONE #3: ENJOY LIFE'S SIMPLE PLEASURES AGAIN. With the years, your life has become more complicated and also much more sophisticated. It's time to relearn to enjoy simple pleasures again, and the best part of all is that they're free. A walk hand-in-hand on the beach, a cup of coffee pleasantly shared on the patio, relaxing before a roaring fire, or sitting close to watch the sun go down are all examples. These kinds of experiences keep you in touch with yourself and your Special Person. They also become the memories that you both will fondly look back on in years to come. Money simply can't buy what you get from these pleasant moments sharing simple pleasures.

STEPPING STONE #4: SHARE THE HARD TIMES. Perhaps the number one benefit of intimacy is knowing that you are not alone when the chips are down. It's easy to share the good times, but getting through the hard times together means revealing a vulnerable part of yourself. When you take the risk, you can confront life's problems with the strength of two. You don't have to find a solution or perform in any way when your Special Person needs you. All you have to do is be there, attentive and supportive. Sharing the hard times deepens your ability to share the good times because you know you're really together. It is comforting to know that through thick or thin, you will always be there for one another.

STEPPING STONE #5: PLAN REGULAR "BREAKOUTS." Before life got so complicated, you and your Special Person had fun times together because of your spontaneity. Gradually, getting away became more difficult and required detailed advance planning. The net result is that you've been getting away less and less. You know that routines at work can trap you, but so can routines at home. Breakouts are escapes out of town together — for a day, overnight, a weekend — on a regular basis. During Breakouts, you have time to talk and relax and be alone with your Special Person in a way not possible at home. Making regular Breakouts a part of your lifestyle, without the children if possible, helps build intimacy *and* relieve stress.

STEPPING STONE #6: A LITTLE ROMANCE GOES A LONG WAY. Romantic moments are one of the most exciting parts of courtship and still can be the "spice of life." These days, you may feel so burned out that even sex seems to be too much effort, and besides it's become routine and less than fulfilling. A sad but common sign. When you bring back romance, things will change. Create the setting: candlelight, dinner for two, relaxed conversation, a glass of wine, moonlight, gentle touches, and whispered "sweet nothings" all count. Remember, no goals. Just enjoy the time together. With just a bit of practice, rusty skills return and you'll soon be making love again, not just having sex.

STEPPING STONE #7: BRING BACK "PLAYFUL BANTER." In the good old days, you and your Special Person had lots of fun together, just horsing around and playing affectionate word games. This kind of pleasant, playful banter is an important signal of intimacy because it communicates trust and positive feelings. There are many varieties of Playful Banter; private terms of endearment, outrageous nicknames, special ways of kidding, sharing fantasies or even acting them out by adopting special roles (*i.e.*, the "he man" and the "seductress"). Don't forget to keep sarcasm, indirect put-downs, and negativity out of it. Make sure you smile so your intentions won't be mistaken when you begin to express your personal warmth and playful sense of humor once again.

STEPPING STONE #8: DEVELOP "TOUCHSTONE" AC-TIVITIES. It is truly amazing how two individuals can live together, yet lead totally separate lives. Making the time to be together with a Special Person as part of your regular routine is important to intimacy maintenance. Regular walks (or jogs) together, tackling home projects, shared cooking and cleaning up, or involvement in an interest or sport you both enjoy go a long way toward creating that together feeling. These kinds of activities encourage you to chat comfortably and keep in touch as part of your life together. Without them, you easily drift apart and don't know what's going on with your Special Person until there's a problem.

STEPPING STONE #9: CULTIVATE YOUR SENTIMENTAL SIDE. The essence of sentimentality is remembering what you have shared with your Special Person. Fond memories of where you've been together along life's path help you to face the present and the future with a shared strength. Take the time to periodically recall special memories together: the tender moments, the laughs, the hardships overcome. This is your "couple heritage" that builds a sense of togetherness and confidence. And, take the time to really celebrate birthdays, anniversaries, or other days special to you both. When you trade your future orientation for some warm sentimentality, you will have an anchor in the past and more intimacy in the present.

STEPPING STONE #10: STRIVE FOR "COUPLE COM-PLEMENTARITY." For intimacy *and* compatibility, developing a complementarity between you helps you to relate to one another in a healthy "check and balance" fashion. You may be an impulse buyer, and your partner may be skilled at long-term financial planning. You may have more skill in disciplining the children, but your Special Person may be a pro at handling problems with parents and in-laws. With mutual acceptance of areas of personal strength and weakness, you and your Special Person can compensate for one another in areas where skills are not strong. However, without self-confidence and trust, such differences easily become sources of conflict in your relationship instead of areas of complementary strength.

Fear of Being Known

Any discussion of intimacy could not be complete without some focus on the deep, personal fears that often inhibit closeness. When such fears are present, they result in a myriad of psychological defenses to prevent the vulnerability of intimacy. Beyond the pervasive fear of betrayal already discussed, there are several other kinds of fears that you may have to work on for intimacy to reemerge and deepen your relationship.

1. FEAR OF REJECTION. Deep down, many individuals with intimacy conflicts have a fearful question: "If I really let someone know me, will they like me?" If there is enough insecurity, no one may be permitted beyond your various facades to really know, to love, and to accept you. The question and the fears then remain intact. The only way to overcome the loneliness and isolation of life without intimacy is to take the risk to be known. Do it gradually and you'll find warm acceptance instead of cold rejection. You'll also feel more complete.

2. FEAR OF DEPENDENCY. Another common fear underlying intimacy problems is anticipated loss of autonomy or independence if too much closeness develops. To cope with this fear, a "defensive independence" becomes a style of relating. The fear is that if suppressed dependency needs ("Take care of me") are permitted even minimal expression, then they will become overwhelming with loss of personal identity and consequent inability to function. However, maintaing interpersonal distance from others is not only painful, but a maladaptive way to cope. Instead, face your dependency as a challenge to personal growth so you can have *both* autonomy and intimacy.

(**NOTE:** Some individuals are uncomfortable with closeness because of fears that *their partner will become dependent on them.* Sometimes this fear is warranted, as any support or nurturance given brings insatiable demands for more. In a good relationship, both partners will recognize this problem and work on it together so intimacy without dependency can develop.)

3. FEAR OF LOSS OF MASCULINITY. In men, an old-fashioned conception of masculinity is associated with stoicism, lack of emotional support, and an independent, domineering demeanor. Such a way of relating to a Special Person is not fertile ground for intimacy to flourish. There is a new generation of men who are sensitive, expressive, and caring, but who still retain a strong masculinity. These men get along better in the world, they make much better mates, and they have fewer stress problems because of the intimacy in their relationships. If *your* "manhood" is standing in the way of a better and closer relationship, now may be the time to trade in your outdated masculinity for a new and more functional model.

Young At Heart, Alive Within

True intimacy is without question the most precious quality that can exist in a relationship. Intimacy is also so vulnerable that it must be constantly guarded and protected. It slips away so easily that you don't realize it until you become aware of a void within and a diminished capacity to really enjoy life. An important emotional resource has been weakened and your stress increases. The result is that material success just isn't as fulfilling as it used to be. Inside, you now realize that intimacy is something you need more than you thought.

Keep these points in mind as you make the decision to rebuild intimacy with your Special Person. First, take the initiative. As you take the lead, be consistent in the changes you make. Second, recognize that you're out of practice in being close and you may feel a bit awkward at first. Of course, you'll get better with time. Intimacy returns slowly, so do give it a chance. Third, and most difficult, make every attempt to forgive the past. Put resentments and hurts you've been holding inside behind you. Without this kind of forgiveness, rebuilding intimacy will be virtually impossible. As part of your relationship renewal, give one another room to make some mistakes as your relationship becomes closer.

At its root, intimacy is a special kind of loving friendship. It's such a shame to let a potentially close relationship with a Special Person turn into an "acquaintanceship" with a little sex thrown in. You both lose. A wit remarked that "the best rule of friendship is to keep your heart a bit softer than your head." A whole lot softer is more like it. For that complete feeling, try an intimate involvement with a Special Person. There is no *real* success without it!

Chapter 14

A New Bedtime Story: Romantic Responses and Loving Libidos Make Interesting Interludes!

Sadly, you may be among the many quite accomplished men and women who awaken one day to find that their once-satisfying physical relationship has deteriorated to a once a week (or less) obligatory ritual. Your energy is constantly dissipated juggling the responsibilities of a demanding career, managing a household, and responding to the needs of children. Before you is a never-ending stream of problems and hassles that must be faced.

As you begin to look more closely at what has happened, you also discover to your dismay that intimacy has waned, and romance has virtually disappeared. These days, there's no time and little energy just for the two of you. You get what's left over after everything else is done and that's not much. The more you think about the unfairness of it all, the less you like it. Welcome to middle-class America!

These changes have resulted from the hectic pace of your life and your corresponding neglect of Lifestyle Management issues. Needless to say, these negative lifestyle changes have spilled over into your physical relationship. You may see yourself and your Special Person in one or more of several common Sexual Slippages. If you do, then it's time to confront some of the underlying Lifestyle Management issues directly. It's also time to embark on a process of renewing this important part of your relationship with your Special Person.

SEXUAL SLIPPAGE #1: THE ENERGY CRISIS. Your physical relationship is diminished because you're just too tired. You find yourself avoiding sex because it takes just too much energy. It doesn't seem worth the effort anymore. You want to sleep instead, but you don't feel good about it.

SEXUAL SLIPPAGE #2: SAME TIME NEXT WEEK. Sex is too predictable these days to be exciting so you don't particularly look forward to it. "Same time, same place, same way" is the tedious theme of your physical relationship as you go through the motions — again.

SEXUAL SLIPPAGE #3: THE QUICKIE SYNDROME. Because there's so little time available, you and your Special Person cooperate in fast sex. The "quickie" has become a disappointing standard fitted into a few spare moments here and there. It's over so quickly, it's hardly satisfying.

SEXUAL SLIPPAGE #4: BAD VIBRATIONS. Because you're so irritable and grouchy in the living room, your relationship in the bedroom is sorely strained with hidden resentments. Because it's difficult to relax even in bed, you and your Special Person have become subtle adversaries there.

SEXUAL SLIPPAGE #5: APPLAUSE NEEDED, PLEASE! You find yourself performing in the bedroom because you relate to sex as a technical skill and an achievement. You've got goals in mind and a task at hand. The real you has disappeared. Now there's an actor who wants applause.

Your physical relationship with your Special Person is very important, but easily pushed aside as you respond to more immediate demands on your time. It is unique in its ability to bring together all of the qualities that make a relationship deep and good: intimacy, communication, emotional sharing, trust, self-esteem, validation of you and your Special Person, self-expression as a man or woman. At its best, sexual relating is a bonding that not only symbolizes, but affirms again and again the unity in your relationship. Without care and attention, however, truly making love can easily become "just plain old sex" that isn't particularly fulfilling.

As you've advanced in your career, its probably true that your physical relationship has slowly slipped to become less satisfying. You may feel old beyond your age and very tired, but age is not the problem at all. It's just plain neglect. You haven't been taking care of yourself. Adopting some of the strategies of Lifestyle Management will help you learn to relax and take more time for leisure activities and family life. Then, relearning some of the sensual skills that you and your Special Person once so pleasurably shared will enhance the renewal of your physical relationship. Here are some common sense suggestions for you both to consider as you bring your "sensuous selves" back to life.

The Bedroom as Arena

You've probably heard the tongue-in-cheek dictum: "Don't go to bed mad, just go to bed!" Actually, there is a great deal of truth in this seemingly flip advice. It is quite likely that if you are experiencing problems keeping work and your Life After Work in balance that your sexual relationship has been negatively affected as well. From your "friends and lovers" relationship of the past, you and your partner have slowly become adversaries. Your physical relationship easily becomes the arena where all kinds of relationship problems that have nothing to do with sex become manifest. Power, guilt, manipulation, obligation, dominance, anger, martyrdom, and self-righteous indignation may now be alive and well and living in your bedroom.

With your many responsibilities at home and at work, it's hard to find the time to make love in a relaxed and spontaneous way. Add the conflicts that are carried from other parts of your life to the bedroom, and this important part of your total relationship quickly begins to deteriorate. If you want a New Bedtime Story, one of your first commitments must be to take the conflict out of your bedroom. To accomplish this, both you and your partner must share responsibility. The renewal of your physical relationship cannot proceed until this spirit of cooperative change and caring compromise is a solid pact between you. Only then have you set the stage for your sexual relationship to become an affirmation of the depth of your caring instead of an index of your differences.

There are many subtle and not so subtle indicators that you have developed an adversary relationship with your partner where sex is concerned. Check yourself on the following kinds of responses that may now be part of your sexual relating. Be particularly concerned about the kinds of responses that have become patterned scenarios in which you each play out your respective parts, with negative feelings the inevitable result. Here are some sample Sexual Adversary Scenarios to consider.

_____ 1. When your partner doesn't submit, you have a temper tantrum and accuse your Special Person of being sexually repressed with Victorian attitudes.

_____ 2. After sex that is not satisfying to you, you later find little ways to hurtfully put down your partner's "performance" as inadequate.

_____ 3. You give in to sex only when your partner has been "good" and has done what you want.

_____ 4. When your partner doesn't respond quickly to your physical needs, you threaten to leave and find "gratification" somewhere else.

_____ 5. You make your partner feel very guilty and selfish for denying you sex when you want it.

_____ 6. You give in to your partner and then play martyr for days.

_____ 7. You refuse to cooperate with anything your partner wants because there was no cooperation with you when you wanted a sexual encounter.

_____ 8. You eventually have sex because of your partner's insistence, but as a way to get back you refuse to actively participate or enjoy it.

_____ 9. You make a play for sympathy and physical discomfort until your partner responds to your sexual needs.

_____ 10. You do everything you can to gratify your partner so you can get it over with quickly because sex has become no more than an obligation.

In long-term relationships, the above vignettes are replayed again and again as they evolve into destructive patterns that create deeper conflict, seriously impair intimacy, and damage the self-esteem of you both. Counselors are fond of saying that the bedroom reflects what goes on in the living room. There is undeniable validity to this perception. Couples who are secure enough to respond positively to a partner's needs and preferences have developed a mutually satisfactory way to resolve differences that extends to the bedroom as well. It's a fact of life that such differences can and do occur in the healthiest of relationships. However, when the capacity for creative compromises disappears, then life in the living room is surely diminished, and as adversaries in the bedroom, it's even worse!

Some Caring Compromises

Your sexual relationship is really part of an evolving process of give and take between you and your partner. It is fraught with individual differences in moods, emotions, and modes of response. Typically, early in their relationships, couples make allowances for these differences with understanding and Caring Compromises. However, as work and career and family responsibilities consume ever more time and energy, the sexual relationship, once high priority but now vulnerable, often begins to decline. With the "me versus you" stance of an adversarial relationship growing, you both begin to suffer.

To reactivate your Sensuous Self and bring back your once emotionally fulfilling physical relationship, your first major step is to begin to make those Caring Compromises with your partner once again. As a way to start, consider some Who, What, Where, When and Why (Not) questions as they pertain to your present sexual relationship. As you proceed to resolve these issues, you'll again become cooperative allies instead of angry adversaries.

CARING COMPROMISE #1: RESOLVING THE "WHO" QUESTION. An imbalance in "who" initiates sex is the crux of your first Caring Compromise. A commonly encountered, but negative situation is one in which one partner consistently initiates sex and the other just as consistently rejects or resists advances. The end result is development of an oppressor-victim relationship in which power plays, guilt, and manipulation become intricately associated with lovemaking.

YOUR COMPROMISING POSITION: A first positive step is to talk about the initiative problem. Then agree on a way to create more balance. You might take turns initiating sex. Or, you might just as easily agree to give one another clear and consistent signals that you are open to lovemaking. Along with the agreement to move toward balance in initiating sex is a corresponding commitment to spend regular quality time together in nonsexual activities.

CARING COMPROMISE #2: RESOLVING THE "WHAT" QUESTION. "What" kind of sexual relationship you each want is a second point of potential conflict. Foreplay, after talk, positions and variations, and attitudes toward experimentation are all aspects of lovemaking that must be comfortably and creatively worked out between partners. Past experiences and personal preferences all affect what is desirable in a physical relationship now. "Our way" instead of "my way" must be the byword here.

YOUR COMPROMISING POSITION: Learning about yourself and about your partner is crucial for establishing a loving and lasting physical relationship. Avoid your partner's vulnerabilities and aspects of lovemaking that create discomfort. And, be willing to give of yourself to your partner as a way to invite loving reciprocity. If you can't talk openly about preferences, let your partner guide you. With these changes, sexual renewal will be your reward.

CARING COMPROMISE #3: RESOLVING THE "WHEN" QUESTION. "When" is the preferred time for a sexual relationship is often a focus for contention between partners. Perhaps you're a morning person and your partner is definitely a night owl. Your daily cycles of moods and routines are just not similar. For women, the time of the month may significantly affect libido and sexual receptivity in either direction. With busy schedules and different routines, deciding amicably "when" to have sex is important to you both.

YOUR COMPROMISING POSITION: First of all, make sure that at least some of the time there is plenty of time available for leisurely and relaxed lovemaking. "Sex on the run" as the norm is hardly fulfilling. Next experiment a bit. Try sexual liaisons at different times of the day or night. Or, if your daily cycles are different, alternate morning and night as part of your Caring Compromise. On days off or weekends, let spontaneity be your guide whenever the mood strikes.

CARING COMPROMISE #4: RESOLVING THE "WHERE" QUESTION. A major reason for the stagnation of a sexual relationship is lack of variety. Not infrequently, sexual liaisons take place at the same time each week in the same way and in the same place. They become a chore and an obligation because of the monotonous routines you've established. Anything repeated over and over in exactly the same way is bound to become dull after awhile. Breaking out of these "bedroom blahs" can stimulate your libido and revive your interest.

YOUR COMPROMISING POSITION: Decide as a couple to be just as creative and spontaneous in your physical relationship as your sense of decorum permits. At the very least, take some of your sex out of the bedroom. Those same four walls can get awfully old after awhile. Try making love before a roaring fire, in a motel room, or parked on a secluded road. Deciding "where" to spend this part of your intimate life together can be fun and exhilarating.

CARING COMPROMISE #5: RESOLVING THE "WHY (NOT)" QUESTION. The "why not" question reflects the right of refusal that each partner shares in a solid and healthy sexual relationship. It is when refusal becomes excessively one-sided that conflicts develop and worsen with time. While it is entirely legitimate to tactfully decline sex now and then, constant refusal becomes avoidance of your partner. Hurt, resentment, and conflicts that spill over into the rest of your life are the result.

YOUR COMPROMISING POSITION: First of all, make sure that when you do decline sex that it is done in a fashion that is not ego-shattering to your partner. Second, it is entirely possible to substitute another satisfying activity in lieu of intercourse. For example, taking a walk, snuggling, or another way of just being together can help you both feel close and open the door for more sexual relating later. Third, examine just how often you are refusing sex with your partner and why. If there are other issues involved, address them. Fourth, practice accepting a sexual refusal in a gracious and mature way. You'll both feel better in the long run!

Stop "Working" at Sex!

One of the greatest sexual vulnerabilities that achievement-oriented individuals face is subconsciously transforming a good physical relationship into task-oriented psychological work. Although these changes occur slowly over time, there is an eventual awareness that the relaxed closeness, pleasant playfulness, and intimate sharing that once made the relationship fulfilling aren't there anymore. The spontaneity and fun you used to have in bed are also gone. Instead, there's now a success-dominated need to achieve and perform. Sex has inadvertently become an extension of the mental work you do all day.

It seems almost absurd to talk about "working" at sex, but it's a most common part of the deterioration in fulfillment so characteristically found in the physical relationships of successful individuals and couples. It's a fact that you can't psychologically work and relax at the same time. If your sexual relationship isn't particularly satisfying these days, then it just might be that a destructive combination of your success motivation, hurry sickness, contaminated leisure, and a highly pressured lifestyle have conspired to short circuit the good times. You and your Special Person both lose.

To remedy this problem, it is first necessary to again define the *psychological* nature of work. Psychological work goes on in your mind and has nothing to do with where your body is or what it is doing. Too much of this mental work, which also consumes tremendous amounts of energy, results in a "draggy" emotional fatigue that is with you morning and night and that you can't sleep away. In addition, psychological overwork may add to the frustration and stress you experience each day. No question about it. You can easily work at sex. There are always four qualities present when you are working. Look for them in your bed.

WORK QUALITY #1: YOU HAVE A STRONG GOAL-ORIENTATION. From the very beginning, you set your sights on a defined end point. Then you focus and direct all your energy toward successfully attaining that particular goal.

WORKING IN BED: Your goal is to have the best possible climax (or bring your partner to one). Sometimes "multiple" and "simultaneous" become part of your goal-orientation. (**NOTE:** These days, there seems to be a definite trend toward "goal inflation" that adds great stress to your work in bed!)

WORK QUALITY #2: YOUR EGO IS HEAVILY INVOLVED IN THE OUTCOME. Your self-esteem is so heavily dependent on success that you create tremendous pressure for yourself. You're Okay if you make it; you're personally negated if you don't.

WORKING IN BED: Your masculinity or femininity is directly linked to how consistently and successfully you attain your goals in bed. Your self-esteem demands that you succeed, but you're also driven by fear of sexual failure.

WORK QUALITY #3: THERE IS ALWAYS A PRODUCT THAT RESULTS FROM YOUR EFFORTS. You need some kind of tangible evidence that you have attained your goals and not wasted your time. Your work product serves both of these purposes. Any activity without such a "product" creates discomfort.

WORKING IN BED: Your climaxes or your partner's demonstrate successful task completion as does verbal praise that is given to you as a lover. You count on these "products" to validate your skill and bolster your masculine or feminine ego.

WORK QUALITY #4: YOU CRITICALLY EVALUATE YOUR WORK AFTER THE FACT. Without fail, you critically examine the work you have completed. Then you assign an evaluative label (good-bad, success-failure, Ok-not OK). You're also particularly concerned with how you could improve your work product in the future.

WORKING IN BED: After it's all over, you analyze what happened in bed. It might have been good, but it could always be better. You focus on aspects of performance that need improvement in you *and your partner.* Then you attach your good/bad grade to the experience.

Relaxing into Romance

It's hard to be romantic when you're in a hurry and when you're under pressure. It's no wonder then that romance has faded with the kind of lifestyle you've got these days. Basically, romance is a "pleasant, sensory-based togetherness that encourages creative sharing, openness, spontaneity, and the affirmation of caring between two people." As such, romance is imaginative, adventurous, fanciful, and fun. On one hand, romance is the best possible context for physical union. On the other hand, a sexual encounter does not necessarily follow from romance at all. When you assume that it does, you've begun to put the "work" back in.

Emotionally rejuvenating relaxation is a deep and pleasant involvement in *any* activity in which the experience itself is the primary reward. It goes almost without saying that true relaxation is the antithesis of psychological work. So is romance. In fact, romance is a way of pleasantly relaxing together. It is a creative and spontaneous process of being together and sharing experiences. Romance has no goals, no success-failure ego-involvement, and no products. It's just the *process* of pleasantly enjoying yourself and your Special Person. "Whatever will be, will be!" is the best theme for this kind of experience.

By recovering your ability to relax into romance, you are also taking a major step toward improving your physical relationship. To help you break down your tired old routines, here's a Recipe for Romance for you and your Special Person to try together.

ROMANTIC RECIPE I: BEGIN WITH A GENEROUS HELPING OF IMAGINATION. Creative innovation is the key here, but don't go too far too fast. Avoid "romantic" changes that are directly geared to sex or your efforts may backfire. Finding fun new ways to relate and be together outside the bedroom is the essence here. A bit of seductive teasing is just fine, though!

START-UP SUGGESTIONS: Call your Special Person to coyly ask for a date. Dress in a new way that emphasizes your masculinity/femininity. Arrange a "clandestine" meeting to discuss your impending "affair of the heart." Seclude yourselves in the corner of an out-of-the-way restaurant with a romantic atmosphere. Try a picnic for two with a glass of wine, a loaf of bread, and thou.

ROMANTIC RECIPE II: ADD A DASH OF ADVENTURE. Romantic adventure is a new and exciting experience you can share together. A subtle element of "danger" makes it especially stimulating. Sharing adventures bring you together and help you move beyond your too-passive way of relating to one another. Such experiences need not be expensive and may lie just beyond your doorstep.

START-UP SUGGESTIONS: Dress down and go "slumming" in some totally classless joints. "Impulsively" take an afternoon off for a special treat. Go "parking" together; remember the old days? Try a new sport or game at which you are both complete novices (no heavy competition, please). Drive to a nearby city and rent a motel room "just for the day."

ROMANTIC RECIPE III: STIR IN SENSORY STIMULA-TION TO PERSONAL TASTE. Titillating as many senses as possible is one of the most pleasurable aspects of romance. It enhances your ability to relax and enjoy yourself by reveling in sensory experiences instead of analyzing them. Creating and sharing a sensual togetherness adds depth and intimacy to your relationship.

START-UP SUGGESTIONS: Have dinner by candlelight. Try massage using scented oils. Dance in the moonlight. Relax before a roaring fire. Listen to some romantic or sensual music together. Touch one another in caring (but nonsexual) ways. Cook an especially aromatic meal together. Scrub one another's back in the shower or tub. Snuggle in a hammock.

ROMANTIC RECIPE IV: MIX TO CREATE A PRIVATE WORLD FOR TWO. The ability to enter a timeless, joyful world just big enough for two is important to romance. You're emotionally together even in a crowd. You create the feeling that you're alive and well and together, and that's all that matters as the problems of the world are forgotten. This skill can't be taught directly, but here are some pointers to help you "let go" in this special way.

START-UP SUGGESTIONS: Take your time with everything you do (no tight schedules). *Do not* discuss work, problems, the children, or what you have to do tomorrow. Look at one another constantly. Stay close together. Don't be distracted by other people. Reminisce about good times you've shared. Share a dream or fantasy of the future. Sit quietly together to experience a sunset.

ROMANTIC RECIPE V: SPRINKLE WITH SOME PLEAS-ANT PLAYFULNESS. "Couples who can play together, stay together" is an axiom with great validity. Playfulness is a light, airy, mischievous state of mind. Horsing around, sharing some laughs, playing word games, and just being silly together signify enough trust to drop defenses and facades to become just two people having fun.

START-UP SUGGESTIONS: Go fly a kit together. Romp in the surf. Play tag in the park. Tell jokes and humorous anecdotes. Use as many "lines" on one another as you can think up. Play some interesting roles with one another. Make up some word games (twenty questions, trivia). Get some quarters and go to a video arcade. Pretend you're naive adolescents for a night.

Beyond Performance in Bed

Now that you're taking the time to create a relaxing, romantic context for your physical relationship, you're ready to tackle what goes on between your ears in the bedroom. Learning to be together in a fun way and breaking old patterns will help a lot. Then getting rid of your destructive work patterns in bed will complete the process of "letting go." As you do, you will experience once again all the emotional and physical fulfillment that making love used to bring.

As a successful and motivated person, you are used to "making it happen." The only problem is that you can't direct and control your body's sexual responses like you direct and control your work. Your body knows how to respond sexually, but you've got to relax with enough trust to "let it happen." Your analytical, anticipatory, evaluative, competitive, and goal-oriented responses are functional at work. In your bedroom, they've got to go! The bottom line for good sex is to experience it, not intellectualize it. Expect nothing. Go with the flow. Then all you want to happen, will.

Now that you understand some of the basics, here are some Sensual Suggestions to help you and your Special Person relax and enjoy being together when you're actually in the bedroom.

Each suggestion is a way to help you take the work out, take the pressure off, and put the fun back into making love.

SENSUAL SUGGESTION #1: SET NO GOALS FOR YOUR SEXUAL EXPERIENCE. How can you possibly enjoy the *process* of making love if you're focusing all of your attention and energy on attaining a goal? Instead, do what comes naturally with no pre-conceived end point. You don't have to have intercourse. You don't have to climax (or bring your partner to one). You don't have to be the best. Forget everything that "should happen" if you're a *real* man or woman. Relax. Take the pressure off. You don't have to do anything except be together comfortably.

SENSUAL SUGGESTION #2: DIRECT YOUR ATTENTION TO YOUR SENSORY PLEASURE. If you have a work orientation to sex, you may relate to making love as a technical exercise. It's not! Analyzing everything that's going on or focusing on your partner's responses are part of the problem. Instead, train your attention on *your* five senses and the pleasurable stimulation emanating from them. It's easy and fun and you can do it without making your physical relationship one-sided or selfish. Just step back and pleasantly experience your body responding naturally.

SENSUAL SUGGESTION #3: EXPRESS YOURSELF MORE FREELY IN BED. When you stifle or inhibit outward expression of your sexual responses, you also cognitively short-circuit some of your body's ability to function naturally. Your need to control your responses in bed may reflect your self-consciousness and your inability to deeply accept your own sexuality. Loosen up in little ways. Your body functions best sexually if you're not trying to inhibit it while it's trying to respond. Breathe more heavily. Let your body move in a comfortable rhythm. Express your pleasure verbally as you free yourself.

SENSUAL SUGGESTION #4: CREATE SENSUAL VISUAL IMAGES FOR YOURSELF. Visual images can enhance your freedom to "let go" sexually. While imagining yourself to be with someone else may be destructive, other sensual possibilities are limited only by your imagination. Sometimes it's possible (and fun) for you and your Special Person to create a shared fantasy to be experienced together. Remember, the most powerful erogenous zone you have lies between your ears. Close your eyes and integrate a sensual image with the rhythm and flow of making love.

SENSUAL SUGGESTION #5: TRY THE "RHYTHM METHOD" OF LETTING GO. Rhythms strike a deep chord in the human psyche. This almost instinctual responsiveness facilitates abandoning yourself to an easy and pleasing rhythm. You find yourself "letting go" listening to certain music, hearing the surf, or dancing. By extension, rhythms can also enhance your body's sexual responses. As you relax, you can let a rhythm pleasantly carry you. Internal rhythms (your breathing, body movements, or pulse), fantasy rhythms (riding a wave, rocking on a cloud), or external rhythms (music, your partner's body) all work very well.

SENSUAL SUGGESTION #6: CREATE AN ORGASMIC DISTRACTION FOR THAT CRITICAL MOMENT. Many otherwise fulfilling sexual experiences are thwarted at the last moment by destructive thoughts that "kill the climax." These are *negative* orgasmic distractions and may be thoughts as innocuous as "I'm almost there" or "It's going to happen." Creating a *positive* orgasmic distraction helps solve this problem. As you feel your body approaching the critical moment, try focusing on a particular body sensation (what's going on in your knee), lock into a vivid visual image (a giant wave about to break), or even repeat a word over and over ("I love you"). By doing so, you will "forget" to cognitively monitor your body's responses and thus let it function naturally.

Growing Together Again

Learning to relax and enjoy your physical relationship with your Special Person is an important part of Lifestyle Management. There is no question that you have neglected this part of your total relationship. There's little joy of living left because everything else takes precedence over quality time spent together. Life has become a too serious matter and the results are predictable. You and your Special Person suffer from emotional neglect and lack of physical fulfillment.

It is well-known that your sexual energy (libido) is very vulnerable. It quickly disappears when you are tired, frustrated, under pressure, burned out, or angry. The consistent absence of sexual energy ("I just don't seem to feel like it anymore.") combined with a decline in the quality of your physical relationship are danger signs. Something important is missing that helps you stay alive inside and excited about life. Your sexuality doesn't disappear with age, only with neglect. Part of the danger is that with continued neglect, this loss may become permanent. "Use it or lose it!" takes on special meaning here.

To help you in your commitment to renewal of your physical relationship with your Special Person, here are three decisions to make and then to protect judiciously. Each is part of the bedrock of a fulfilling physical relationship that lasts.

BEDROCK DECISION #1: TO CONSISTENTLY MAKE QUALITY TIME AVAILABLE TO BE TOGETHER. A good relationship takes time of the highest possible quality. Quality time is alone time. It is doing interesting things together. Without distractions. Without children. Without pressure. A positive relationship in the living room carries over into the bedroom.

BEDROCK DECISION #2: TO MAKE YOUR PHYSICAL RELATIONSHIP A HIGH PRIORITY. Studies have shown that in good relationships that last, maintaining a good sexual relationship is a priority for *both* partners. It is a part of the relationship that deepens and improves with time because the affirmation and renewal that it represents never ends.

BEDROCK DECISION #3: TO MAKE LOVE INSTEAD OF HAVING SEX. Making love is not a physical act, but sex is and that's why it's not very fulfilling to mature people. Making love is defined by the deep emotional communication that becomes the most fulfilling part of physical sharing in your relationship. It is an expression of caring and acceptance that makes each of you a Special Person to the other.

With characteristic insight, Ralph Waldo Emerson noted that "though we travel the world over to find the beautiful, we must carry it within us or we find it not." Feeling good about yourself as a man or woman is an inner beauty that is shared in a fulfilling physical relationship. Such inner beauty has a powerful charisma that communicates significant statements about you. "I know who I am." "I like who I am." "I don't have to prove my adequacy to anyone." "I can relax and be me." "I do not fear expressing myself." "I want you to know me." These feelings are part of your beauty, and you can't really make love without them!

It must be obvious by now that renewing your physical relationship with your Special Person is actually a process of self-renewal. It signifies an important step you have taken toward personal fulfillment and emotional health. It means that you've decided to stay alive inside by enjoying more of the good things in life because you deserve them. As you make your renewal a reality, your tired old "bedtime story" will soon change in positive ways for you both. You will be delighted to find that with new Romantic Responses, two Loving Libidos will get together for some most Interesting Interludes!

Chapter 15

Positive Parenting for Professionals: How to Raise HEALTHY Achieving Children!

Question: "What is creative, spontaneous, fun-loving, emotionally expressive, naturally loving, intuitive, and creative all at the same time?" The answer to this riddle is simple: "Any child." Your children. It was also you before you learned how to be so successful. Ask yourself how many of these same qualities live strongly within you today. It's quite likely that you've traded spontaneity for structure, emotional openness for rationality, sensuality for objectivity, and set routines for creative innovation. Sometimes you find yourself wishing you could be more like the kids.

These days, you carry a heavy burden of responsibilities. And, you've lost much of your ability to really "let go" to enjoy yourself. Although you're definitely successful and an achiever, you're not as happy as you think you should be at this point in your life. You want to do the very best for your children to help them become successful, but sometimes you wonder if it's possible to raise HEALTHY Achieving children. The answer to this question is a resounding "YES" *if* you guard against some of the parenting vulnerabilities that strong achievement motivation, success, and a career-orientation bring.

By the time a child is ready to leave home, eighteen years of parental modeling and the kinds of responses the child has received from you has determined not only the basis for that child's self-esteem, but also how self-esteem is related to work. Raising a HEALTHY Achiever takes awareness and know-how. The HEALTHY Achieving child has a strong positive sense of self and does not avoid challenge, can handle failure and setbacks well, and thrives on personal accomplishment. It is also a child who is caring and sensitive, who retains emotional openness, and who knows how to enjoy leisure time and friendships.

Ultimately, you cannot take full responsibility for what your child becomes. However, by learning about and practicing some common sense techniques for Positive Parenting, you can maximize the opportunities for each of your children to become a HEALTHY Achiever within the context of their personal interests and the innate limits of individual potential. By examining closely some common, but subtly destructive parenting patterns, you may also gain insight into your own development. You will discover some of the roots of your present dissatisfaction and find directions for positive change. Then you *and* your children will grow toward happier, healthier, and more productive lives together.

Parenting Response Patterns to Avoid

Children who have become UNHEALTHY Achievers (and there are many of them) are unhappy and insecure as adults. A remarkable number have attained high levels of success and are quite accomplished. Within, however, and amid all the accoutrements of success, they lead stressful and unfulfilled lives. When the roots of this paradox are traced backward in time, one characteristic stands out above all others. The parents of these children were UNHEALTHY Achievers, too! Through the years, they managed to transmit their UNHEALTHY Achieving style to the children who then in turn became UNHEALTHY Achievers themselves.

These parents responded inappropriately to their children, sometimes to motivate, often without thinking of the long-term implications. In either case, these consistent response styles reflected the parents' unhealthy way of relating to work and to success. These parent-to-child reinforcements shaped the child's self-esteem and relationship to work in the same destructive mold as the parents. Three problem-producing patterns are frequently seen. Each stems from an unhealthy parental need for a child to achieve and a corresponding fear that the child will not!

PROBLEM PATTERN #1: RESPONDING EXCLUSIVELY TO ACHIEVEMENTS. Examples:

● "What a good little boy/girl you are for making such a beautiful finger painting. Daddy (Mommy) really loves you for making it."

• "Everybody thinks it's just wonderful because you are on the winning team."

• "You've made us so proud that you got into the Honor Society. So many other parents can't be as proud as we are."

All of these statements sound very appropriate, don't they? Parents are expressing directly to their child approval for success and achievements. And they should! The problem here is subtle, quite common, and very telling in its effect over the eighteen years a child is in the home. The negative part of this pattern is that *parents only respond with positive reinforcement and approval when there has been a success or an achievement.* A child who is not achieving gets little or nothing in the way of parental approval. Such parents tend to rely too heavily on their own successes and achievements as a basis for self-esteem and develop the easy habit of doing the same with their children.

The effect of this very selective and narrow form of approval on the child's self-esteem is enormous. Over time, the child comes to believe that parents' love and acceptance is contingent upon achieving, reaching goals, and succeeding. Conversely, there is insecurity and a sense of being inadequate and unloved *without* continued successful achievement. Gradually, the child's self-esteem becomes heavily linked to doing well, but without any other basis for self-validation. The result of this unhealthy parenting response style is that a negative introject is created within the child. An introject is a deeply internalized belief about oneself that stems from consistent experiences with important people and that becomes a basis for self-esteem (or lack of it).

THE FAILURE INTROJECT: "What is important is what I produce and achieve, not who I am as a person. If I don't keep producing, no one could possibly love or accept me."

PROBLEM PATTERN #2: SETTING PERFECTION AS THE CRITERION FOR ACCEPTANCE. Examples:

• "You got four A's and one B+ on your report card. I want to know why you didn't come home with straight A's"

• You only made the semi-finals in the tennis tournament. The problem with you is that you've got a lazy streak."

• When you beat Andy in computer class, then I'll know you're *really* trying. Your score is OK, but you *can* do better."

These statements are characteristic of the perfectionist's "You can always do better than you did" response pattern. There are just two guidelines for this destructive parental reinforcement pattern. First, always ignore or gloss over what your child has done right or correctly. In other words, ignore your child's strengths. Second, cue in immediately on an area of performance weakness or one that could stand improvement. Let your child know how disappointed you are because of the child's failings and lack of effort. It's true that perfectionist parents frequently produce perfectionist children, and this is the kind of parental response pattern that will do it.

Basically, a child subjected to this unfortunate parental response pattern is denied any real kind of approval. The implicit message is that approval can come only when the child achieves a standard of perfection. Clearly, that's an impossible task. The child, when this message has been internalized (introjected), begins to set unreasonably high personal standards for *self-acceptance*. The result is a continual push for perfection, without ever being able to consistently achieve it. The child experiences frequent failure because of unrealistically high expectations and is perennially unhappy and dissatisfied as a consequence. It is well-known that perfectionists are some of the most unhappy and failure-oriented people in the world!

THE FAILURE INTROJECT: "I am inadequate and an unloved failure if I make any mistakes at all and don't maintain a standard of perfection in all that I do."

PROBLEM PATTERN #3: CONSISTENTLY REINFORCING COMPETITIVE INADEQUACY. Examples:

• "You'd better shape up. All the kids on the block are going to leave you behind, and you'll never catch up if you don't get on the ball."

• "Why can't you be more like your brother/sister. He (she) is really going places and you'll never amount to much if you don't do some changing."

• "You know how hard you have to work just to keep up. Don't ever forget that you'll be with some really smart kids in college."

The nucleus of this Problem Pattern is a negative comparison of your child to specific others or to a group. Quite frequently, such consistent and negative comparisons stem from parents' fears that a child will not perform or achieve up to their expectations. These kinds of statements are in fact a distorted attempt to motivate a child to try harder by making negative comparisons constantly. What is actually being communicated, however, is a parents' sense of disappointment and a vote of no confidence in a child's capabilities. The child hears the *real* message and internalizes it.

On the child's part, what is continually heard is, "You're not good enough." The child perceives that parental approval and acceptance is contingent upon doing well. At the same time, at a more subtle level, the parents are communicating that they don't believe that the child has what it takes to really make it. No wonder a child who receives this kind of consistent reinforcement usually has a poor self-concept. How can you feel good about yourself when you are hit all the time with this self-esteem "double whammy." These children sense (correctly) that parents see them only in negative contrast to others who are perceived to be bright, motivated achievers!

THE FAILURE INTROJECT: "I am not as capable as my peers and I must always work extra hard to make up for my deficiencies to feel good about myself . . . if I can do it at all!"

The Emotional Backlash

When one of these Problem Patterns is the dominant response mode of parents to a child over the course of development, personal insecurity and a nagging sense of inadequacy become major impediments to positive self-esteem. The fear of failure and the need to succeed to stave off feelings of low self-worth become strong, but negative, sources of motivation to achieve. The fear of failure and the need to succeed is the nucleus of Performance-Dependency. A Performance-Dependent child has few internal resources to deal with failures and setbacks because self-worth is so highly contingent upon success as measured by external criteria.

Because failure is such a powerful negation of the self, the Performance-Dependent child lives in fear of its impact. Yet, the possibility of failure can never really be eliminated. In fact, it is necessary to learn to deal well with failure to become a HEALTHY Achiever, which the Performance-Dependent child is not! With Performance-Dependency created by the Problem Patterns of parental response, a child may react in several different ways. Each is the hallmark of an UNHEALTHY Achieving child and carries with it a high and unnecessary price in emotional pain, fear, and low self-esteem. Here are brief descriptions of the three major response patterns of the Performance-Dependent child.

PERFORMANCE-DEPENDENT STYLE #1: THE WORK-AHOLIC ACHIEVER. The workaholic child grows up accepting parental achievement values and lifestyle hook, line, and sinker. Often the Workaholic Achiever is a first child who excels in secondary school, college, and later in a career. Such children are typically bright and motivated with a need to succeed to support their externally dependent self-esteem that immediately drops with any setback or failure. For this kind of child, the attachment of self-worth to achievement is so strong that even minor setbacks (*e.g.*, a temporary drop in grades) may precipitate a severe emotional crisis. Frequently, social skills are neglected in lieu of ever higher levels of success and accomplishment. Needless to say, these children receive massive social support for their accomplishments. In reality, they do all the right things for the wrong reasons. Behaviorally, they are likely to become driven Type A individuals who are unable to relax and enjoy life because of the internal void that is experienced when they stop achieving. Relationship problems often develop later in life because of their excessively high achievement needs, and they are also prone to serious stress-related health problems.

PERFORMANCE-DEPENDENT STYLE #2: THE CON-FLICTED ACHIEVER. This child reacts to the high performance expectations of parents with severe emotional conflict and resulting high anxiety. With time and continuing parental pressure to achieve, performance anxiety mounts to near paralytic levels. The inevitable result is impaired ability to perform. In demanding performance situations, for example, tests or employment interviews, there is extreme anticipatory anxiety, physical symptoms of stress, mental blocking, and other problems that diminish performance. It is not uncommon for Conflicted Achievers to develop a pattern in which physical symptoms or other avoidance behaviors permit them to escape performance situations. Within, there is a deep emotional need to be reassured of a parent's or spouse's love "no matter what." Translated, this need is really a critical question: "Will you still love me even if I can't perform well?" Conflicted Achievers may be very bright, but low self-esteem and high performance anxiety severely limit fulfillment of their considerable potential.

PERFORMANCE DEPENDENT STYLE #3: THE STUB-BORN NONACHIEVER. The third kind of response to excessive performance demands by achievement-oriented parents is so prevalent that it might easily be termed the "later child syndrome." A combination of high achievement expectations and constant negative comparisons to a more highly achieving older brother or sister leads this child to give up at an early age. Feeling unable to compete successfully (parents constantly reinforce lack of successful competition), this child soon refuses to compete at all! The psychological result is minimal performance in school and determined opposition to anything even remotely academic. The Stubborn Nonachiever may choose a career direction that cannot possibly result in comparison to other siblings by parents. For their part, parents typically disapprove of such career choices (*e.g.,* clerk, rock musician, construction work) because of the marginal economic security provided by such employment. Parental disappointment is manifested in intense pressure to choose a career direction more acceptable to them.

This "achievement conflict" between parents and a later child causes great emotional damage that does not heal, even long after this child has left home. What really hurts such achievement-oriented parents is the total rejection by the Stubborn Nonachiever of all they stand for. The child has learned that it is better not to compete at all than to compete and lose. At another level, this child may be quite intuitive. Often such a child perceives early in life that the parents' lifestyle, filled as it is with status needs, constant pressure to succeed, and making more and more money, simply does not bring contentment. This child makes an early decision (often subconsciously) to pursue personal happiness (albeit in a somewhat naive way) despite powerful parental objections. The price is high. A sense of being different and unacceptable to the family develops within. Although the relationship to parents may eventually become more cordial, the deep hurt resulting from early parental rejection may never be completely reconciled or forgiven.

Rounding Out: The 3-P Method

Children raised with these three Problem Patterns of parental reinforcement frequently develop very disturbed relationships to work. All feel insecure and inadequate and any positive feelings of self-worth are inordinately tied to successful performance. In contrast, HEALTHY Achievers most often have parents who model a lifestyle balanced between work and leisure interests and provide their children with a consistent balance of positive responses to PERSON, to PROCESS, and to PRODUCTS. Reinforcing your children positively in each of these three areas is the essence of the 3-P Method. It a way of insuring that your children are receiving healthy parental responses from you.

POSITIVE RESPONSE MODE #1: REINFORCING UNCONDITIONAL ACCEPTANCE OF PERSON. *The* most important way for you to respond to each child is with unconditional positive acceptance. You might say, "I love you just because you're you" or "I'll always love you no matter what happens" or "It really makes me feel good to know that you're my son/daughter." This kind of consistent parental response, spontaneous and combined with a big hug, powerfully reinforces a sense of being loved and accepted in a child. It helps the child develop a source of inner strength that enables healthy coping with the later vicissitudes of life. With the sure knowledge of unconditional parental acceptance, a child is better able to confront challenges, take risks, and has no need to always "prove" acceptability by performing as UNHEALTHY Achievers do. To be effective, this kind of parental response *should not* be attached to any kind of accomplishment. It is sad to realize how many successful adults grow to maturity with deep feelings of inadequacy because parents didn't communicate unconditional acceptance during development. It's so easy and so important to do so.

POSITIVE RESPONSE MODE #2: POSITIVE REINFORCEMENT FOR ACCOMPLISHMENTS. Your child must survive in a very competitive world (as you do), and it is important to respond to your child's achievements consistently and positively. However, there are three cautions to keep in mind when you relay your good feelings about your child's accomplishments. First, make sure you respond to what the child has done well, not what could have been done better (the perfectionist's mistake). Second, make it a point *never* to compare any of your children to one another. Each child is unique and comparisons are destructive to the self-esteem of both children involved. Third, support your children through the inevitable setbacks and failures. Make these learning experiences instead of castigating them for goofing up. If you follow these simple guidelines, your child will grow in inner confidence and mastery skills, and you will be an important part of it!

POSITIVE RESPONSE MODE #3: MODELING AND GIV-ING POSITIVE SUPPORT FOR PROCESS EXPERIENCES. "Play" is the active form of relaxation that everyone needs for full and healthy living. All children find play natural and fun. It is basically the ability to become pleasantly involved in any activity where the primary reward is the experience itself. Many very successful and upwardly mobile parents develop the very bad habit of psychologically "working" at leisure. Their "play" is actually work because it has a strong goal-orientation, significant ego-involvement, a necessary product that results from the experience, and the need to later evaluate what happened as a personal success or failure. When children are taught this orientation to "play," then it is no longer real leisure, nor do the satisfying benefits of relaxation occur. In your strong need to encourage "success," you may be inadvertently teaching your child to contaminate leisure at an early age. Perhaps it's time to decontaminate *your* leisure and with your child learn to "let go" and play together in healthy ways. To do this, model and reinforce slowing down and enjoying the *process* of experiences, instead of focusing solely on the outcome.

Positive Parenting: New Directions

As you have become busier with your career and the demands of many responsibilities, you may have slowly slipped into patterns of benign neglect of your children's emotional needs. The neglect is easy because your children may not complain or can't articulate what they are missing in their relationship with you. However, they *feel* the loss in ways that shape how they will live, love, and work later in life. By learning how to meet your children's emotional needs now, you help prepare them for later success. You also build a relationship with each one that will last a lifetime. Here are seven New Directions for you to put into practice with your children.

NEW DIRECTION #1: AFFECTIONATELY TOUCH EACH ONE OF YOUR CHILDREN EVERY DAY. "Have you hugged your child today?" reads the familiar bumper sticker. It's good advice because it's a fact that children need lots of physically affectionate touching for healthy development. There is no other way to as powerfully communicate your emotional bond to a child as through affectionate touching. Snuggling together, a caring pat on the head, an arm around a shoulder or waist, dancing together, or even a friendly wrestling match all communicate your acceptance and positive regard. It's a good idea to be very spontaneous with touch and combine it with verbal expressions of your unconditional love. When you do, you will be literally "keeping in touch" with your children, and you will feel more complete as well.

NEW DIRECTION #2: MODEL INTIMACY AND HEALTHY CONFLICT RESOLUTION FOR YOUR CHILDREN. In your relationships with your spouse and children, you are a model observed for years. You simply can't hide from your children no matter how hard you try. From you, they learn how to relate to others, values to guide behavior, and strategies to deal with problems. Far too frequently, highly achieving individuals develop problems with intimacy at home and also have trouble dealing with conflict. Two of the finest gifts you can give to your children are to model for them emotional intimacy and openness in relationships and methods to solve problems and conflicts in healthy ways. Like it or not, you are perhaps the *primary* influence that shapes your child's ability to get along with others, as well as to be successful. A true source of pride in parenting is to be modeled later *by* your children, not rejected for all you stand for.

NEW DIRECTION #3: CREATE OR PRESERVE FAMILY TRADITIONS FOR YOUR CHILDREN. Some of the fondest memories of childhood begin with, "Remember when we always . . .?" The emphases are on *we* and *always*. This emotionally important kind of tradition is a predictable family event occurring on special days or at particular times. It is annual, it is family-oriented, and it is fun. Dressing up to go Halloweening together, seeing cousins each year at family reunions, going to grandparents for Thanksgiving dinner, or *always* spending the second week in August at a particular beach cottage are all examples. These traditions, repeated each year throughout development, provide a pool of happy memories that result in a sense of stability later in life. If you don't have such family traditions now, be creative and begin them. You will be making warm memories for you and for the kids.

NEW DIRECTION #4: SET AND ENFORCE LIMITS FOR YOUR CHILDREN. Far too many successful parents grant destructive permissiveness to their children in lieu of spending quality time with them. Children, no matter what age, need clearly defined limits that are consistently enforced with consequences meted out fairly for violation of those limits. It is from reasonable external limits that a child learns internal control (that is, to set personal limits) and develops self-confidence. Children raised without consistent limits frequently feel unloved and that parents really don't care about them. Over the years, an undisciplined child becomes demanding, impulsive, and selfish with ever more expensive tastes. Setting limits and enforcing them, however, does take time and energy. The payoff in life skills will be of immense help to your child later, though. And, your relationship with your child almost always improves when you set reasonable limits and enforce them consistently. There is no better way to love your child then to take the time for caring discipline.

NEW DIRECTION #5: EAT A MEAL EVERY DAY WITH YOUR CHILDREN. It's surprising how many busy families are never all together for even a few moments from week to week. A good ground rule is to eat at least one meal together as a family each day. No matter what meal is chosen, it should be a high priority within the family. Mealtimes should be pleasant experiences where family members can daily touch base with one another, discuss recent events or family issues, and to generally learn to know one another through casual conversation. Under no circumstances should the television set be on while the family is eating! It's a distraction that is easy, but it cuts off communication. It's a sad statement that one shared meal may be virtually the only opportunity for the modern family to be together on a daily basis. Make this minimum time together an absolute must.

NEW DIRECTION #6: TEACH YOUR CHILDREN WORK RESPONSIBILITIES. Recent evidence has clearly indicated that children who had chores and other family responsibilities during development were better adjusted and became more successful as adults. Successful parents are prone to shower their children with material wealth without demanding anything in return. The child learns to expect things to come easily and without much personal effort. It is important to have each of your children accept chores and other regular responsibilities around the house. Working at odd jobs for neighbors or childhood and adolescent entrepreneurial enterprises should always be encouraged, as should regular part-time work once they become of age. Through such activities, the child learns the realistic relationship between effort and reward and begins to adopt healthy work habits as well. It's easy to give your children all you didn't have as a child, but it's a mistake that you *both* will pay for later!

NEW DIRECTION #7: ALWAYS "BE THERE" FOR YOUR CHILDREN. Emotionally "being there" for your children has both psychological and physical dimensions. When there are problems, hurt feelings, or emotional upset, "being there" means supportive caring and helping in a positive way. It is easy to withdraw or blame or become angry when your child has encountered a difficulty, but such responses are helpful to no one. At another level, participating in the important events and milestones of your child's development is also a critical aspect of "being there." Attending a scout induction ceremony, a piano recital, graduation day, school plays, or sports events in which your child is a participant is most important. When you aren't there consistently and other children's parents are involved, the deep hurt and resentment that is generated often persists well into adulthood. By caring enough to "be there" for each child, you help build a strong self-concept and an inner security that would not otherwise be possible.

The New Empty Nest

The "empty nest" syndrome is said to occur in women whose personal identities are focused solely on motherhood. Inevitably, children grow up and depart. According to the script, the end result is a mother left alone at home with few personal interests, an "empty nest" and no clear identity or life role anymore. The departure of the last child precipitates this period of depression, emotional turmoil, and inner struggle to forge a new identity and new directions. At worst, some women are not able to move beyond the loss of the central mother role.

These days, this stereotyped version of events is much less valid. The woman of the house today is much more likely to have her own personal interests, a career direction, and an active social life. Parenting remains an important and critical role, but identity and self-esteem don't stem exclusively from motherhood. As a result, the "empty nest" signals a transition for the modern woman, but not a highly traumatic one. In fact, it is more likely to be viewed as a positive event. Today's woman is looking forward to the point where more time is available for leisure activities with a spouse or friends, more time to devote to career development, or more time to become involved in other personally meaningful activities. In short, the new woman looks forward to a new role and new freedom after the trying years of child rearing are over.

There is a *new* "empty nest" problem, however, that primarily strikes men. Men tend to be most busy establishing themselves in successful careers during their late twenties and thirties, even into the early forties. During this same period, young children need time and attention and involvement from *both* parents — including Dad. Because of career involvements, Dad may be less available during these years than at any other time during a child's development. The result is an absent father during the children's most critical years of physical and emotional growth. Day after day, week after week, month after month, Dad makes choices in little ways to place career concerns over Positive Parenting. Suddenly, the years mount up. The children are grown! It just doesn't seem possible.

The emotionally shocking realization that the children are grown brings on Dad's "empty nest" syndrome. It is somewhat different from the outmoded feminine version of years past where a woman loses a life role and a personal identity. In the masculine version, the awareness that children are grown triggers intense regret and guilt over years of involvement that could have been — but wasn't. The years of sharing with children simply can't be recaptured. The joys, the disappointments, the problems, the family times spent together aren't there as fond memories. Now "the kids" are grown and gone. Sometimes, relationships do become closer after the fact of the children's departure, but involvement all through adulthood just can't be regained in adulthood when it is more convenient for Dad. The early sharing is an opportunity lost forever. It is an emotional void that Dad must live with forever.

Being Something Special

The most fulfilling kind of parenting success occurs when each of your children grows into adulthood *thinking of you* as "something special." And, the feeling should be mutual. Each child should be *seen by you* as "something special." These kinds of positive feelings simply don't happen by accident. They are the result of consistently taking the time to care, to teach, to discipline, to talk, and to play with your children. With your positive involvement, each child matures into adult life with a sure knowledge of your unconditional acceptance. Each knows that individual differences are valued and respected. Each one also knows that there will always be support for growth and development in personally meaningful directions.

Unfortunately, you cannot protect your child completely from all the pressures and problems of life. If you have been a positive model, however, you have helped each child build healthy coping skills, strong and adaptive life values, and a reservoir of inner strength to help through the tough times. These are the buffers that will enable your child to succeed and to practice Lifestyle Management to preserve health, happiness, and career longevity in a highly stressful, competitive world. Children raised in families where there was Positive Parenting are far ahead of those who were raised amid affluence in families that are fragmented, interpersonally distant, and full of subtle and not-so-subtle conflict.

Before leaving this discussion of strategies for Positive Parenting, there are three very negative habits that it is wise to completely eliminate from your interactions with your children. Each of them diminishes Positive Parenting and discourages open communication between parent and child.

TURNOFF #1: TELLING "HARD LIFE" STORIES. Like a broken record, you tell your children over and over how hard you had it growing up, how easy they have it now (thanks to you), and how little they appreciate it. Instead, in a positive way help them learn the same values that you have learned on your way to becoming successful, rather than preaching your "hard life" and "lucky stars" routines to them.

TURNOFF #2: TURNING EVERY CONVERSATION INTO A DISCUSSION OF MONETARY COSTS. Because you're so money-oriented, you may have developed a habit of bringing "cost" into every talk, no matter what the subject. When you do, you communicate that all you really value is money and material wealth. Instead, talk with your children about all manner of interesting things and teach them how to emotionally live richly and fully each day by modeling it for them.

TURNOFF #3: INSTILLING A NEGATIVE PERCEPTION OF OTHER PEOPLE. In many not always obvious ways, you may be inadvertently teaching your children through your responses that other people are basically bad, not to be trusted, or not as good as they are. Keep it up and that perception will eventually include *you*, too! Instead, teach them to always respect others, to focus on their strengths, and to maintain a solidly optimistic personal viewpoint on life and living.

As a Positive Parent, treat your children as your greatest legacy because that's just what they are. Keep in mind that your children must grow up in a world far more complex and difficult than the days of your youth. Take the time to be involved and to know each one of your children deeply. They need all the help they can get. You'll benefit, too. Your children are naturally loving, and their feelings for you will grow deeper and stronger and more fulfilling unless you systematically stamp them out with cynicism, inaccessibility, and neglect of their emotional needs. With deep insight, a very wise parent observed that "there are only two lasting bequests that we can hope to give our children. One of these is roots; the other, wings." Roots and Wings. Each of your children deserves no less from you!

Chapter 16

Getting Your ACT Together. Motivational Strategies for Surviving Your Career!

Over the years, you've clearly become wiser and more competent in your work. You've experienced success firsthand and your standard of living has risen accordingly. You're comfortable economically, and you're confident that with your dedication, you will continue to progress. You're satisfied that you're about where you should be at this point in your career. The problem is that you're not feeling so good about it. You used to be challenged by your work, stimulated each day, and easily excited by anything new and interesting. Now you're still doing all you need to do, but it seems that something inside you has turned off. You've caught a case of the Doldrums.

You are among many thousands of talented and career-oriented individuals who experience the Doldrums each year. The signs are universal. The feelings most distressing. Here's a quick checklist of the symptoms of the Doldrums, that uncomfortable state of listlessness and despondency that occurs all too often. Look at yourself through them.

_____ 1. At work, you feel that you are just going through the motions.

_____ 2. Your life has become humdrum with each day no more than a boring replica of the one before.

_____ 3. You feel lethargic and don't seem to have your usual energy.

_____ 4. Deep within, you feel unsettled and deeply dissatisfied.

_____ 5. Practically nothing these days gives you the big kick that you used to get from something new and exciting.

_____ 6. You are completely overwhelmed by what you must get done each day.

_____ 7. Your life has become so complicated that it's almost impossible to keep everything straight.

_____ 8. You are resentful because you give and give, but seem to get so little back.

_____ 9. You feel directionless and disorganized and not sure what you're working for anymore.

_____ 10. You have frequent urges to run away and start a whole new life.

The facts are that although you're continuing to do reasonably well at work, personally you just don't feel good about you. Looking at yourself a bit more closely, you realize just how much things have changed over the last several years. You don't feel like that peppy, inner-directed, HEALTHY ACHIEVER you once were. In fact, in addition to the symptoms of the Doldrums, you have the telling characteristics of an individual who has lost control from within. In a nutshell, you're feeling terrible because . . .

• your SELF-ESTEEM is diminished. These days you feel more like a victim than anything else. One painful result is . . .

• a deep inner FRUSTRATION as life has become a never-ending series of major and minor hassles that you must face each day. It just doesn't go away and it causes you to feel . . .

• DOWN and DEPRESSED. You grit your teeth and manage to hold your own at work, but it's getting harder and harder to do so. There is an elusive contentment within that you are seeking, but can't seem to find.

It is certainly in your best interest to stay alive inside so that you can not only continue in a long and productive career, but also remain reasonably happy and healthy while you are doing so. These days, for whatever the reasons, you've lost that HEALTHY ACHIEVING part of you and the personal meaning that is part of it. It's time to begin looking for the causes. And, there are causes. You will not find them anywhere in your environment. They lie within. That's where your search must begin.

Beginning Your ACTing Career

You used to row your own boat in a direction you chose for you. Now you're floundering in the riptides of your life that randomly push you this way and that. Incessant pressures, daily problems, and mounting responsibilities have conspired to rob you of your sense of purpose and that essential feeling that you are the master of your own destiny. As a once-healthy achiever, you have lost your Center Within. However, this loss need not be permanent. You can become a HEALTHY ACHIEVER again by understanding what has happened and taking the necessary steps to rebuild the inner foundations of your self-esteem.

You know that it's about time for you to get your ACT together again. As a start, here are the three interrelated foundations of your Center Within that are at the core of every HEALTHY ACHIEVER. You can start rebuilding them today. As you do, you start ACTing healthy again.

"A" Stands for ACCEPTING Your Adequacy. It is almost axiomatic that unhealthy achievers push constantly for success as a means to demonstrate their adequacy to themselves and to others. Power, wealth, status, and possessions all become external symbols of success that say "See, I *am* adequate." The problem is that within such individuals there is a void that can never be filled. External successes temporarily keep personal insecurities at bay. But, the unhealthy achiever must continue to do more and more in bigger and better ways to gain the reassurance that success brings. Life becomes a drive for success that is really a series of "quick fixes" that don't stick.

The HEALTHY ACHIEVER, on the other hand, is psychologically much different. This individual has already made a positive decision about personal adequacy. The result is that there is no great insecurity within, nor is there a need to constantly prove anything to anybody. The HEALTHY ACHIEVER does achieve, however, but achieving for this individual is a means for creative self-expression from within instead of a drive to fill an insatiable need for reassurance. And, because the HEALTHY ACHIEVER has made a decision about personal adequacy from within, setbacks, problems, and even failures are handled with the grace that stems from the strength of personal adequacy.

"C" Stands for CONTROL from Within. In short, the unhealthy achiever has lost control. Because of the need to achieve to allay personal insecurity, priorities become skewed in the direction of work because that is where the rewards of success are most easily obtained. Leisure activities, quality time with the family, and friendships are slowly compromised as priorities become skewed. The unhealthy achiever is not only victim to expansive ego needs, but also prone to manipulation through flattery. The net result is that the unhealthy achiever says "yes" too much for questionable reasons and easily becomes overinvolved in work without respect for personal limits or the quality of Life After Work.

By contrast, the HEALTHY ACHIEVER is never out of personal control. This individual preserves the prerogative to make healthy choices from within. There is acceptance that people and situations can't always be controlled, but there is also the ability to *choose how to respond to any situation.* Because of personal acceptance of adequacy within, the HEALTHY ACHIEVER has healthy priorities that include much more than work and more work. At the same time, a healthy perspective on problem situations and a respect for personal emotional needs help to insure Lifestyle Balance. And, choices are constantly made to meet these needs in day-to-day living. The HEALTHY ACHIEVER never permits external chaos to erode healthy inner choices.

"T" Stands for TRAINING Your Talents. As the unhealthy achiever gives up control from within, life quickly fills to overflowing with the extraneous details of daily living and a myriad of responsibilities. Life becomes a game of "catch up," with inability to separate the important from the mundane, the meaningful from the minutiae, the innovative from the routine. As these changes take place, the unhealthy achiever succumbs to the Doldrums. In the midst of success, life begins to lose its meaning as energy drops and zest for living disappears. There is a distressing feeling of being trapped as a personal orientation to life increasingly centers on how to get everything done that must be done today.

Just the opposite of these trends is found in the HEALTHY ACHIEVER who is always moving forward in directions that are personally meaningful. Because there is strong personal acceptance and comfortable control from within, the HEALTHY ACHIEVER is free to discover new parts of the self, to bring them out into the open, and then to develop them. The HEALTHY ACHIEVER lives a well-rounded life and has many interests. It is this way of living that makes the HEALTHY ACHIEVER a talented individual and a most interesting person. No day is boring and routine because new awarenesses and learning are taking place all the time. The ongoing process of mastery and maturation is the hallmark of this creatively involved individual who enjoys living fully every day.

Losing Your ACT Is Painfully Normal

It is not uncommon to find HEALTHY ACHIEVERS pursuing a personally meaningful career and experiencing a positive sense of direction for years at a time. However, a point usually comes when a significant decline in happiness and emotional well being is recognized. All of the symptoms of the Doldrums become manifest. Previous self-acceptance, the crucial sense of inner control, and the excitement of training personal talents slip away. When this occurs (as it does from time to time for most individuals), it is important to understand that ACTing in your career is rarely permanent. Developing your Center Within is not something you do once and then forget. In fact, losing your ACT occurs so frequently that it must be considered a normal part of personal and career development.

When you experience an erosion of your positive feelings about life and living and begin to pick up the signs of the Doldrums, you can proceed in two basic directions. The negative option is to find someone to blame or some other scapegoat for your unhappiness. This relieves you of responsibility for yourself and helps to convince you that you are truly not in control of your life and never will be. Under such circumstances and with time, you become a resentful, bitter, and pessimistic victim of circumstance.

A much better alternative is to see the Doldrums as an emotional message. The symptoms of the Doldrums are your body's way of communicating that you are not adequately meeting your basic emotional needs at this time in your life. Change is clearly indicated, and you will have to take control of your life by making some key decisions *for you* to restore your Center Within. Tackling the Doldrums head-on with personal insight and a positive attitude toward change is a tremendous advantage in solving the existing problem. When you do, even the Doldrums become an impetus for personal growth and maturation. The HEALTHY ACHIEVER wins again!

There are five frequently encountered reasons for the Doldrums and when you understand them, you become aware of yourself in deeper and more meaningful ways. By closely examining each of these psychological underpinnings of the Doldrums and relating them to your experiences, you can pinpoint emerging issues within you and also define clear-cut directions for change.

Remember that not one of these reasons is mutually exclusive of the others. Several may be present in any individual experiencing the distressing personal and career plateau reflected by the Doldrums. Here are the five possibilities to consider.

POSSIBILITY #1: YOU HAVE BURNED OUT. In short, you have been pushing too hard for too long, and you just don't have the energy to keep up the pace. The Doldrums you are experiencing are just part of the broader depressive state characteristic of Personal Burnout. Over the years, you have let your strong achievement needs overwhelm everything else in your life. As this has occurred, you have slowly lost the ability to relax and psychologically "get away from it all." Now that you're successful, you find yourself emotionally exhausted and personally unhappy as well. You just don't know how to stop anymore.

DECISION DIRECTION: Your critical decision is how to immediately begin to enhance the quality of your Life After Work. Regaining Lifestyle Balance will be necessary as you learn to temper your achievement needs to enjoy life. Recovering relaxation skills and decontaminating your leisure will be a key part of this decision. Be patient because it will take time.

POSSIBILITY #2: YOUR WORK IS SECURE, BUT TOO EASY. If your work is not challenging, even boring these days, it is quite possible that you have been seduced into lethargy by work that is too easy, but highly secure. Basically, you have outgrown your work, but you are in a bind because you are faced with a difficult decision. The "go-getter" part of you is stagnating, but giving up the security of your present position is risky. A key characteristic of this problem is that you wish you were in a new position where you could use all of your talents and continue to grow, but you're stopped because that would take energy that you're not sure you have.

DECISION DIRECTION: You can always opt for security and stay where you are. Many individuals do. A more positive resolution is a decision to create new stimulation in your present position or to overcome your negative inertia to find new work that will challenge and excite you. Sometimes lateral transfers help. However, the responsibility to make things better is yours alone.

POSSIBILITY #3: YOU HAVE MOVED FROM "HANDS ON" TO MANAGEMENT. Career ladders almost inevitably lead to administrative or managerial responsibilities. Those motivated individuals who demonstrate excellence in the direct application of "hands on" skills are most likely to be promoted. On the other hand, many very good managers (and just as many poor managers) are not emotionally suited for such positions. The toll is high in terms of chronic frustration and unhappiness. Often the Doldrums result when individuals talented in the direct application of their skills are moved to positions that require solving more abstract production and "people" problems.

DECISION DIRECTION: The two sides of your decision coin are clear in such circumstances. To make more money at the price of a chronic case of the Doldrums is one. The other is to find a new position where you can move forward by directly using your "hands on" skills. Even stepping down from management in your present firm is worth it if it brings peace of mind.

POSSIBILITY #4: YOUR NEEDS HAVE CHANGED WITHIN. As you mature, what you need from your work to feel personally satisfied and fulfilled may periodically change. With age, most individuals move from being highly stimulated by the accumulation of possessions and demonstrating competency in the marketplace to an undeniable need to find contentment within. That requires a reorientation of your relationship to work as you become more interested in enjoying what you do instead of the material rewards that you get from it. In a nutshell, "what makes me happy" begins to take precedence over success and more success just for success' sake.

DECISION DIRECTION: It is imperative to respond to your emerging need to enjoy what you do at work. That means training yourself to focus on the process of what you do instead of the products. Many individuals easily make this change within the context of their present position. If that is not possible, look for a strong avocational interest that will provide you with at least a modicum of the kinds of inner satisfactions that you now seek.

POSSIBILITY #5: YOU ARE TRAPPED BY BAD PRECEDENTS. With success, your life has slowly grown into a monstrous collection of obligations, responsibilities to others, and details to which you must attend each day. These myriad expectations of you extend far beyond your work, and they are now totally out of hand. You've played the "nice guy" too many times by saying "yes" when you should have said "no." You've also set some awful precedents along the way that lead others to take your efforts for granted. The tail is now wagging the dog, and you are paying the price. No wonder you're feeling bad. At home and at work, there's nothing left for you.

DECISION DIRECTION: To solve this painful dilemma, you must sort out the important and drop the unimportant. You must also learn to say "no" to protect the time you need to do satisfying things just for you. Shift responsibility back where it belongs as you slowly take control of your life once again and reverse the precedents that have trapped you. Stick to your guns so it doesn't happen again!

Characteristics of HEALTHY ACHIEVERS

Defining the characteristics of HEALTHY ACHIEVERS is actually outlining the psychological methodology for maintaining your Center Within. Together these qualities constitute a strategy for maintaining control and direction in your life despite what is going on around you. Each one of these characteristics is based on developing only a single product throughout life—YOU! By following these guidelines, you not only strengthen your Center Within, but you also begin to do the right things for the right emotional reasons. Use each one of these guidelines not only as a diagnostic tool, but also as the basis for new directions that will create a happier, healthier, and more productive *you.*

THE HEALTHY ACHIEVER #1: YOU WORK FOR YOURSELF, NOT OTHERS. No matter who provides your paycheck, as a HEALTHY ACHIEVER you are psychologically self-employed. In every facet of your life — including your career — you work toward a wiser and more mature you. In fact, you do not work directly for money or other material rewards because you know that they will come to you as you strive for excellence and mastery in all that you do. Instead, it is the inner satisfaction of learning and the fulfillment of doing well that you seek. It is from developing all of your potential for you that your motivation arises. And, because you psychologically work for yourself, you are in a strong position to maintain and further develop your Center Within.

THE HEALTHY ACHIEVER #2: YOU COMPETE WITH YOURSELF, NOT OTHERS. It is very easy, but a mistake, to measure your self-worth in relationship to the performance of others. Then it's only a short step to start "keeping up with the Joneses" as a way to feel good about yourself. The problem is that the Joneses' activities then determine your self-worth, and you make decisions based on what they are doing so you can keep up. The HEALTHY ACHIEVER avoids this easy trap by making decisions based on personal well-being and on what is good for the family. If there is competition at all, the HEALTHY ACHIEVER strives to beat a "personal best." Because of this orientation to living, the internal control that stems from the Center Within is easily maintained by the HEALTHY ACHIEVER.

THE HEALTHY ACHIEVER #3: YOU TAKE THE INITIATIVE TO CREATE INTERESTING CHALLENGES FOR YOURSELF. You know that some children never learn to entertain themselves. Instead, they depend on others to keep them stimulated. There are also many adults who have not learned this critical skill. Not so the HEALTHY ACHIEVER. This individual has two basic motives: to keep on growing and to keep life interesting. The HEALTHY ACHIEVER has the ability to create personally meaningful and challenging things to do and does them all the time. If work is boring, this individual finds an area for personal development. If Life After Work becomes routine, variety is created. The HEALTHY ACHIEVER never depends on others for stimulation because there is a strong and healthy and creative Center Within.

THE HEALTHY ACHIEVER #4: YOU SET REALISTIC GOALS TO GUIDE YOUR DEVELOPMENT. In other words, as a HEALTHY ACHIEVER you know where you are going and feel good about it because you have decided on a positive direction for yourself. You never let yourself sink into living day by day without direction as unhealthy achievers are prone to do. Neither are you a dreamer who chronically escapes into fantasies of the future, but who is reluctant to pay the price to make dreams come true. The HEALTHY ACHIEVER sets realistic three-year plans with a commitment to revising them annually as personal changes in self or life circumstances occur. As a result, the HEALTHY ACHIEVER is always moving in a direction defined from within that insures personal development and a strengthened sense of self.

THE HEALTHY ACHIEVER #5: YOU MAKE FAILURES AND SETBACKS INTO LEARNING EXPERIENCES. As a rule, it's hard to be really successful if you can't handle failure. Unhealthy achievers have a strong tendency to take their failures personally and as a result, they lose the tremendous learning potential in these experiences. In a nutshell, the unhealthy achiever is driven to succeed and fears failure because self-esteem is so heavily linked to achieving. The HEALTHY ACHIEVER is much less vulnerable because self-esteem and adequacy are not as dependent on external successes. Because there is a healthy Center Within based on a positive decision about personal adequacy, setbacks are kept in perspective and used to produce insights that result in greater self-awareness and mastery. In this way, even failures strengthen the HEALTHY ACHIEVER'S forward movement.

THE HEALTHY ACHIEVER #6: YOU NURTURE A CREATIVE EXCITEMENT ABOUT LIFE AND LIVING. It's tough to stay emotionally alive and excited when you are struggling each day just to keep up. As you look around you, so many of your peers have become bored cynical individuals who just plod along to the deadening routines of their lives. The HEALTHY ACHIEVER is different. Such an individual finds it easy to get "turned on" and excited about all kinds of things and does! And, the excitement of the HEALTHY ACHIEVER is highly contagious. Others gravitate to this special person because of it. The HEALTHY ACHIEVER also finds it easy to generate "team spirit" in group endeavors and provides stimulating encouragement to others' projects as a zest for living from the Center Within emerges each day.

THE HEALTHY ACHIEVER #7: YOU MAINTAIN A SUPPORT NETWORK OF HEALTHY PEERS. The HEALTHY ACHIEVER has lasting power, and part of that power results from ongoing relationships with *healthy* peers. Unhealthy achievers are often loners who have little time for relationships. Or, they may associate only with workaholic colleagues who reinforce the need to work even more. The HEALTHY ACHIEVER is aware of these destructive extremes and seeks out peers who strive in a healthy way for mastery, but who also appreciate the benefits of leisure activities, family life, and friendships. Leaving naysayers and complainers behind, this individual easily goes beyond a personal work environment to find other HEALTHY ACHIEVING friends, each with a positive Center Within.

THE HEALTHY ACHIEVER #8: YOU HAVE A STRONG CAPACITY FOR SELF-AFFIRMATION. The HEALTHY ACHIEVER is a principled individual with a healthy sense of self-esteem not dependent on externals. One result is that there is little fear of moving along a personally defined path even when it means being a bit different when necessary. The HEALTHY ACHIEVER seeks out advice when it is needed and uses it in positive ways to help smooth the path ahead. However, the doubts or perhaps even the overtly negative reactions of others do not stop the HEALTHY ACHIEVER, nor does fear of failure. Life is seen as a personal path negotiated each step of the way, but defined from the Center Within. Because of this internal capacity for self-affirmation, combined with a sensible approach to living, the HEALTHY ACHIEVER ultimately goes farther than the unhealthy one who is limited by insecurity within and fear of disapproval without.

THE HEALTHY ACHIEVER #9: YOU POSSESS EMOTIONAL SELF-AWARENESS AND INTERPERSONAL SENSITIVITY. The HEALTHY ACHIEVER doesn't spend life chasing after the external symbols of success. Rather, focus is on developing a more competent, alive, and wiser person within. Time is taken to contemplate what is really important in life, such as continuing relationships, sharing good times, and giving of oneself. The HEALTHY ACHIEVER then begins to respond in ways that meet these needs and material rewards usually come along the way. And, because of emotional self-awareness that results from nurturing the Center Within, the HEALTHY ACHIEVER develops compassion for others and sensitivity to their well-being. Helpful support comes naturally because the HEALTHY ACHIEVER finds "being there" for others emotionally satisfying.

THE HEALTHY ACHIEVER #10: YOU KNOW HOW TO "GET AWAY FROM IT ALL" AND YOU DO. Work at home, work at work, work with hands, work with mind—all without cease—are the hallmarks of the unhealthy achiever. And, such an individual is usually found sleeping when not working. How do you spell relief under such conditions? The fact is, you don't. Because of the Center Within, the HEALTHY ACHIEVER is able to keep work in reasonable perspective. Work is a form of personal expression that remains interesting and challenging, but this individual does not do too much of it. In short, the HEALTHY ACHIEVER practices Lifestyle Management. By making "getting away from it all" a priority, the HEALTHY ACHIEVER preserves the capacity not only to enjoy work, but also Life After Work. By doing so, the HEALTHY ACHIEVER adds deeper meaning to success and enjoys the fruits of labor in ways that unhealthy achievers simply cannot.

Tips for Turning the Tide

It is neither unusual nor uncommon for a HEALTHY

ACHIEVER to lose a personal Center Within now and then. In fact, it's more likely to happen than not. What is critical is the awareness to recognize the signs of the Doldrums and then to move in constructive directions that will reverse them. Making a commitment to Turning the Tide in your favor when you lose your Center Within is actually a decision to take control of your life once again. The alternative is to continue to be buffeted mercilessly by the powerful crosscurrents that you are exposed to each day.

Here are seven decisions to help you start Turning the Tide to recover your Center Within. Each one represents a decision *for you because you are important.* Each also helps put the personal characteristics of the HEALTHY ACHIEVER into context.

TURNING THE TIDE #1: CHOOSE YOU INSTEAD OF OTHERS. Chances are that if you are feeling out of control these days, you are responding excessively to others' needs and neglecting your emotional self in the process. The fact is that you can't really give to others unless you feel good about yourself. Because you count too, it's time to reverse this trend. It's time to take the time, make the time, to do some of the things that you enjoy. Your interests. Your friends. Your family are all an important part of living fully each day. By choosing to take care of yourself a bit more in lieu of taking care of others, everyone will benefit because you'll be a more pleasant and giving you.

TURNING THE TIDE #2: CHOOSE QUALITY OVER QUANTITY. Part of feeling out of control is trying to do too much. Slowly your life becomes filled with more tasks to get done each day. You can't really enjoy doing anything because you are chronically overwhelmed. External demands have forced you to choose quantity over quality. Your new directions are obvious. You must choose to do fewer things, but you must also choose to do them well. Making this choice involves removing the extraneous and the mundane from your life. Beware of filling the new time available with new responsibilities geared to others. Doing fewer things well and enjoying them is great for self-esteem.

TURNING THE TIDE #3: CHOOSE SIMPLICITY OVER COMPLEXITY. One inadvertent product of success is that your life gradually becomes immensely complicated. You nostalgically look back to the "good old days" when life was simple and straightforward. Life will never be quite that way again, but you can take steps to move in that direction by uncomplicating your lifestyle now. You must make decisions for a simpler life. Some decisions may be major (a move to a smaller and more manageable home) and some relatively minor (to remove the hassles of a rental home and reinvest the money elsewhere). Cutting out those activities that are not particularly fulfilling is also helpful. By taking these steps, you not only simplify your life by removing worries and problems, but you also create more time to enjoy yourself.

TURNING THE TIDE #4: CHOOSE INNER SATISFACTION OVER EXTERNAL REWARDS. It is seductively easy to begin orienting your life excessively toward tangible rewards of achievement with the hope that if you get enough of them, happiness will follow. As you may have already found, beyond the basics, the more possessions you have, the more time (and money) must be spent in upkeep. Mere possession of "things" becomes progressively meaningless if you don't have time to relax and enjoy life. It is important to Turning the Tide that you begin to work for personal satisfaction and inner fulfillment instead of external rewards. As you do, your successes become deeper and more meaningful than your tangible assets can ever be.

TURNING THE TIDE #5: CHOOSE PROCESS OVER PROD-UCTS. To put this decision another way, SLOW DOWN so that you can enjoy and value experiences. Right now, you are product-oriented. You rush from morning to night to get everything done. Relaxation and emotional rejuvenation come from permitting yourself to become deeply and pleasantly involved in a given activity and valuing the experience over anything you might get out of it. It's true that in your work, you must strive for tangible products. In your Life After Work, however, choose experiences that provide you with personal satisfaction even if there are no tangible products to show for the time spent! When you do, you'll find that contentment is a new "product" you'll really like.

TURNING THE TIDE #6: CHOOSE DIRECTION OVER DESPAIR. The Doldrums reflect a trapped, unsatisfying despair in your life. Living day-by-day using every bit of your energy just to keep up isn't much fun. Choosing a personal direction for yourself is critical to breaking this downward spiral of inner turmoil, boring daily routines, and directionless living. By choosing a direction that is meaningful to you and moving along the path that it creates, you regain control of your life. Then you can cope with the frustrations and hassles that are part of life. Without direction, the inevitable minor irritations in your life become an oppressive force that makes you its victim. As a rule, *any* direction is better that no direction at all.

TURNING THE TIDE #7: CHOOSE EXCELLENCE OVER MEDIOCRITY. This decision is deceptive because it doesn't mean becoming a perfectionist in all areas of your life. Such a goal will truly drive you (and others) to distraction. Rather, it is choosing to develop every bit of potential you have in *one* area of your life and thereby become excellent. And, this area of excellence need not necessarily be your work at all. It can involve becoming the best parent you can be, a gifted piano player, a great windsurfer, or a very savvy coin collector. By choosing to develop excellence in one area of your life, you not only choose direction, but your self-esteem rises and there is a positive and enduring effect on everything else you do, too!

Developing Products from Within

Maintaining a strong and postive Center Within these days is difficult, but certainly not impossible. At the core of the good life is a commitment to you. The HEALTHY ACHIEVER has made this commitment to inner fulfillment and sound priorities. Decisions are made that keep each day creative and interesting, growth enhancing, and chock full of zest for life. In a world obsessed with products, the HEALTHY ACHIEVER has an enduring interest in only one kind. That is to develop healthy products from within. It is only when you decide to do so that everything else begins to make sense.

Think about it for a minute. You live in a world full of unhealthy pressures and seductive expectations. Many times each day, advertisers link your self-esteem to their *products*. Your employers (or clients) want you to work extra hard every day to produce *products* for them. Along the way, you have developed strong achievement needs, so you direct your energies toward creating the *products* that reassure you of your adequacy and your ability to "make it" in the marketplace.

Sooner or later, however, you begin to realize just how much your life has become oriented toward mindlessly producing for the sake of producing. As you are subtly maneuvered over the years in the direction of a product-dominated lifestyle, you slowly lose your grasp on who you are as a person, as a man or woman, and as a professional. In a nutshell, you lose the *essence of you* that lies buried beneath the layers of your many responsibilities to others. Nothing seems to mean much anymore. The painful price of your losses? A good case of the Doldrums. Don't make the mistake of waiting until you feel better to become a HEALTHY ACHIEVER once again. The longer you wait, the more likely it is that you will feel even worse.

You can begin to strengthen your Center Within right now. Instead of rushing through life on a schedule tightly packed with people to meet, things to do, and places to be, turn it around by making some key decisions for you. Then you will find that you will have people to care about and enjoy, personally interesting things to do, and pleasant places to be that will give you the deeper satisfactions and the fulfillment that you need to sustain life within. Abraham Lincoln sagely observed that "people are about as happy as they decide to be." Undoubtedly true. On the other hand, it's a whale of a lot easier to make that decision when you have a strong Center Within and you're a HEALTHY ACHIEVER in all that you do!

Caveats and Carrots: Making Lifestyle Management Work for You!

Now you know what Lifestyle Management is all about. You know a lot about the changes that have slowly occurred in you over the years as you became more successful. You are also acutely aware of how these changes have adversely affected virtually every aspect of your life as you live it each day. Your leisure activities, the way you communicate, your closeness to loved ones, your relationship with the kids, even your love life has been seriously contaminated with work-related attitudes. You realize how these subtle habits have interfered with enjoying the good life that is rightfully yours. You know because you've been there. You know because you've suffered from success.

Along with your understanding has come hope. You know that just as these many habits have been learned, they can also be unlearned. Without effort on your part, however, nothing at all will change because you are responsible for yourself. You are in control. You realize that there will never be a right time to make the needed changes so you're willing to start today. Right now. You are ready to make *Real Success* a meaningful part of your life, but you are also aware that you must find it within yourself, rather than seeking it in the work world. You are also sadly aware of just how much personal vitality and zest for living you've lost as you pushed yourself hard to "make it."

Perhaps one of the most distressing aspects of your success at work is the realization that your personal world has become very shallow and superficial. You analyze, anticipate, compete, work toward long-term goals, evaluate, and remain objective so much of the time that you've forgotten how to live. Deeper priorities have slipped away. As a result, your success no longer has the emotional depth to make it personally meaningful to you. You may have many material things, but there isn't much joy in your life anymore. You may have great stature in the community, but you may not have closeness in your relationships. You may be doing great things, but you aren't personally fulfilled. You may be promoted, but you don't share in your children's growth and development. You may be succeeding at great heights, but there isn't time to enjoy life's small pleasures these days.

A deeper part of yourself has been neglected for years while you were busy moving up in the world. Now, as the saying goes, you're "up agin' it." Have you paid your dues or haven't you? Do you deserve more out of life than you're giving yourself or don't you? Are you going to enjoy life now that you've arrived or aren't you? Are you going to keep work success in perspective or aren't you? You know the options. You understand the consequences. The choice must be yours. Each of you must decide within that you have paid your dues. When you do, *Real Success* with emotional depth and personal meaning will soon be yours.

Keep in mind that no matter what your chosen life's work, if you're motivated and interested and involved, the distressing problems that come with a work-dominated lifestyle are substantially the same. Striving engineers, accountants, managers, teachers, homemakers, and clerks are all vulnerable. Recently, after a seminar on Lifestyle Management given to a group of ministers, several approached afterward to express how well various Lifestyle Management concepts fitted into their spiritual lives. Later, in a thank you note, one sent a poem that well exemplified the negative consequences of neglecting deeper parts of yourself in the pursuit of success. Here it is, obviously written by someone who's been there.

"If you put your nose to the grindstone rough,
And hold it down there long enough,
You soon will say there is no such thing,
As a brook that babbles or a bird that sings.
These three will all your world compose:
Just you, the stone, and your ground down nose!"

Having It All: Heroic Highs and Magic Moments

To bring home an even deeper awareness of how you're living these days, here's a simple exercise. Ask several of your busy colleagues to recall happy memories. Do the same yourself. More than likely, the answers will be surprisingly consistent. What you will hear (and recall yourself) are descriptions of deeply meaningful experiences found midst a hectic and pressure-packed lifestyle. These are Magic Moments, filled with wonderful sensations and pleasant feelings of contentment. During these times, you've been truly able to "get away from it all." If you think about it, most happy moments are recalled vividly through your senses. In other words, they are not intellectual experiences. An idyllic fishing trip. Moonlight on the beach. Chatting on the veranda at a spring dance. A mountain vista stretching away from you. The examples are innumeable. Add a few yourself.

What is so characteristic of these Magic Moments is that they represent one important type of Natural Experience. They reflect specific times and settings in your life when you were able to deeply "let go" to enjoy the *process* of whatever you were doing. You didn't try to make anything happen. You didn't have to. You just relaxed into the experience. In a nutshell, you were able to let yourself "be," and that experience kindled a fond memory. Now ask yourself how many of these special kinds of experiences you've had lately. Probably not many, as your Life After Work has been overwhelmed by your many responsibilities and by your work-contaminated attitudes toward living.

Now, if you go beyond this special kind of Natural Experience, you will also realize that there is another kind of happiness. In addition to Magic Moments of being in a sensual setting, you have also experienced Heroic Highs from time to time. This kind of inner joy comes from mastery. It has its roots in the achieving part of yourself. It is the emotional boost that comes from successfully meeting new challenges, from attaining personal goals, and from "making it" in a competitive world of work. You used to regularly experience this kind of happiness too, but that was way back when work was fun and you were growing instead of just trying to survive. You notice that you haven't had many of these kinds of highs recently either. You've been down and unhappy at work *and* at home. Now you know why and you're ready to do something about it.

These ideas about happiness reflect a simple fact of your emotional life that you must recognize. Without the ability to "get away from it all" regularly, *both* kinds of joy disappear from your life. When your success-oriented way of relating dominates all else, work isn't much fun anymore because you can't get away from it. And, because you can't get away from work, your ability to "let go" to enjoy Natural Experiences is seriously compromised. The net result is that life becomes a daily drag with little joy and even less relief from the grinding pressures you face each day. Economic success is little more than a hollow victory because you can't enjoy it. While successful, you no longer have the ability to experience the personal contentment that is the essence of *Real Success*.

As you begin to practice Lifestyle Management and make it stick for you, both Magic Moments and Heroic Highs will return. It will be a signal that you are beginning to experience *Real Success* because you now have Lifestyle Balance. Don't forget that Lifestyle Management (one last time) is learning to creatively balance work and achieving and success on one hand with satisfying involvements in leisure activities, family life, and friendships on the other. As you recreate a healthy Life After Work, the pleasure of challenge *and* those special moments that become fond memories soon begin to return.

A solid bit of wisdom that reflects the basic strategy underlying Lifestyle Management has been succinctly put into words by an unknown, but knowing, individual. It goes something like this. Keep it in mind.

"If you want to experience fulfillment in your life's work over the long term, three qualities must be present. First, you must have a basic aptitude for what you do. Second, you must experience success in it. Third, and most important, YOU MUST NOT DO TOO MUCH OF IT!"

Your Prime Time Priorities

No matter what your chronological age happens to be, if you're not happy, it isn't prime time for you. And, if you're not experiencing the positive feelings that come from successfully meeting new challenges as well as moments of deep peace and inner fulfillment, then the probability is that you do not yet have enough Lifestyle Balance. You know that the changes that must be made are all possible and all within you. Because of these facts, you also realize that how you are living each day is ultimately up to you. You are never without choices. For better or for worse, *It's All in Your Head!*

As you exercise the power within you to choose a more balanced lifestyle, here are some of the signs that are positive indicators that you are moving in the right direction. Keep on making changes for you until every single one of them is both natural and an important part of how you choose to live each day.

1. It has become a personal priority for you to HAVE YOUR SHARE OF FUN EXPERIENCES NOW because you realize that you can't save good times for later like you save money in the bank.

2. You now REGULARLY RELAX IN YOUR HOME (not just rest there) instead of distorting homelife into little more than an extension of your other work.

3. Life's LITTLE FRUSTRATIONS DON'T BOTHER YOU AS MUCH these days because you have developed perspective on what is important and what is not.

4. You SEE PEOPLE AS PEOPLE and respond positively to who they are instead of perceiving them solely in terms of what they do and how well they're doing it.

5. The time you spend WATCHING TELEVISION HAS DIMINISHED markedly because you have so many other interesting things to do.

6. There is MUCH MORE NON-SEXUAL TOUCHING in your relationships with those you care most about these days.

7. Because you have DEFINED YOURSELF AS ADEQUATE FROM WITHIN, you aren't driven to constantly prove yourself anymore.

8. You ENJOY LIFE'S SIMPLE PLEASURES (which cost nothing) because you are taking the time for them instead of constantly rushing hither and yon each day.

9. You can now PLAY FOR FUN WITH OTHERS because you have moved beyond the aggressive competitiveness that used to turn off other people.

10. Recently, you have become MORE PATIENT AND UNDERSTANDING because you have slowed your pace and can accept the flow of life around you.

11. You UNCONDITIONALLY EXPRESS YOUR LOVE AND CARING to your loved ones each day instead of assuming that they know how you feel.

12. You have LEARNED TO LIKE YOURSELF AS A PERSON so you can let others know you without wasting energy playing roles or maintaining an image.

13. You have REESTABLISHED RELATIONSHIPS WITH FRIENDS and now spend quality time with them after the neglect of years.

14. You are again INVOLVED IN LEISURE INTERESTS OR A HOBBY as you were years ago before you became too busy.

15. There is MORE CREATIVE CHALLENGE AND INTEREST IN YOUR WORK because you are now regularly "getting away from it all."

16. You can SIT DOWN AND DO NOTHING IN PARTICULAR without guilt about being non-productive because you know what you deserve for you.

17. Your PHYSICAL RELATIONSHIP IS MORE FULFILLING for both of you now because you are "really there" making love instead of just having sex.

18. You are MORE OPENLY EXPRESSIVE AND YOU SHARE MORE OF YOUR THOUGHTS AND FEELINGS these days as you have overcome Personal Burnout and the emotional withdrawal that goes with it.

19. You are a MEANINGFUL PART OF YOUR CHILDREN'S LIVES because it is important to you instead of finding excuses to share experiences with them "later."

20. An important SPIRITUAL DIMENSION IN YOUR LIFE HAS RETURNED as you have become more in touch with the real you within instead of living solely in a superficial world of competitive work.

The Happy Ending

Every story should have a happy ending, and this one certainly can have a wonderful final chapter for you. You know just how to go about it. There is no question, though, that to emotionally survive in a pressure-packed world of work and heavy responsibilities is not easy. The choices are tough. And, because the nature of your work is so highly cognitive these days, new skills are needed. You know what these skills are and with your new armamentarium of survival strategies, you have positioned yourself to begin to enjoy the "good life" that you have earned and that is so rightfully yours after years of striving and sacrifice. Remember little Pogo Possum from down in the Okefenokee Swamp? His famous off-the-cuff remark was right on target: "We have met the enemy and it is us!" True. True.

A final word. It is so easy to forget that you are important. How you live each day is a sure indicator of just how deeply you believe in your worth. Life is simply too short not to live it in a fulfilling and personally meaningful way for you. That's the rock bottom line of it all. You will find it most difficult to keep giving and giving your all if you're not important enough to give to yourself along the way too. You are the most important product that you will ever have the chance to develop, and a well-rounded life full of inner satisfaction and joy of living is a sure sign of quality in that endeavor. You will see that quality return right before your eyes as you make it a priority. You will feel it in your heart as it becomes an emotionally satisfying reality.

A Personal Note

As a psychologist and a person profoundly interested in preserving the quality of life of achievers, the involved doers of this world, it is my pleasure to bring this book on Lifestyle Management to you for no other reason than because you are important and because you are more than the work that you do each day. It is my deepest hope that these concepts and strategies will make a positive difference in the life of each and every reader. And, in case you're wondering, I've been whereof I speak. Over the years, these important lessons in Lifestyle Management have been gleaned from personal experience and from professional involvement with many achieving clients who sought help in learning how to emotionally survive their careers and live well with their successes. The genius Albert Einstein once thoughtfully quipped to a colleague: "If you can't say it simply, you don't understand it well enough."

I hope I did so you can too.

INDEX

NEED ANOTHER COPY?

Would you like another copy of IT'S ALL IN YOUR HEAD for . . .

> . . . a friend who is burned out and down in the dumps?
> . . . a spouse who doesn't know how to stop working?
> . . . a colleague who is living in a pressure-cooker?
> . . . a boss who is experiencing health problems?
> . . . an over-achieving child who doesn't enjoy life?
> . . . a parent who needs to slow down but can't?

IT'S ALL IN YOUR HEAD is a personally meaningful gift for a Special Person on a special occasion. Or anytime. Just use the handy coupon below to order your additional copies today.

IT'S ALL IN YOUR HEAD can also be purchased at substantial discounts when ordered in quantity. This book is excellent for use in management meetings, as part of business or sales promotions, in training programs, as a text for college courses, or as a corporate gift for staff members. Write or call DIRECTION DYNAMICS for information on quantity discount rates.

DIRECTION DYNAMICS 309 Honeycutt Drive Wilmington, N.C. 28412

Telephone: (919) 799-6544

Please write for your FREE CATALOG of DIRECTION DYNAMICS' books and cassette tapes.